Breaking Through Bytes

Breaking Through Bytes: Women Shaping the Digital World celebrates the indomitable spirit of women who redefined technology. Divided into 9 iconic chapters, the book provides vivid portraits of 18 female pioneers who cracked the digital code, women who dared to question, create and conquer, describing the evolution of technology through an inspiring lens.

The book spans millennia, tracing the impact of trailblazing women in technology. In early chapters, meet historical figures from the first century to the early 1800s, whose contributions laid the groundwork for today's advancements. Dive into stories of mixed digital artist Thea Baumann, actress and inventor Hedy Lamarr, and pioneering programmer Betty Snyder alongside virtual reality specialist Claire Blackshaw. Discover modern innovators like Kayleigh Oliver, a woman of colour waving the flag for programming all whilst balancing motherhood and tech, and Rocio Evenett, a fashion technologist revolutionising the supply chain. Whether through games, music, or Artificial Intelligence (AI), women from diverse backgrounds have continually defied conventions and reshaped industries.

Breaking Through Bytes uniquely explores women's contributions to STEM and digital technologies, focusing on underrepresented innovators across the centuries. It blends detailed technical achievements with personal stories to inspire readers interested in the history of technology, gender diversity, and modern digital innovations.

Kelly Vero is a tech writer and researcher with a passion for uncovering the hidden stories of women in technology. With a focus on innovation, gender equity, and digital transformation, Vero brings historical and contemporary achievements of women in STEM to light through detailed, scholarly writing.

Breaking Through Bytes
Women Shaping the Digital World

Kelly Vero

CRC Press
Taylor & Francis Group
Boca Raton London New York

CRC Press is an imprint of the
Taylor & Francis Group, an **informa** business

Designed cover image: © Kelly Vero

First edition published 2025
by CRC Press
2385 NW Executive Center Drive, Suite 320, Boca Raton FL 33431

and by CRC Press
4 Park Square, Milton Park, Abingdon, Oxon, OX14 4RN

CRC Press is an imprint of Taylor & Francis Group, LLC

© 2025 Kelly Vero

ISBN: 9781032935676 (hbk)
ISBN: 9781032934228 (pbk)
ISBN: 9781003566465 (ebk)

DOI: 10.1201/9781003566465

Typeset in Minion
by KnowledgeWorks Global Ltd.

Contents

Preface

BORN WITH TWO BRAINS (AND THAT'S GOOD)

When I was a kid, I had a penchant for pulling ballpoint pens apart, laying them on the kitchen table in their constituent parts, and rebuilding them again. The ecstasy of knowing that they were useless alone yet a vital tool for creativity when assembled was exciting for me. This fascination perfectly describes my brain. On one side, I crave reason, logic, order, and routine. I want to know how things work and to refine what seems *unrefinable*. I'm mathematical, yet hopeless at maths. The other side of my brain is exploding with creativity. Creativity and logic must work in tandem to bring about innovation.

The women featured in this book embody that balance. They don't merely exist in rigid roles of technical proficiency or artistic genius—they navigate the intersection of both, finding harmony between logic and creativity. Claire Blackshaw's work in gaming blends a deep understanding of code with the art of storytelling, while Thea Baumann's augmented reality work brings new worlds to life through both visual creativity and technical precision. These women are living proof that to innovate, one must embrace both sides of the brain.

Ada Lovelace was my first role model, and she had been dead for over 150 years when I first discovered her. She saw potential in machines that went beyond calculations—envisioning them as tools of creativity, capable of composing music and art. It was her vision of the Analytical Engine that made me realise that logic and creativity are not opposites, but partners in progress. Lovelace was the first to truly combine the two, showing us that innovation can come from imagining the impossible and making it logical. But she wasn't there to support and foster the new generation of left and right brains working together to solve complex problems.

I found nine women like me, but incredible; and I asked them about their challenges and achievements. I was curious about who was there to support them and how they overcame societal expectations to create magic. Kate Edwards, the geopolitics expert for video games, balances the cold, hard logic of data with thoughtfulness, respect and the human creativity needed to build immersive digital worlds that reflect real human experiences.

Because women often hide their intellectual capabilities, they feel they must choose between being seen as logical *or* creative but not both. The title of this preface is exactly a question posed to me as I was leaving school and preparing for a career or tertiary education. And as I explored the stories of these women, I felt that I wasn't alone. Rocio Evenett, for example, works to streamline the fashion supply chain using computer-aided design (CAD) and precision-driven design, yet her work is as much about aesthetics and creativity as it is about technicality. These women don't just straddle two worlds—they redefine them.

In my own career, I've always felt that tension between logic and creativity, but I found a way to let both thrive. Game development and novel writing are often seen as unrelated disciplines, but to me, they're two lovers, each offering something different when the other grows cold. Marion Mulder's work in ethical AI speaks to this same balance—her dedication to ethical design draws on both creative empathy and logical precision. Like Mulder, the women in this book show that the intersection of logic and creativity is not only possible but necessary for innovation.

The philosopher Hegel once posited that thesis and antithesis can synthesise into a higher level of truth. The women in this book exemplify that idea, blending creativity and logic into something greater than the sum of their parts. They don't just code or paint—they create systems and art that reflect the duality of the human mind (Hegel, 1807). Kayleigh Oliver's successful FOBBs app blends gameplay mechanics with immersive storytelling, proving that technology can be both a technical and artistic endeavour.

The historical women I've included in this book—like Delia Derbyshire and Hedy Lamarr—also embody this duality. Derbyshire revolutionised music by blending electronic pulses with artistic vision. She saw music where others saw only machinery, proving that creativity is alive and well in the logical manipulation of sound (Pinch and Trocco, 2004). Hedy Lamarr, pioneered the frequency-hopping technology that paved the way for modern Wi-Fi. She used her intellect to solve practical, logical problems, while her creativity fuelled her vision of what technology could achieve. Her life, tormented by two parts she had to play—beautiful or intelligent, but never both, the public wouldn't stand for that.

Yet, it is impossible to talk about these women without acknowledging the gender divide that has long persisted in technology and science. In many ways, this book is an exploration of that divide and how women have been forced to navigate it (Beyer, 2012). Society has long placed an unnecessary apartheid between men and women, boxing us into roles that limit our potential. Why should we have to choose between logic and creativity, beauty, and intelligence, or even gender and role?

I've been going grey since I was 17. I used to look across the living room at my mother who had befallen the same fate. One day whilst watching an advert for Lady Grecian 2000 or similar (this was the 80s) she turned to me and said, "there has to be a better way to colour our hair." She asked for a pencil and a piece of paper and drew a tube with a comb placed at the end of it; she handed it to me, and we set about looking for ways we could create a hair dye distribution design that pushed the correct amount of hair dye onto the comb. The next time I saw that design before it was commercially available was in the bin in our living room. My mother, dyslexic and who left school aged 14 did not feel worthy of following her idea through when it had taken her so long to spell her own name correctly.

Our mothers are our first role models, and I still see her as a very smart woman who held the family together with three jobs and though she may have been influenced by other role models compared to mine that doesn't denigrate her intelligence. Today, as a neurodivergent woman in my fifties, I am fairly sure that my neurotype comes from her rather than her from my father, the engineer. Our mothers are not just caregivers, they are providing us with the tools we need to survive. In doing so we may or may not learn to cook (my father taught me to cook), but mother will tell us what we should or shouldn't eat to stay alive. She teaches us how to present ourselves to other people (our fathers tell us we can't go out looking like that). Our mothers want us to be better than them, in every way and with each generation our mothers strive for us to be the change that they wanted to see. If we become mothers ourselves, we are to repeat the same fate without ever expecting different outcomes.

A few years later my mother found an advertisement on the back of a magazine which called her to action in bold black letters: "Would you like to patent your invention or idea? We can help."

"It's too late isn't it, Kelly?" She lamented.

"It's never too late, mum."

She didn't do it. She will never do it.

Our mothers, often unsung heroes of creativity and practicality, teach us lessons about resilience and ingenuity that shape who we become. My mother was not formally educated in the way society seems to value, but her intellect—her ability to problem-solve creatively—was undeniable. I see the same strength in the women I interviewed and the stories I uncovered from history.

For women like Betty Snyder, who was debugging the ENIAC computer in her dreams, or Joan Clarke, who quietly helped crack the Enigma code, the challenge has always been to balance creativity with cold, hard logic—while the world often refused to recognise their contributions. These women didn't just solve equations or design new systems. They broke the barriers society placed on them, redefining what it means to be both brilliant and female.

Each of the women in this book, whether historical figures like Dani Bunten Berry or modern innovators like Thea Baumann, show us that creativity and logic are inseparable. They've succeeded not by choosing one over the other but by embracing both in ways that defy convention. In a world that often tells us to pick a lane, they've taken both roads and paved new ones along the way.

In writing this book, I've come to realise that the duality of creativity and logic is not something to be feared or compartmentalised but embraced. The women here have taught me that balancing both sides of the brain isn't a weakness but a strength. They've harnessed the power of both, creating systems, art, and technologies that shape our world. The gender roles assigned to us are arbitrary, outdated constructs that often stifle innovation (Margolis and Fisher, 2002). As I delved into the lives of these women, I saw repeatedly how they pushed beyond those boundaries, refusing to be limited by them.

The future of technology lies in breaking down the walls that divide us—whether those walls are between creativity and logic, gender, or societal roles. The women featured here are proof that when we embrace the full scope of our abilities, we can achieve the extraordinary.

REFERENCES

Beyer, K. (2012) *Grace Hopper and the invention of the information age.* Cambridge, MA: MIT Press.

Hegel, G.W.F. (1807) *Phenomenology of spirit.* Bamberg and Wuerzburg: Joseph Anton Goebhardt

Margolis, J. and Fisher, A. (2002) *Unlocking the clubhouse: Women in computing.* Cambridge, MA: MIT Press.

Pinch, T. and Trocco, F. (2004) *Analog days: The invention and impact of the Moog synthesizer.* Cambridge, MA: Harvard University Press.

CHAPTER 1

Hello World

I'M STARING AT A blank screen listening to a song from a playlist I created specifically for this book. A blank screen doesn't always signify a writer's block though, sometimes it's a white space, waiting for words to jump into it or a blank canvas waiting to be painted. In my case, it's usually a flashing command prompt cursor and I want to fill it with the joy and pain of challenge and achievement through problem and solution.

At which point do the synapses in our brains urge us to do something, motivating us towards more enzymes or more cell reproduction? My curiosity for what happens when has always been around understanding why I'm curious. Why do I want to know more than my brain can handle and who else feels like this? I like to think it's you.

Where women's intelligence and curiosity transcend cultural and temporal boundaries, we jump into white spaces, blank canvases, and command prompts making us early architects of scientific thought and technological innovation as much as anyone else. This chapter focuses on the early females, and how, despite societal constraints, our legacies laid the groundwork for future generations of ours. This chapter honours those who broke new ground long before technology became digital and widespread.

Aganice (also known as Aganike) of Egypt lived around 1900 BCE during the Middle Kingdom period. She was one of the earliest recorded women in history to engage in the field of astronomy and natural philosophy. As a princess of Egypt, she belonged to the elite class, which afforded her unique access to education, a privilege typically denied to most women of her time. Her royal status likely enabled her to engage with scholarly pursuits, particularly in fields dominated by men, such as astronomy. This access to learning would have provided her with the rare opportunity to observe celestial phenomena, contributing to the ancient Egyptians' profound understanding of the stars, planets, and other celestial events. Royal women in ancient Egypt sometimes held powerful positions, both politically and religiously, which further facilitated their engagement with scholarly and intellectual activities (Robins, 1993).

Aganice's work in astronomy is particularly significant in the context of the Middle Kingdom's scientific advancements. During this period, the Egyptians refined their calendar system, which relied heavily on astronomical observations, such as the rising of the

DOI: 10.1201/9781003566465-1

star Sirius to predict the flooding of the Nile. It is plausible that Aganice contributed to the knowledge that helped shape these systems, participating in the observation and recording of celestial events that were crucial for both agricultural planning and religious rituals. The Egyptians viewed the movements of the stars and planets as divine messages, and her understanding of these phenomena would have positioned her as a figure of influence, not just within the royal court but also in broader society, which deeply revered astronomy for its practical and spiritual significance (Clagett, 1995).

In addition to her contributions to astronomy, Aganice can be seen as a natural philosopher who engaged with the fundamental questions of the universe. She asked why and more importantly, due to her position in society, she was allowed to ask why.

The ancient Egyptians' worldview combined scientific observation with theological interpretations, and as a woman of both royal and intellectual stature, Aganice would have been immersed in this cultural blending of science and religion. Her observations of the heavens may have informed the religious narratives of the time, linking celestial phenomena with the divine and influencing the ways in which the ancient Egyptians understood their place in the cosmos. Although historical records of her life are sparse, Aganice's legacy as an early female astronomer underscores the importance of royal or higher-caste women during this time (Ogilvie and Harvey, 2000).

It feels almost too early to speak of the unbelievable subjugation that women experienced in ancient times, yet here we are. In the moments of research and reflection, I leaned upon my Greek and Roman Mythology degree in which it was never enough to just know your Scylla from your Charybdis. I also needed to know my Pliny from my Plebeians; I already knew that Pythagoras was a bit of a joke in the classical world. His theorem might have been fake news because it wasn't his theorem at all. Though we don't know exactly who brought the theorem to bear, we can dive into the life of Theano for some of the answers. She was a prominent philosopher and mathematician from approximately 500 BCE, and one of the few women recorded in ancient Greek history to engage in intellectual pursuits at the Pythagorean school of thought. As the possible wife or at least a close associate of Pythagoras, she is believed to have played a significant role in the school, both as a philosopher and a mathematician. In the male-dominated world of Ancient Greece, opportunities for women to engage in scholarly activities were rare. Theano's involvement in the Pythagorean school highlights her exceptional position as a woman who not only participated in but also contributed to the preservation and promotion of the teachings of Pythagoras after his death. This role indicates that, within the Pythagorean community, women were granted unique access to intellectual discourse, emphasising the school's departure from typical gender restrictions of the time (Waithe, 1987).

Pythagoras, or at least the cult of Pythagoras is an unusual one: it's problematic because he's neither a god nor barely a mathematician; so, who did the maths? Theano is often credited with work related to the concept of the Golden Mean, a mathematical principle concerning the harmonious proportions of parts to a whole, which has applications in art, architecture, and nature. This theory, central to the Pythagorean understanding of the universe, exemplified the integration of mathematics and philosophy, where numerical relationships were seen as reflections of the natural order and cosmic balance. Theano's involvement in mathematical theory, especially the Golden Mean, would have had significant philosophical implications, tying mathematics to ethical and metaphysical ideas about balance and harmony in life. Her contributions further suggest that she was deeply involved in expanding the intellectual legacy of Pythagoras, ensuring that mathematical principles were studied not merely as abstract concepts but as essential elements of a broader philosophical inquiry into the nature of reality (Deakin, 2013).

After Pythagoras' death, Theano is said to have played a critical role in maintaining and preserving the Pythagorean school. This was no small feat, considering the challenges faced by women in ancient Greece. Societal norms largely confined women to domestic roles, no surprises there. Theano's leadership in promoting Pythagorean teachings ensured that the school's doctrines survived through turbulent times, with her writings contributing to the school's philosophy and ethics. Theano's influence demonstrates that, within specific philosophical communities, women were able to attain positions of respect and intellectual authority. Although many details about her life remain uncertain, Theano's legacy as a Pythagorean philosopher and mathematician endures, underscoring the vital role she played in preserving one of ancient Greece's most influential intellectual traditions (Lloyd, 1999).

As one age ends, another begins. If the Egyptian age of women in technology began and ended with Aganice, then presumably tech gets hotter in a new age. Remember that during this time there was a fire in Alexandria which made record keeping either extremely problematic or completely useless given the desire to push knowledge out of those who were not the inheritors of the new age. What did Aglaonice, a pioneering female astronomer in Ancient Greece during the 2nd century BCE, know?

She holds a special place in history as the first recorded woman to study and practice astronomy. She is most famously known for her ability to predict lunar eclipses, a feat that, during her time, earned her both awe and suspicion. Aglaonice was often described as a sorceress by her contemporaries, with her predictive abilities being seen as mystical rather than scientific. This blending of science with myth reflected the ancient world's deep associations between women and magic, particularly when women possessed knowledge that appeared to defy the ordinary understanding of the universe. The male-dominated scientific community of the time often conflated her accurate astronomical predictions with supernatural powers, underscoring the challenges women faced in being recognised as legitimate scholars (Waithe, 1987).

Despite the mystical aura surrounding her name, Aglaonice's work in astronomy was grounded in an understanding of celestial mechanics. Her ability to predict lunar eclipses suggests that she had knowledge of the regular patterns of the moon's orbit and its relation to the Earth and the sun. These patterns, when studied carefully allowed astronomers to anticipate when the moon would pass into the Earth's shadow, leading to an eclipse. Aglaonice's success in making these predictions demonstrates her grasp of basic astronomical principles, even if her male contemporaries framed her knowledge within the context of magic and sorcery. Her work signifies an early instance of women making significant contributions to science, even when those contributions were not always understood or respected as scientific achievements.

Aglaonice's legacy is intertwined with both science and myth. Her association with a group of women known as the "Witches of Thessaly," who were rumoured to have the power to "pull the moon from the sky," further illustrates how women's intellectual pursuits were often linked to supernatural phenomena in the ancient world. This mythical framing, however, did not diminish Aglaonice's place in history as a groundbreaking astronomer. In fact, it highlights the complex role of women in science during antiquity, where their contributions were both celebrated and obscured by the cultural narratives of the time (Lloyd, 1979).

The fear of knowledge or people who attain knowledge is unbelievably strong. It's attractive and magnetic. It repels and draws us closer to the parts of us that discredit our intellect. The miscommunication of curiosity as some form of witchcraft cannot be discounted and well, well, well it would have to be women at the centre of this confusion, right? We can't just go about our business being curious. And this is why we can't have nice things.

These witches were a group of women in ancient Greek mythology and literature who were reputed for their knowledge of magic and witchcraft. Thessaly, a region in northern Greece, was particularly famous in the ancient world for its association with powerful sorcery and supernatural phenomena. These witches were often depicted as having the ability to control the natural elements, including the moon and stars, and they were believed to possess special powers to summon or manipulate celestial bodies (Ovid, 1955). In ancient Greek literature, Thessalian witches were notorious for their ability to "pull the moon down from the sky." But what does that mean? This phrase was not meant to be taken literally but symbolised their supposed power over lunar and celestial forces, often connected with practices of divination and necromancy. Thessalian witches were frequently associated with using herbs, potions, and incantations to achieve their magical feats. Thessaly's reputation as a hub of witchcraft and magic became a common trope in Greek mythology, and its witches were typically portrayed as figures who wielded dark and forbidden knowledge (Johnson, 1999).

One of the most famous literary references to these witches comes from the Roman poet Lucan's epic poem *Pharsalia* (also known as *De Bello Civili*), where the character Erictho, a particularly malevolent Thessalian witch, is portrayed as performing dark rituals, including necromancy. She calls upon the spirits of the dead and communes with the forces of the underworld, cementing her status as one of the darkest representations of a Thessalian witch (Lucan, 1992).

The connection between the Witches of Thessaly and the moon likely stems from their association with the goddess Hecate, who was linked to magic, witchcraft, and the night. Hecate was a deity associated with the moon and was often depicted as a protector of witches. The mystical practices attributed to these women reflected broader cultural fears and fascinations with the unknown, particularly the unexplained movements of celestial bodies, which were interpreted through the lens of magic before they were scientifically understood. Aglaonice's life and work seem enigmatic to the early presence of women in scientific fields, even in the face of societal limitations that sought to frame their knowledge in terms of magic rather than empirical understanding.

Though astronomy and philosophy were a gateway to what might become the pioneering state of curiosity in and of technology; Theano seems to have the upper hand in a transferable working understanding of the Pythagoras theorem. She was close to it and would have taught it extensively in her later life. Aganice and Aglaonice may have been more hobbyists than chasers of truths and formulae comparatively. Don't you think? When do we stop being curious and move from the rabbit hole of Wikipedia to the practice of the lab, or in this case, the writing of a book about women I've never met, I know, and who I cherish deeply?

Pandrosion, a Greek mathematician active in Alexandria during the 4th century CE, made significant contributions to the field of mathematics, particularly in the realm of algebra. Although much of her work is lost, later mathematicians like Hypatia and Pappus of Alexandria acknowledged her efforts. Pandrosion is best known for her method of solving cubic equations, which was an early attempt at systematically addressing higher-degree algebraic problems. Her work in approximating cube roots, while not completely preserved, marks her as one of the earliest known contributors to the study of algebra and geometry. According to Pappus, she utilised geometric methods to solve these equations, aligning with the Greek tradition of addressing algebraic problems through geometrical constructions (Cuomo, 2001).

Pandrosion's contributions are mainly known through critiques by Pappus of Alexandria, who commented on her techniques in his *Mathematical Collection*. Know her name. Despite the limited records of her contributions, Pandrosion's presence in the historical record highlights the role of women in early mathematics. Alexandria during late antiquity offered a rare environment where women like Pandrosion and her contemporary Hypatia could engage in scholarly pursuits. However, much like many women of her time, Pandrosion's intellectual contributions were under-recorded and often overshadowed by male contemporaries. Although Pappus criticised her approach as not fully rigorous, his mention of her work indicates that it was important enough to be part of the academic discourse of the time. Pandrosion's methodology involved geometric constructions to approximate cube roots, an approach common in the ancient world but still innovative for her era. Her work laid the groundwork for future mathematical advancements, even though Pappus' critiques suggest that mathematical rigour was still developing at that point. The fact that her work was preserved, albeit through critique, underscores its significance in the mathematical community of the time (Pappus of Alexandria, *Mathematical Collection*, 1921; Becker, 1986).

Her work with cubic equations exemplifies the involvement of women in mathematics during a period when their scholarly achievements were typically marginalised or erased from history. Nevertheless, her legacy persists through the records of many scholars just like Pappus, revealing that women were active participants in developing early mathematical techniques.

They must have been friends, right? There's no way that Pandrosion and Hypatia of Alexandria, born around 355 CE, could have at least known about each other. But sadly, there is no direct historical evidence to suggest that Pandrosion and Hypatia were friends or even contemporaries. Hypatia was a pioneering figure in mathematics, astronomy, and philosophy during late antiquity. She is widely regarded as one of the most prominent female intellectuals of the ancient world, contributing significantly to the preservation and development of classical knowledge.

As a respected scholar, Hypatia took on the role of head of the Neoplatonist school in Alexandria, where she taught mathematics and philosophy. She is credited with commentaries on works by major thinkers such as Diophantus and Apollonius, providing explanations and expansions on their geometric and algebraic theories. Although none of Hypatia's original works survive, her contributions to the understanding of mathematics, particularly in the study of conic sections, helped preserve these classical texts for future generations (Dzielska, 1995).

Hypatia's leadership in academia was unusual for a woman in the male-dominated world of ancient intellectual life. Her appointment as the head of her own academy in Alexandria signified her extraordinary intellect and the respect she garnered from her contemporaries. She became a highly influential public figure, offering lectures to a wide audience, including students, scholars, and government officials. As an educator, Hypatia embraced the Neoplatonic philosophical tradition, which sought to reconcile Plato's ideas with religious and ethical concerns. Her wide-reaching influence, however, also made her a target during a period of increasing tension between Christian authorities and the pagan intellectual elite of Alexandria (Deakin, 2007).

Hypatia's tragic death in 415 CE marked a brutal end to her scholarly life and has come to symbolise the clash between science and religious extremism. In the volatile atmosphere of religious conflict in Alexandria, Hypatia's pagan background and association with the city's secular political leadership placed her at odds with rising Christian powers. A mob of Christian extremists, led by a group of monks called the *parabalani*, attacked Hypatia as she was riding in her chariot through the city. They dragged her to a church, where she was brutally beaten and killed. According to some accounts, her body was dismembered and burned. This act was not just a personal tragedy but also represented the broader decline of the classical intellectual tradition in Alexandria, as religious orthodoxy grew hostile to the scientific and philosophical pursuits once encouraged under Roman rule (Watts, 2017). In the early 5th century, tensions between Christians and pagans in the city escalated. The city's Christian bishop, Cyril, was engaged in a bitter power struggle with the Roman prefect of Alexandria, Orestes, who was a supporter of Hypatia. Although Hypatia was a neutral philosopher, some Christian factions perceived her as an obstacle to Cyril's authority and as a symbol of paganism. The exact motivations behind her murder are debated, but religious fanaticism played a significant role. Hypatia's death marked the decline of classical pagan philosophy in Alexandria and symbolised the increasing dominance of Christianity in the city. Her legacy, however, as a pioneering woman of science and philosophy, has endured through the centuries as a martyr for the pursuit of knowledge.

Due to the limited records about Pandrosion and the lack of overlap in their time periods, it is unlikely that they were personally acquainted which is a shame because they really needed each other. Gender should not be a driver in how we lead a good life, but it can help us to be better advocates for each other and lift each other up.

If both women were part of the broader tradition of female scholars in Alexandria, a centre of intellectual activity during their respective lifetimes, it is possible that Hypatia, as a prominent mathematician and philosopher, was, at the very least, aware of the work of earlier mathematicians like Pandrosion. Hypatia was known to work on and expand the mathematical ideas of earlier scholars, so it is conceivable that she may have been influenced by Pandrosion's methods, even if indirectly. Nonetheless, the historical record does not provide clear connections between the two figures. Let's pretend that they rooted for one another.

The Islamic Golden Age, which spanned from the 8th to the 14th centuries, was a period of remarkable intellectual achievement in mathematics, astronomy, and medicine. Scholars from the Islamic world translated and built upon the works of ancient Greek, Roman, and Indian scholars. Can you imagine that women were as much a part of this movement towards the future as men? As with Aganice's story, the role that higher caste and royal women played during this time is acceptable for this part of history, especially from a cultural and religious perspective where perhaps we wouldn't see as many women driving the narrative as we do today. Al-'Ijliyyah, sometimes known as Mariam Al-'Ijliyyah, flourished in the 10th century as a renowned maker of astrolabes in Aleppo. She worked under the patronage of Sayf al-Dawla, a ruler of the Hamdanid dynasty in Syria. Astrolabes were intricate scientific instruments used for solving problems related to time and the position of stars and planets, playing a critical role in astronomy, astrology, and navigation. Al-'Ijliyyah's contributions are particularly noteworthy because very few women from this period are recorded as makers of such scientific devices. Her work highlights the role of women in the Islamic scientific tradition during the mediaeval period, despite the challenges they faced in participating in the scientific community (Rashed, 1996).

Astrolabes, such as the ones crafted by Al-'Ijliyyah, were vital tools for these scholars. They were used to calculate prayer times, find the direction of Mecca, and study the stars. The court of Sayf al-Dawla in Aleppo became a centre of scientific and intellectual activity during this period, drawing mathematicians, philosophers, and artisans, including Al-'Ijliyyah. Her presence at the court is a testament to her skill and the recognition she garnered in the world of mediaeval Islamic science (Saliba, 2007).

Al-'Ijliyyah's involvement in the creation of astrolabes underscores the unique role that some women were able to play in the scientific courts of the Islamic world. While women were often excluded from formal education in many parts of the world during this period, Islamic culture allowed for some notable exceptions. In scientific and intellectual circles, especially within royal courts like Sayf al-Dawla's, women like Al-'Ijliyyah could contribute meaningfully to the advancement of science and technology. Her work ensured that crucial knowledge about the stars and their movements was preserved and expanded during this critical period in history. The legacy of Al-'Ijliyyah remains a vital example of how women participated in shaping the intellectual landscape of the Islamic world (Saliba, 2007).

Adelle of the Saracens, a female physician of Arab descent and of Islamic heritage was active in 12th century Italy, teaching at the renowned Salerno School of Medicine; one of the most prestigious medical institutions of mediaeval Europe. The school, located in southern Italy, was a centre of medical learning and one of the few places in mediaeval Europe where women could participate in formal medical education and practice medicine. Known as the *Trotula*, a term that came to be associated with female practitioners and their medical works, Adelle and other women at Salerno contributed significantly to medical knowledge, particularly in the areas of gynaecology and obstetrics. Their work focused on women's health, which was often overlooked in medical treatises written by men at the time (Green, 2008). Can we say Adelle was a femtech pioneer? She wouldn't have been the only woman focused in this area of medicine; women at the Salerno School of Medicine, including Adelle, played an essential role in disseminating knowledge about women's health and medical treatments. These women practised medicine, taught students, and contributed to the body of medical literature, which was quite rare for the time.

Adelle was a key figure in passing on medical knowledge, despite the restrictions placed on women in other parts of Europe. The Salerno School's progressive stance on women's participation allowed figures like Adelle to flourish and contribute to the advancement of medical science. Her teachings, like those of other female physicians of the time, focused on practical treatments derived from experience, a tradition that had been passed down through generations of women (Green, 2008).

Humanism, as a philosophical and cultural movement, emphasises the value and agency of human beings, individually and collectively, and it prioritises human welfare and the potential for human growth. Originating during the Renaissance, humanism placed importance on reason, ethics, and the development of knowledge to improve life. Humanism's focus on human-centred approaches is particularly relevant to fields such as medicine, as seen in Adelle's time at the Salerno School of Medicine, where the treatment of individuals, especially women, reflected a compassionate, holistic approach to health and well-being.

Drawing a connecting line from the principles of humanism to modern technology, especially in fields like User Experience (UX) design, the influence of human-centred thinking is profound. UX design is essentially the practice of crafting digital products and experiences that are intuitive, accessible, and designed with the user's needs in mind. It places the human experience at the core of the design process, aiming to create technology that enhances human capabilities, solves problems, and improves overall quality of life.

Here's how humanism directly relates to UX design and modern technology:

1. **Human-Centred Focus**: Just as humanism focuses on human welfare and development, UX design prioritises the user's experience and interactions with technology. Instead of designing solely for efficiency or technical superiority, UX designers focus on creating solutions that are easy to use, intuitive, and satisfying for humans. This mirrors the humanist ideal of valuing human experiences and emotions as central to the design.

2. **Empathy and Ethical Considerations**: Humanism encourages empathy—understanding and considering the perspectives of others. In UX, this manifests as empathising with users and designing products that address their real-world problems

and frustrations. Designers often use techniques like user interviews, personas, and journey mapping to get closer to the human side of the technology, ensuring that the final product reflects the users' needs and values. Like humanism, UX encourages a reflection on ethics—ensuring that technology serves a meaningful, positive purpose in people's lives.

3. **Iterative Learning and Growth**: The humanist tradition places value on learning and continuous improvement, a principle that also defines UX design. UX involves iterative processes of testing, learning, and refining based on user feedback. This cycle of learning mirrors humanism's belief in the continuous betterment of society and individuals through knowledge, understanding, and innovation.

For example, when designing for healthcare apps, UX designers must deeply consider the human condition—whether they are creating an app for chronic illness management or mental health support. The goal is to create something that works harmoniously with human behaviour and cognitive patterns, minimising frustration while providing clear and accessible solutions to very real, human problems.

Adelle's role at the Salerno School underscores the limited but impactful presence of women in early medical science. Women like her were able to work within the confines of a male-dominated society and carve out a place in the world of medicine, particularly in treating and understanding women's health. The school became famous for its treatment of women, and this focus on women's medicine reflected the significant contributions of female practitioners such as Adelle. Although women were generally barred from the medical profession in most of mediaeval Europe, the exceptional environment of Salerno allowed women to study, teach, and practice medicine, leaving a legacy in medical history (King, 2001).

The Western Roman Empire collapsed. The more I try to understand our role in expanding technology, the more I see cycles of humans, not just gender-specific, but most people engaging in ways to destroy culture, learning, and knowledge. It's as though every generation or so, we're ready to kill any sense of understanding to make way for darkness. After all, the Middle Ages weren't dark (though sometimes we call them thus): the opposite was true. Some of the brightest and most incredible thinkers, scientists, and texts were created during this time. But this section of history is also problematic. As civilisations make way for new civilisations that usually means peace is followed by war. The paradox of human stories and accounts of intellectual wonder and domination, freedom and control, serenity and violence; humility and extremism are captured in the images of a thousand documentarists and the words of all languages. How do we condense all that we know into something we can all understand?

Herrad of Landsberg (1130–1195) was an Alsatian abbess who compiled the *Hortus deliciarum* (*Garden of Delights*), an educational and encyclopaedic work between 1167 and 1195 while serving as abbess of the Hohenburg Abbey. The *Hortus deliciarum* was a monumental achievement, serving as an illustrated compendium of scientific, philosophical, and theological knowledge. Herrad's work reflected the comprehensive education she provided to the young nuns under her care, spanning topics such as natural philosophy, astronomy, ethics, and religious doctrine (Newman, 1982). The codex was designed as a teaching tool, using illustrations and writings to explain complex concepts, which was particularly revolutionary in a time when such opportunities for women were rare.

Herrad's work illustrates the unique role convents played during the mediaeval period as intellectual sanctuaries where women could pursue education and scholarship, an opportunity not readily available elsewhere in society (Ferrante, 1982). Her work combined visual, auditory, and kinaesthetic learning methods, which bear resemblance to modern-day multimodal education. For example, the *Hortus deliciarum* contained strikingly detailed illustrations that visually represented scientific phenomena and religious concepts. These images were not just decorations; they were an integral part of the educational experience that Herrad fostered, complementing the oral and written instruction that was typical in convent life (Newman, 1982).

Convents in the mediaeval period, such as the Hohenburg Abbey, provided one of the few places where women could engage in scholarship and intellectual pursuits. Unlike in Renaissance society, where women's roles became more restricted and formal educational opportunities decreased, convents remained centres for learning where women could contribute to religious and scientific knowledge. Herrad's *Hortus deliciarum* has a subtext where the knowledge women produced a compendium of information to preserve and teach in these spaces. By focusing on theological teachings alongside scientific knowledge, Herrad's work demonstrated the intellectual versatility women could achieve, even when confined to the religious sphere (Ferrante, 1982).

In a way this is a little like playing *Assassin's Creed* (2008) or exploring the world of *The Elder Scrolls V: Skyrim* (2011); the elements of everything we desire from history are there. In some cases, such as role-playing video games; if we desire a design for life we can access it in a very visceral way. We would have to wait a further 300 or 400 years before Hieronymus Bosch brought a similar garden to our senses and expanded our universe further in more ways than Herrad might imagine from the comfort of her abbey. Herrad started something, and that was the ability to disseminate information attuned to however people learn.

Anna Maria van Schurman (1607–1678) was a Dutch polymath who made significant strides in advancing women's access to formal education during the 17th century. She was the first woman to attend university lectures in Europe, specifically at Utrecht University, though she had to sit behind a screen to avoid distracting her male peers. Van Schurman's education was extraordinary for her time, as women were typically excluded from higher learning. By mastering several languages, including Latin, Greek, Hebrew, and Arabic, as well as studying theology, philosophy, art, and science, she demonstrated that women could excel in academic fields traditionally reserved for men (Pope-Hennessy, 1909). Her presence at Utrecht University marked a symbolic breakthrough for women in academia during the Renaissance period.

Van Schurman was also a highly respected theologian and philosopher. Her writings advocated for the intellectual capabilities of women and argued that women deserved the right to education, particularly in the study of theology. In her most famous work, *Dissertatio de Ingenii Muliebris ad Doctrinam et Meliores Litteras Aptitudine* (1641), she argued that women were just as capable as men when it came to intellectual pursuits, especially in religious and philosophical studies (Schurman, 1641). Her argument was radical for the time, as it challenged the widespread belief that women's primary roles were domestic, and she actively engaged in debates with male scholars who opposed her views. Van Schurman's works inspired later generations of women to pursue education and intellectual careers, even in the face of societal constraints.

During the Renaissance, the hurdles women faced in accessing formal education were monumental. Academic institutions, including universities, were exclusively male domains, with religious and societal norms reinforcing the idea that women should not engage in scholarly pursuits. For Anna Maria van Schurman, however, her remarkable intellect and determination allowed her to break through these barriers, even if only in a limited capacity. Her attendance at university, though hidden behind a screen, was a symbolic victory against the gender-based restrictions of her time (Pope-Hennessy, 1909). Despite these challenges, van Schurman became a leading intellectual figure of the Dutch Golden Age, known not only for her theological and philosophical contributions but also for her skill in art, music, and science.

Anna Maria van Schurman's fight for academic recognition extended beyond her own personal achievements; she advocated for a broader cultural shift in the understanding of women's roles in society. Her ability to master so many disciplines, coupled with her insistence on women's right to education, set the stage for future generations of women intellectuals. Her polymathic approach—integrating art, science, theology, and philosophy—demonstrated that women's contributions to knowledge could be just as multifaceted and valuable as men's. Her persistent fight for intellectual equality and the unyielding spirit required to overcome societal barriers (Schurman, 1641) makes learning for women, and let's be serious, we do take it for granted. Anna teaches us that we all have a right to learn.

The Enlightenment, spanning the late 17th and 18th centuries, was a period of profound intellectual growth and scientific discovery. It was marked by the application of reason, empirical evidence, and scientific methods, all of which significantly shaped technological advancements during the era. Margaret Lucas Cavendish (1623–1673) was one of the pioneering women who contributed to this intellectual revolution. Known for her work as a philosopher, poet, and scientist, Cavendish was an unconventional figure in Enlightenment circles, attending meetings at the Royal Society and engaging in debates with prominent male philosophers such as Thomas Hobbes and René Descartes (Whitaker, 2002). Her involvement in such esteemed intellectual spaces challenged societal norms and expectations, particularly in an era where women were often excluded from scientific and philosophical circles.

During the Enlightenment, technology evolved as scientific experimentation and rational thought gained prominence. In this period, the emphasis shifted from religious and metaphysical interpretations of the world to a focus on observation, experimentation, and mathematical analysis. The rise of mechanical philosophy—epitomised by figures like Descartes and Newton—laid the groundwork for technological innovation. Cavendish, though often sceptical of the more mechanical interpretations of the natural world, engaged deeply with these ideas. She challenged the prevailing scientific views, particularly those that promoted a mechanistic understanding of nature, arguing instead for a more holistic approach to the study of the natural world (Cavendish, 1666). Her contributions are particularly significant because she was one of the few women of her time to actively participate in the philosophical and scientific discussions that drove technological and intellectual progress.

Margaret Cavendish's involvement in the intellectual circles of the Enlightenment was an extraordinary feat, given the significant gender barriers of her time. Women were largely excluded from formal scientific education and intellectual societies, and their contributions to science were often disregarded or underappreciated. However, Cavendish defied these conventions by writing extensively on natural philosophy, and she became the first woman to attend a meeting at the Royal Society of London in 1667 (Whitaker, 2002). Although she did not perform experiments herself, she actively engaged with the scientific ideas of the time, questioning and critiquing the work of some of the most prominent philosophers and scientists. Cavendish's writings—such as *Observations upon Experimental Philosophy* (1666) and *The Blazing World* (1666)—demonstrated her deep interest in science, politics, and metaphysics, and they stand as early examples of feminist thought in science and technology (Cavendish, 1666).

Cavendish's challenges to gender norms extended beyond her participation in intellectual debates; she also used her writing to critique the male-dominated scientific establishment. She questioned the mechanistic worldview becoming prevalent among Enlightenment thinkers, arguing instead for a more interconnected understanding of nature (Whitaker, 2002). Cavendish was also critical of the limitations placed on women's intellectual capabilities, advocating for women to be given more opportunities to engage in scientific inquiry and intellectual discourse. Her ability to navigate these male-dominated circles and assert her voice in scientific discussions was groundbreaking and paved the way for future generations of women in science and philosophy.

The Enlightenment period was, for the most part, a male-dominated intellectual landscape. Women, like Cavendish, who managed to break into these circles, often faced intense scrutiny and marginalisation. Despite these challenges, Cavendish's prolific output and fearless engagement with the leading intellectuals of her time made her a prominent figure in the Enlightenment. She is considered by some as one of the first proponents of scientific feminism, advocating for women's intellectual potential and critiquing the exclusion of women from scientific knowledge (Whitaker, 2002). Her work during the Enlightenment challenged the very foundations of gender and intellectual hierarchy, offering a new perspective on the role of women in scientific and technological progress.

Margaret Cavendish's life and work exemplified the struggle for women's inclusion in the intellectual and scientific advancements of the Enlightenment. Her boldness in challenging contemporary gender norms and her contributions to philosophical debates were extraordinary for her time. Cavendish's influence can be seen as part of a larger trend during the Enlightenment, where reason, individualism, and the pursuit of knowledge became central, opening the door, however slowly, for greater inclusion of women in intellectual fields.

Belonging is so important to women who feel marginalised or excluded from their area of interest because of gender, ableism, or more. I've felt like this a million times in my career. I am neurodivergent so it can also be frustrating to either be heard or understood. In the last 5 years I have been working in artificial intelligence (AI); and though the playing field is much more level, it's still a place where I want to belong, and I still don't feel accepted yet. Now, that's possibly because of my career in video games, or it could just be because these days our intellect is measured by the company we keep on social media. However we shape up, we want to fit in, and if we do fit in, we don't want to disappear.

In 1675, Marie Desprast made history as the first woman to be officially recognised as a *maîtresse couturière* and accepted into the French fashion guilds, marking a pivotal moment in the evolution of high fashion. During the 17th century, the Parisian guilds, traditionally male-dominated institutions, were the gatekeepers of craftsmanship and industry standards in various professions, including tailoring and fashion. The fashion industry at the time was increasingly significant due to the court of Louis XIV, known as the Sun King, which set trends across Europe. Desprast's admission into the guild as a *maîtresse couturière* was revolutionary because it formalised the role of women in the fashion industry, granting them professional status and the ability to operate as independent couturiers (Lapham's Quarterly, 2017). This allowed Desprast and other women to legitimise their skills and establish themselves in what was quickly becoming a vital economic sector (Steele, 2005).

The Parisian fashion guilds were highly regulated, with strict rules governing membership, apprenticeships, and production. The guilds acted as institutions that both protected and regulated the profession, ensuring that only those with the highest skills could claim the title of *maître* or *maîtresse*. Marie Desprast's acceptance into the guild was significant not only because her approval broke gender barriers but also because it set a precedent for other women to follow. Her work as a *maîtresse couturière* involved mastering the art of tailoring and clothing design, using techniques that required a deep understanding of fabrics, textiles, and the scientific properties of materials available at the time (Ogilvie, 2019). The recognition of her skills and the subsequent inclusion of other women into the guilds elevated women's contributions to fashion from informal labour to recognised and valued craftsmanship. This period marked the beginning of a more formalised industry that combined artistry with technical skill, paving the way for future innovations in fashion technology (Steele, 2005).

The significance of Marie Desprast's achievement extends beyond fashion and speaks to the broader social changes of the time. The late 17th century was a period of immense technological and scientific development, and while many of the contributions of women were under recognised, Desprast's inclusion in the guild system highlighted the possibility for women to enter previously inaccessible professions. This intersection of craftsmanship, science, and technology in the fashion industry allowed for the introduction of more sophisticated methods of garment construction and design, blending artistry with the emerging technological advances of the era (Steele, 2005). Desprast's work set the stage for future developments in *haute couture* and established a legacy of women's leadership in the fashion industry, which continues to influence modern fashion technology (Lapham's

Quarterly, 2017). Her success demonstrated that women could excel in technical and creative fields and fostered an environment where the talents and skills of women in fashion could be professionally recognised and nurtured (Steele, 2005).

In 1680, Jeanne Dumée, a French astronomer, emerged as a passionate defender of the Copernican theory of heliocentrism, which posited that the Earth and other planets revolved around the Sun. Nicolaus Copernicus first proposed this model in the 16th century in his work *De revolutionibus orbium coelestium* (1543), directly challenging the widely accepted geocentric model. The geocentric model, most notably formalised by Ptolemy in *Almagest* (c. 150 CE), had dominated Western thought for centuries. The geocentric view, which placed Earth at the centre of the universe with all celestial bodies orbiting it, aligned with both the philosophical teachings of Aristotle and the religious doctrines of the Christian Church, which perceived Earth's central position as reflective of humanity's unique status in creation (Lindberg, 2007).

The controversy surrounding heliocentrism stemmed from its contradiction of both scientific and religious beliefs. The geocentric model was not only scientifically entrenched but also supported by the Church's theological view that Earth occupied a special, immovable position. By proposing that Earth revolves around the Sun, Copernicus' model suggested that Earth was no longer the centre of the universe, undermining the anthropocentric views of Christian theology (Kuhn, 1957). In 1616, the Catholic Church declared heliocentrism as "formally heretical" and placed Copernicus' writings on the Index of Forbidden Books (Fantoli, 1994). This opposition culminated in the infamous trial of Galileo Galilei, a proponent of heliocentrism, who was found guilty of heresy by the Roman Inquisition in 1633 and forced to recant his support for the theory (Shea, 1972).

Scientific scepticism also delayed the acceptance of heliocentrism. The Ptolemaic system had accurately predicted planetary positions for centuries, making it difficult for the new model to gain traction. Copernicus' heliocentric model, while mathematically elegant, did not immediately offer better predictive capabilities than Ptolemy's geocentric system (Lindberg and Numbers, 1986). However, the later contributions of Johannes Kepler, who refined the heliocentric theory by introducing elliptical orbits, and Isaac Newton, who formulated the law of universal gravitation, provided the critical evidence that eventually led to the widespread acceptance of the heliocentric model and the advancement of modern astronomy (Finocchiaro, 1989).

Despite these religious and academic challenges, Dumée published a detailed summary of the arguments in favour of the Copernican theory. In her writings, she boldly stated, "between the brain of a woman and that of a man, there is no difference," emphasising that women, like men, were capable of understanding and contributing to complex scientific ideas. Dumée's defence of heliocentrism was not only a significant scientific contribution but also a courageous assertion of women's intellectual abilities during a time when their participation in academic discourse was heavily restricted (Ogilvie and Harvey, 2000).

Dumée's work is especially remarkable given the social context of 17th-century Europe, where women faced substantial barriers to education and scientific engagement. Women were often excluded from formal academic institutions and scientific societies, leaving them to pursue their intellectual interests in more informal and private settings. Dumée, however, did not shy away from engaging with the prevailing scientific debates of her time. Her defence of heliocentrism was rooted in meticulous research and a thorough understanding of astronomical observations, which she used to challenge the geocentric views that still dominated European thought. (Ogilvie and Harvey, 2000). This intellectual rigour positioned her as a key figure in the growing acceptance of heliocentrism even though her contributions were often overshadowed by her male counterparts.

The necessity for women like Dumée to defend their ideas was largely a result of the scepticism they faced from the male-dominated scientific community. Women were often viewed as lacking the intellectual capacity to engage with complex scientific theories, and their work was frequently dismissed or ignored. For Dumée, defending the Copernican theory was not only about advancing scientific knowledge but maybe also about proving that women could contribute meaningfully to the scientific revolution. Her perseverance in the face of societal doubt exemplifies the broader struggles that women in science have faced throughout history. Dumée's legacy lies not only in her support of heliocentrism but also in her role as an early advocate for the intellectual equality of women in the sciences (Ogilvie and Harvey, 2000).

Can we have it all? Absolutely. Should we pursue it? Without a doubt. Will we achieve it? That's a journey we'll explore in the final chapters. Looking back at figures like Dumée and Aganice, though separated by centuries, they share more in common than meets the eye—both fought to prove themselves in a world that wasn't ready to listen, even if one of them was royalty.

History tells women to sit down, shut up, and fall in line, and many do. But it's the outliers, the ones who don't fit neatly into those constraints, who change the game. These outliers aren't always rebellious by nature; sometimes they're simply curious and driven, like Herrad, Al-'Ijliyyah, or Van Schurman—women who sought to challenge ideas and forge their own paths. Cavendish and Theano remind us that when we're onto something important, we must lead with conviction, regardless of opposition. Leadership in innovation requires courage, and not everyone is willing to take that stand. Hypatia did, and though her story ended in tragedy, it serves as a powerful reminder of the risks inherent in pushing against the status quo. Sometimes, standing up for what we believe comes with great costs, but it's those moments that drive progress forward, especially in technology.

REFERENCES

Becker, A.S. (1986) 'Pandrosion, pappus, and Hypatia: Women in ancient mathematics', *Classical Quarterly*, 36(2), pp. 478–491.

Cavendish, M. (1666) *Observations upon experimental philosophy*. London: A. Maxwell.

Clagett, M. (1995) *Ancient Egyptian science: A source book*. Philadelphia: American Philosophical Society.

Cuomo, S. (2001) *Ancient mathematics*. London: Routledge.

Deakin, M.A.B. (2007) *Hypatia of Alexandria: Mathematician and martyr*. Amherst, NY: Prometheus Books.

Deakin, M.A.B. (2013) 'Theano: The world's first female mathematician?', *International Journal of Mathematical Education in Science and Technology*, 44(3), pp. 350–364.

Dzielska, M. (1995) *Hypatia of Alexandria*. Cambridge, MA: Harvard University Press.

Fantoli, A. (1994) *Galileo: For Copernicanism and for the church.* Vatican City: University of Notre Dame Press.

Ferrante, J.M. (1982) 'Women's education in the middle ages', *Signs: Journal of Women in Culture and Society,* 7(4), pp. 741–762.

Finocchiaro, Maurice A. (1989) *The Galileo affair: A documentary history.* Berkeley: University of California Press.

Green, M.H. (2008) *Making Women's medicine masculine: The rise of male authority in pre-modern gynaecology.* Oxford: Oxford University Press.

Johnston, S.I. (1999) *Restless dead: Encounters between the living and the dead in ancient Greece.* Berkeley, Los Angeles and London: University of California Press.

King, M.L. (1991) *Women of the renaissance.* Chicago: University of Chicago Press.

Kuhn, T.S. (1957) *The Copernican revolution: Planetary astronomy in the development of Western thought.* Cambridge, MA: Harvard University Press.

Lapham's Quarterly. (2017) *When women ruled fashion.* [online] Available at: https://www.laphamsquarterly.org/fashion/when-women-ruled-fashion [Accessed: 18 August 2024]

Lindberg, D.C. (2007) *The beginnings of Western science.* Chicago: University of Chicago Press.

Lindberg, D.C. and Numbers, R.L. (1986) *God And nature: Historical essays on the encounter between Christianity and science.* Berkeley, Los Angeles and London: University of California Press.

Lloyd, G.E.R. (1979) *Magic, reason and experience: Studies in the origin and development of Greek science.* Cambridge, UK: Cambridge University Press.

Lloyd, G.E.R. (1999) *Ancient worlds, modern reflections: Philosophical perspectives on Greek and Chinese science and culture.* Oxford: Oxford University Press.

Lucan. (1992). *Pharsalia,* translated by Susan H. Braund. Oxford UK: Oxford University Press.

Newman, B. (1982) 'Herrad of Landsberg and the Hortus Deliciarum', *Speculum,* 57(4), pp. 751–755.

Ogilvie, S. (2019) *The European Guilds* (Princeton, NJ, 2019; online edn, Princeton Scholarship Online, 23 May 2019). https://doi.org/10.23943/princeton/9780691137544.001.0001

Ogilvie, M.B. and Harvey, J.D. (2000) *The biographical dictionary of women in science: Pioneering lives from ancient times to the mid-20th century.* New York: Routledge.

Ovid. (1955). *Metamorphoses.* Translated by M. Innes. London: Penguin, pp. 567–582 (Book 1), pp. 220–235 (Book 7).

Pappus of Alexandria. (1921) *Mathematical Collection,* translated and edited by T. L. Heath.

Pope-Hennessy, U. (1909) *Anna Van Schurman: Artist, scholar, Saint.* London: Longmans, Green and Company.

Rashed, R. (1996) *Encyclopedia of the history of Arabic science.* London: Routledge.

Robins, G. (1993) *Women in ancient Egypt.* Cambridge, MA: Harvard University Press.

Saliba, G. (2007) *Islamic science and the making of the European renaissance.* Cambridge, MA and London: MIT Press.

Schurman, A.M. (1641) *Dissertatio de Ingenii Muliebris ad Doctrinam et Meliores Litteras Aptitudine.* Utrecht: Utrecht University Press.

Shea, W.R. (1972) *Galileo's intellectual revolution: Middle period, 1610-1632.* Cambridge UK: Science History Publications.

Steele, V. (2005) *Paris fashion: A cultural history.* Oxford UK and New York: Oxford University Press.

Waithe, M.E. (1987) *A history of women philosophers, volume 1: Ancient women philosophers, 600 B.C.–500 A.D.* Dordrecht, Netherlands, Boston, MA and Lancaster, PA: Kluwer Academic Publishers.

Watts, E. (2017) *Hypatia: The life and legend of an ancient philosopher.* New York: Oxford University Press.

Whitaker, K. (2002) *Mad Madge: The extraordinary life of Margaret Cavendish, Duchess of Newcastle, the first woman to live by her pen.* New York: Basic Books.

CHAPTER 2

Mother Earth and the Maths of the Heavens

T HE CURIOSITY OF LEARNING made us leap from the mid-18th century through the early 19th century. We were fuelled by advancing technologies but also by the curious nature of our world. Despite their diverse geographical locations and disciplines, women in technology shared a common thread: they were pioneers who changed the way we understand and interact with the world. Their contributions mark the beginning of modern science and technology, from astronomy and mathematics to physics and early computer science, pushing the boundaries of knowledge at a time when women's participation in such fields was still highly restricted.

Wang Zhenyi and Sophie Germain are exemplary figures of women who defied societal norms and shattered barriers in their pursuit of scientific knowledge. Both women lived in different cultural contexts—Wang Zhenyi in Qing Dynasty China and Sophie Germain in post-revolutionary France—yet their paths were remarkably similar in the ways they overcame obstacles to achieve their goals. Their resilience and brilliance serve as powerful reminders for women today, especially those in fields like technology, where gender disparities persist.

Wang Zhenyi (1768–1797) lived during the Qing Dynasty, a period marked by strict Confucian ideals that emphasised a patriarchal social order. Women were generally expected to focus on domestic roles, such as managing household affairs and raising children. Education for women, if it occurred at all, was typically limited to the "Four Virtues" (fidelity, physical charm, propriety in speech, and proficiency in needlework). Intellectual pursuits like science and mathematics were considered inappropriate for women and were dominated by male scholars (Ko, 1994).

Wang's access to education was unusual for a woman of her time and can be attributed to her family's scholarly background. Her grandfather, who had a vast library, played a crucial role in her education. This library contained books on a wide range of subjects, including astronomy, mathematics, medicine, and literature, allowing her to educate herself in disciplines that were otherwise closed to women.

DOI: 10.1201/9781003566465-2

She was largely self-taught, a remarkable feat considering the complexity of the subjects she mastered. Her learning process would have been characterised by intense personal study, experimentation, and observation. Without formal guidance or access to structured education, Wang would have had to rely on her ability to interpret and understand complex texts on her own. If you've already read the first chapter and choose to read on, this is a pattern which sadly continues throughout all our generations and those of the future (Ko, 1994; Liu, 2011).

Her study environment was likely solitary, involving long hours of reading, calculation, and observation. The physical tools at her disposal were rudimentary by modern standards—she used simple objects like lamps, mirrors, and tables to simulate astronomical events. Despite these limitations, she was able to grasp and explain sophisticated concepts in celestial mechanics, demonstrating an impressive level of creativity and intellectual dexterity.

One of Wang's most notable contributions to astronomy was her explanation of lunar eclipses. She famously used a lamp, a mirror, and a table to simulate the phenomenon, demonstrating how the Earth casts a shadow on the moon, leading to an eclipse. This experiment showed not only her understanding of celestial mechanics but also her ability to convey complex ideas using simple, everyday objects (Liu, 2011).

1. **Lamp as the Sun**: In her demonstration, Wang used a lamp to represent the Sun. The lamp, as a light source, would emit light in all directions, like how the Sun illuminates the Earth and the Moon.

2. **Mirror as the Moon**: She used a small mirror to represent the Moon. The mirror, when placed in the path of the light from the lamp, would reflect light, mimicking how the Moon reflects sunlight to the Earth.

3. **Table as the Earth**: The table was used to represent the Earth. By positioning the lamp (Sun), the table (Earth), and the mirror (Moon) in a straight line, she could demonstrate how the Earth, when it comes between the Sun and the Moon, casts a shadow on the Moon.

4. **Simulation of the Lunar Eclipse**: By carefully aligning these objects, Wang showed how the shadow of the Earth (represented by the table) falls on the Moon (the mirror) when the Earth is directly between the Sun and the Moon. This shadow on the mirror would darken part of its surface, just as the Earth's shadow causes the Moon to darken during a real lunar eclipse. The demonstration illustrated the passage of the Moon through the Earth's shadow, thereby simulating a lunar eclipse.

This setup effectively demonstrated the basic mechanics of a lunar eclipse: the Sun (lamp) shines on the Earth (table), which blocks the light from reaching the Moon (mirror), creating a shadow that represents the eclipse (Ko, 1994; Liu, 1995).

Wang likely demonstrated this experiment to a small, select audience, possibly including members of her family, close friends, and other scholars who visited her family's home.

Given the cultural and societal constraints of the Qing Dynasty, it is unlikely that she had access to a larger public audience or formal academic settings where she could share her work more widely. Her primary audience would have been those within her immediate intellectual circle—individuals who were curious about scientific ideas or who shared an interest in the scholarly pursuits that were common in her family. (Ko, 1994; Li, 1998). This could have included her grandfather, who was a scholar himself and whose library played a significant role in her education. Any demonstration she performed would have been conducted in a private or semi-private setting rather than a public forum.

The response to Wang's demonstration would have depended largely on the attitudes of those around her. Given that she lived in a society where Confucian norms heavily dictated gender roles, with women generally excluded from scientific and intellectual pursuits, the response to her work might have been mixed (Ko, 1994; Liu, 2011).

- **Support and Encouragement**: Within her family, especially from her grandfather and other scholars who recognised her talent, she likely received support and encouragement. Her family's scholarly background suggests that they would have appreciated the intellectual merit of her work, even if it was unconventional for a woman.

- **Scepticism or Dismissal**: On the other hand, outside of her immediate circle, the broader scholarly community, which was male-dominated and steeped in Confucian traditions, might have been sceptical or dismissive of her contributions. It's possible that her work was not widely recognised or appreciated during her lifetime due to the prevailing gender biases.

Despite any immediate scepticism or lack of widespread recognition during her lifetime, Wang's work laid important groundwork for the recognition of women in science. Her ability to simplify and communicate complex ideas like a lunar eclipse using accessible materials was a significant intellectual achievement, demonstrating both her understanding and her capacity to teach others.

In addition to her work on lunar eclipses, Wang wrote extensively on other astronomical phenomena. She produced a series of essays that explained the movements of celestial bodies, the nature of solar and lunar eclipses, and the structure of the cosmos according to the understanding of her time. Her writings were characterised by clarity and precision, making difficult concepts accessible to those who read them.

Wang's contributions to mathematics are an inspiration for anyone who has ever faced barriers in their pursuit of knowledge; especially if they have intellectual prowess which, in Wang's case emerged in piecemeal. In a time when women were largely confined to domestic roles, Wang broke through societal constraints to make significant strides in mathematics, a field dominated by men. Her work remains a powerful reminder of what can be achieved when passion and determination are combined, regardless of the challenges one might face.

One of her most notable contributions was her treatise on the Pythagorean theorem. The Pythagorean theorem, which describes the relationship between the sides of a right-angled triangle, is a fundamental concept in mathematics that forms the basis for much of geometry and trigonometry. Wang didn't just restate this theorem; she expanded upon it, providing her own proofs and methods of understanding that made the concept more accessible. Her ability to break down such a complex principle into simpler terms allowed for a wider audience to engage with and understand mathematical ideas that might otherwise have been too intimidating or abstract.

Trigonometry, which deals with the relationships between the angles and sides of triangles, is essential not just in mathematics, but in fields as diverse as astronomy, engineering, physics, and even computer science. Wang translated and expanded upon existing trigonometric texts, making these crucial concepts more understandable and applicable. She didn't merely translate these works; she interpreted and explained them, adding her own insights and making the subject more accessible to students and scholars alike. In doing so, she played a vital role in the spread of mathematical knowledge in China, ensuring that these ideas could be used by future generations to solve practical problems in various fields.

Her methods for calculating the volume of a sphere further highlight her mathematical genius. At a time when such calculations required advanced understanding and were limited to a small number of scholars, Wang's work provided clear, concise methods for performing these calculations (Liu, 2011). By simplifying these complex problems and presenting them in a way that could be easily understood, she helped demystify mathematics, opening the door for others to engage with and learn from her work.

Today, I think, Wang's legacy is especially powerful. We're travelling much faster through STEM because we're supported as we create an advancing technological world; the foundations of mathematics are more important than ever. Whether interested in coding, engineering, data science, or any other STEM field—the mathematical principles that Wang worked on centuries ago are still relevant and crucial today. Her work is a reminder that understanding and mastering these principles can empower you to break barriers and make your mark in the world, just as she did.

Wang's ability to simplify and disseminate complex mathematical ideas also serves as an inspiration for those who wish to pursue careers in teaching or in any field where knowledge must be shared and communicated. In an era where information is more accessible than ever, the ability to break down complex concepts and make them understandable to others is a highly valued skill. Wang exemplifies how one person's dedication to learning and teaching can have a lasting impact on society.

Her key mathematical works that involved simplifying and explaining methods were vast. Finding the square and cube roots of numbers, a topic that was complex and not widely understood at the time was presented with clarity. Wang's ability to simplify the methods for calculating square and cube roots helped spread these mathematical concepts to those who lacked access to formal education, demonstrating her talent for making complex ideas digestible.

Wang's achievements were made even more remarkable by the societal constraints she faced as a woman. Her ability to make significant contributions to fields dominated by men, despite having no formal education, highlights her extraordinary determination and intellectual prowess. She challenged the Confucian norms of her society, asserting that women were capable of intellectual achievements and deserved the same opportunities for learning as men.

Her ability to produce scholarly work in such a context is indicative of her profound commitment to learning and discovery. Wang's work was a solitary endeavour, often conducted in the privacy of her home, away from the public eye. This isolation, however, may have also afforded her the freedom to explore subjects that were considered unconventional for women without the immediate scrutiny that she might have faced in a more public or academic setting.

Although Wang's contributions were not widely recognised during her lifetime, her legacy has grown significantly in modern times. Today, she is celebrated as one of the pioneers of Chinese science, a woman who defied the limitations of her time to contribute to the understanding of the natural world. Her work serves as a powerful example of the intellectual potential that can flourish even under restrictive conditions, and she is often cited as a role model for women in STEM fields.

Similarly, Sophie Germain (1776–1831) in France faced a culture that actively discouraged women from engaging in intellectual pursuits, particularly in mathematics and science. Her contributions to the field of mathematics, particularly in number theory and elasticity, are not only profound but also serve as a source of inspiration for women interested in STEM fields.

Born in Paris during the tumultuous years leading up to the French Revolution, Germain was the daughter of a wealthy merchant. Her family initially opposed her interest in mathematics, believing that such pursuits were inappropriate for a woman. In a time when women were largely excluded from academic circles, Germain's determination to study mathematics required her to overcome significant obstacles.

Despite her parents' attempts to deter her—by denying her access to books and even removing her candles at night—Germain would secretly study by the light of a hidden candle. This early display of resilience and passion for learning set the tone for her entire career. She managed to gain access to the academic world by adopting the pseudonym "Monsieur LeBlanc," under which she corresponded with prominent mathematicians like Joseph Fourier and Carl Friedrich Gauss (Grier, 2005; Musielak, 2020).

One of Germain's most notable achievements in mathematics was her work in number theory, particularly her contributions to Fermat's Last Theorem. The theorem, which remained unsolved for centuries, postulated that no three positive integers a, b, and c can satisfy the equation $a^n + b^n = c^n$ for any integer value of n greater than 2. (Sampson, 1990). Germain's approach to the theorem was groundbreaking. She developed a sophisticated proof for the case where $n = 5$, and her methods were later expanded by others to cover different cases of the theorem (Del Centina, 2008).

Her work in number theory was significant not only because of the technical skill it required but also because it demonstrated her ability to engage with and advance the work of her male contemporaries. Germain's correspondence with Gauss is particularly noteworthy; Gauss was initially unaware that Monsieur LeBlanc was a woman. When he discovered her identity, he expressed his admiration for her intellect and perseverance, recognising her as an equal in the world of mathematics.

While Germain's contributions to number theory were impressive, her work on elasticity theory arguably had an even more profound impact on both mathematics and applied sciences. In her study of elasticity, Germain extended the work of Leonhard Euler and others, generalising their theories to two-dimensional surfaces. Her work focused on the mathematical modelling of how materials bend and flex—an area of study that is crucial for understanding the strength and stability of structures.

Germain developed what is now known as Germain's equation, a formula that relates the curvature of a surface to its elastic properties. This was a significant advancement in the mathematical theory of elasticity, particularly because it laid the groundwork for later developments in structural engineering, materials science, and even modern physics. Her work was recognised by the Paris Academy of Sciences, where she became the first woman to win a prize from the institution for her contributions to the theory of elasticity.

Elasticity, at its core, is a concept that explains how materials stretch, bend, or deform when a force is applied to them and then return to their original shape when the force is removed. Imagine you have a rubber band—when you pull on it, it stretches (Musielak, 2020; Sadd, 2005). When you let go, it snaps back to its original size. Euler had developed theories about the elasticity of bars—essentially how one-dimensional objects (like beams) would bend under force. Germain's genius lay in her ability to take these ideas further and extend them to two-dimensional surfaces. This was groundbreaking because the world around us is full of complex, curved surfaces, and understanding how these surfaces behave under stress is crucial in fields ranging from architecture to materials science.

In her work, Germain sought to generalise Euler's principles of elasticity and in doing so made elasticity more applicable to practical problems rather than hypothetical arguments. One of her key contributions was relating the concept of elasticity to the sum of the principal curvatures of a surface. For any point on a surface, there are two principal curvatures, which describe how the surface curves in two perpendicular directions. The sum of these curvatures gives you a measure of how the surface is curving at that point. Then, Germain proposed that the elasticity of a surface could be described in terms of these curvatures. Essentially, she was saying that how a surface deforms under stress is related to how it curves naturally.

This idea was a significant step forward because it provided a mathematical framework for understanding how complex shapes (like shells or membranes) would behave when forces were applied to them. Her equations were among the first to describe what we now understand as the elastic behaviour of materials in two dimensions. Understanding elasticity is fundamental in many modern engineering and scientific applications. Elasticity theory helps in designing buildings, bridges, and other structures. Engineers need to know how materials will bend and stretch under loads to ensure that structures are both strong and flexible. Modern materials like polymers, metals, and composites are studied using principles of elasticity to ensure they can withstand forces without breaking. Elasticity is crucial in designing prosthetics and medical implants and in understanding how biological tissues like skin and arteries stretch and return to shape.

Sophie Germain's exploration of elasticity laid the groundwork for understanding how materials behave under stress, which is crucial in a wide range of modern industries. Here's how her discoveries resonate:

1. Germain's work is directly relevant to materials science. The principles of elasticity are foundational in the development of new materials, whether for creating stronger, more durable fabrics for fashion or designing advanced composites used in aerospace engineering. Understanding how materials deform under load helps scientists and engineers develop everything from lightweight sports gear to impact-resistant smartphone cases. When we think about the latest tech gadgets, the design and durability of these devices owe much to the study of material elasticity.

2. Elasticity is closely related to fracture mechanics, which is the study of how and why materials fail. This is particularly important in fields like civil engineering, where the safety of buildings, bridges, and other structures depends on understanding how materials will perform under stress. Knowing how to predict and prevent material failure is key to engineering. Whether designing a skyscraper or a sustainable water pipeline, Sophie Germain's work on elasticity provides the theoretical background needed to ensure that these structures can withstand the forces they'll encounter.

3. In biosciences, the principles of elasticity are crucial for understanding how tissues and organs behave. In biomedical engineering careers or even as a surgeon, it's vital to know how biological tissues stretch, compress, and return to their original shapes. For example, when designing prosthetics or medical implants, understanding the elasticity of materials ensures that these devices move naturally with the body, providing comfort and functionality to patients. In regenerative medicine, elasticity helps in designing scaffolds that can support tissue growth and mimic the mechanical properties of natural tissues.

4. Elasticity is a key factor in product development for cosmetology and dermatology. Elasticity affects how skin responds to ageing, how cosmetic procedures work, and even how products are applied and absorbed. Understanding the elasticity of skin can help to develop better anti-aging treatments, design more effective surgical techniques, or create innovative products that improve skin health and appearance. Germain's principles of elasticity are indirectly at play when choosing materials for applications like facial masks, stretchable beauty patches, or even in the formulation of creams that adapt to the skin's natural movements.

5. The design and manufacture of prosthetic limbs or orthotic devices makes elasticity a critical concept. The materials used in prosthetics must be carefully chosen to mimic the elasticity of natural limbs, ensuring that the prosthetic is both functional and comfortable. Germain's work helps inform how these materials are selected and tested, ensuring that they can withstand repeated stresses while providing a realistic range of motion. Engineers and technicians in this field draw on principles of elasticity to create devices that enhance the quality of life for individuals with physical disabilities.

6. Surgical engineering tools and devices must be designed with a deep understanding of material elasticity. Surgical instruments need to be strong yet flexible, capable of precise movements without breaking under pressure. This is especially important in minimally invasive surgery, where the instruments must navigate the delicate tissues of the body without causing damage. Germain's insights into elasticity help engineers design tools that can perform with the precision required for modern surgical procedures, ensuring better outcomes for patients.

What can women today learn from Wang Zhenyi and Sophie Germain as they challenge the status quo of technology? Their stories emphasise the importance of resilience, self-education, and persistence in the face of adversity. Both women were largely self-taught and sought knowledge beyond the boundaries imposed on them. They were creative problem-solvers who found ways to engage with male-dominated fields by leveraging the resources available to them—Wang through her grandfather's library and Germain through correspondence under a pseudonym. In today's rapidly evolving technological landscape, where women are still underrepresented, their stories underscore the need for women to seek out alternative pathways to education, mentorship, and opportunity (Sampson, 1990; Kett, 1994).

Moreover, their legacy teaches us that breaking into male-dominated spaces often requires a unique combination of passion and innovation. In the same way that Wang used simple everyday objects to simulate celestial phenomena and Germain devised creative methods to participate in academic discourse, modern women can find innovative ways to contribute to and shape the technology industry. Their lives demonstrate that determination, creativity, and a refusal to accept limitations are essential in making strides in fields traditionally closed to women.

Several pioneering women in the 18th and 19th centuries, such as Nicole-Reine Lepaute, Wang Zhenyi, and Huang Lü, made significant contributions to astronomy that helped redefine humanity's understanding of the cosmos. Their work, grounded in observation and calculation, helped decode celestial phenomena and brought precision to a field previously filled with speculation. Through their remarkable achievements, these women altered not only the way we perceived celestial mechanics but also, in a broader sense, how we viewed our place in the universe.

Comets, unlike the predictable movements of planets and stars, appeared suddenly in the night sky and followed irregular, often highly elliptical orbits. This unpredictability made them seem mysterious and unsettling, as ancient civilisations were accustomed to the regular cycles of celestial bodies. The sudden appearance of a comet, often with a bright tail, was seen as an omen because it disrupted the perceived order of the heavens.

Throughout history, comets were often associated with catastrophic events. When a comet appeared, it was frequently followed by disasters such as wars, famines, plagues, or the deaths of prominent figures. This led to the belief that comets were celestial messengers of impending doom. For example, Halley's Comet was linked to the Battle of Hastings in 1066, where it was said to have foretold the fall of King Harold II and the Norman Conquest of England.

Many cultures viewed comets as signs of divine wrath or warnings from the gods. In the absence of scientific understanding, people turned to religion and superstition to explain natural phenomena. The Bible and other religious texts often depicted unusual celestial events as signs from God, reinforcing the idea that comets were portents of significant, often negative, changes. Even respected scholars of the past, such as the Roman historian Pliny the Elder and the philosopher Seneca, contributed to the idea that comets were unnatural and possibly dangerous. Their writings, widely read and respected, spread the belief that comets were extraordinary and potentially harmful events.

My experience of comets was watching Hale-Bopp travel to *perihelion*, or the nearest point of orbit to the sun (which makes the comet brighter and larger to the naked eye), over our skies during an 18-month period from 1995 to 1997. Living in Germany and travelling around Europe in my tiny car, alone, mostly, it loomed large over me like a spectre. I remember a morning after sleeping in my car at a ferry point and seeing it at dawn, hanging in the sky. I could completely understand why comets such as the great comet of 1811, Hale-Bopp and Halley's comet; arguably the most famous comet in our recorded history, wielded such power upon us. However, it's with great sadness that Nicole-Reine Lepaute was not around to see the great comets since completing her work, she would have loved them.

Born Nicole-Reine Étable de la Brière on January 5, 1723, in the Kingdom of France, she came from a family with connections to the French court. Her husband, Jean-André Lepaute, was a royal clockmaker, which gave her access to a network of scientific minds. Her interest in astronomy and mathematics was likely nurtured through her exposure to her husband's work, which involved precise timekeeping—an essential element in astronomical calculations. One of Lepaute's most significant contributions came in her collaboration with the astronomer Joseph-Jérôme de Lalande. Together, they undertook the monumental task of predicting the return of Halley's Comet in 1759. In the late 17th Century, Edmond Halley had predicted the comet's return based on its previous appearances in 1531, 1607, and 1682, but the exact timing was uncertain due to gravitational influences from the planets, particularly Jupiter and Saturn.

Lepaute, along with Lalande and the mathematician Alexis Clairaut, worked tirelessly on the complex calculations required to account for this instability, trying to make unpredictability predictable. Lepaute's role in this project was substantial, as she spent months performing the intricate calculations needed to predict the comet's path. The team's successful prediction of Halley's Comet's perihelion in March 1759 was a significant triumph for astronomy and cemented Lepaute's reputation as a skilled mathematician. More notable because Halley, who was dead at this point, had predicted its return in 1758.

Lepaute was also instrumental in the prediction of solar eclipses. In 1759, she calculated the timing and visibility of a solar eclipse for the region of Paris. Her work was published in the prestigious *Connaissance des Temps*, an astronomical almanac, further solidifying her standing in the scientific community. Her accurate predictions were crucial for both scientific observations and public understanding of these celestial events, which were often viewed with a mix of fear and fascination.

Her contributions went well beyond her calculations, because why stop there? She also participated in translating and editing scientific works, including those of the astronomer

Tobias Mayer. Her ability to communicate complex scientific ideas in a clear and accessible manner made her an important figure in the dissemination of scientific knowledge during the Enlightenment.

Despite her significant achievements, Lepaute's work was often overshadowed by her male counterparts, but not by her husband and it's probably that his standing as royal timekeeper, they would have had more access than most to technology such as clocks, astrolabes, orreries, and other mechanical devices. These tools would have complemented her mathematical calculations, providing a practical way to cross-check her work and refine her predictions. For those who worked closely with her, such as Lalande, simply acknowledged her brilliance and dedication. Lalande himself credited her with performing much of the laborious calculations necessary for their collaborative projects, acknowledging her as an indispensable partner in their scientific endeavours (Bertrand, 2006).

Lepaute's service to cracking the codes of tough formulae and developing or dissecting tables of rich numbers and patterns makes her another in a long line of computers; at a time when such things did not exist. We will look closer at human computers later, but Lepaute's dedication to this came from a curiosity which, when enabled by advocates around her, allowed her to realise some of her dreams. Sure, her husband was a royal timekeeper, but that doesn't make her unremarkable; but it does make her a trophy and perhaps that isn't the road that she wanted to travel. Thank the universe she didn't.

As Wang Zhenyi, in 18th century China had demonstrated how lunar and solar eclipses worked through her innovative experiments using simple objects such as mirrors and lamps, Lepaute looked at mathematical tables to elicit a response to her hypothesis. These experiments not only showed her grasp of scientific concepts but also made the knowledge accessible and understandable to a broader audience. Huang Lü, in the early 19th century, developed a telescope with primitive photographic capabilities, giving people an unprecedented view of the stars and planets Collectively, their work shifted humanity's gaze from an Earth-centric worldview to one that recognised the broader, dynamic nature of the universe.

These astronomers helped humanity transition from a world where celestial events were often regarded as omens or divine acts to a more scientific and structured understanding of the cosmos. Lepaute's precise predictions of Halley's Comet showed that comets were regular phenomena rather than the end of the world. Wang's experiments demystified eclipses, removing the fear that often accompanied them, and showed that they were natural occurrences that could be explained and predicted. Huang's development of telescopic technology offered a new way of observing the heavens, bringing distant objects into clearer view and enhancing our ability to map the skies. These advancements allowed humanity to see the universe as a system governed by natural laws, subject to observation and analysis, rather than one controlled solely by the whims of the gods.

What is particularly striking when we compare the work of these early astronomers to the later chapters of this book is how they set the scene for XR (extended reality) technologies. The astronomers of the past looked up to the heavens, observing and calculating the positions of celestial bodies from their physical place on Earth. Their tools—telescopes, astrolabes, and mathematical formulas—were all designed to extend their senses beyond the limitations of human perception. In a very real sense, these women were using the technology of their time to bridge the gap between human perception and the cosmic reality, creating a form of extended reality within their own capabilities. Wang used tools to explain her principles, Huang created her own equipment, and Lepaute was the computer divining spatial calculations to predict occurrences. In essence, the work of Lepaute, Wang Zhenyi, and Huang represents humanity's first forays into expanding our understanding of the world beyond the immediacy of our perception. Their efforts in astronomy were aimed at understanding the external cosmos, while today's XR technologies bring this sense of exploration inward, creating new realities within our world. Both endeavours—whether decoding the stars or creating immersive digital environments—stem from the same drive: the human desire to push boundaries, extend our sensory limits, and understand more than we are naturally equipped to perceive. In this sense, the work of all these women to this point provides evidence of computational groundwork laid for the scientific and technological innovations that would follow, leading us to the great beyond, because we are not done with discovery.

But we must talk about Ada, mustn't we? For me as an avid technologist, Ada is problematic. I really didn't want to put her in the driving seat of this book. As a role model, Ada is overused. Ada Lovelace was my only role model growing up on a council estate in the 1970s because she was discussed once on a TV show called Tomorrow's World. She was barely mentioned in school. Even in 1986 when Computer Studies classes were introduced into our comprehensive school, she was never mentioned. So, imagine mine and every woman of my age's surprise when we discovered that she had a teacher who was also a woman.

Mary Somerville (1780–1872), a Scottish polymath, made profound contributions to mathematics and astronomy. Mary Somerville's background and largely self-taught education had a profound impact on her approach to learning, lecturing, and her advocacy for other women in her community. Born in 1780 to a modest family in Scotland, Somerville's early life was far removed from the formal education that was typically available to men of her social standing. Her family was not wealthy, but they were landed, and her access to education was sporadic, mostly entailed by her parents' desire for her to learn something "it was thought sufficient for the girls to be able to read the Bible; very few even learnt writing" (Somerville, 1874) in a society where women's education was often neglected or focused solely on domestic skills.

Somerville's early education was accelerated by her uncles; her father, though considered living in genteel poverty, received "naval pay [though] meagre, despite his rise through the ranks" (Somerville, 1874). Her mother sold milk and vegetables from their homestead. Mary's father sent her to an expensive school, but each time she returned, the system would force her back into the expectations that most women of the 18th century would experience. Needlework? The Bible? The boys were learning Latin! She divulged to her uncle that she was secretly learning Latin, and this was where her story began. Instead of being chided for reading by the sewing teacher, she suddenly had access to elementary books on algebra and geometry. She spent the summer learning to play the piano. In addition to the piano, she learned Greek so she could read Xenophon and Herodotus in their original versions (Somerville, 1874).

She was largely self-taught, driven by an insatiable curiosity and a passion for knowledge. This self-directed learning fostered a deep understanding and appreciation for the subjects she studied. Her education was eclectic, spanning various disciplines, which allowed her to make connections between different fields of study and still grab the basics of manners and curtseying (which would have been of the utmost importance at the time but today seems so ridiculous). This interdisciplinary approach was evident in her later works, where she skilfully combined mathematics, astronomy, and physics to explain complex scientific concepts. Studying Euclid's *Elements* to gather perspective on astronomy and mechanical science gave Somerville an opportunity to walk through an open door. She wanted to understand *Elements of Navigation* by John Robertson, she wanted to visit laboratories, and she wanted to know more about everything. As a woman, this wasn't entirely possible. Even during her first marriage, those old expectations of what it was to be a woman in polite society reared their ugly heads again. Her husband was "possessed in full the prejudice against learned women which was common at that time" (Somerville, 1874).

In 1807 her husband died. Leaving her with a healthy inheritance gave her some freedom to pursue her interests as well as to nurse her children. Her world grew once more through trigonometry, natural philosophy, and solving complex equations. She adopted differential calculus, which was still evolving as a branch of mathematics; but it was through her correspondence with William Wallace, father of the eidograph—a fixed-point mechanical tool for copying writing—that she finally found her voice.

Her book, *The Mechanism of the Heavens* (1831), was not her first, but it was her most famous. This book was a translation and expansion of Pierre-Simon Laplace's work on celestial mechanics. Laplace's original work, published in five volumes between 1799 and 1825, was highly technical and mathematical, intended for an audience of experts in astronomy and mathematics. Somerville's *The Mechanism of the Heavens* made this complex material accessible to a broader audience, including those without advanced training in mathematics. This is music to the ears of anyone who wants to feel inspired and motivated but is afraid to take those first steps into a discipline.

Somerville's book translated Laplace's dense and difficult mathematical work into English, but it was more than just a translation. She reorganised and clarified the material, making it more understandable and systematically explaining the principles of celestial mechanics. The book covered the laws of motion and gravitation that govern the movements of celestial bodies, including planets, moons, and comets. It addressed topics such as the stability of the solar system, the motion of the planets, and the perturbations (deviations) caused by their mutual gravitational influences. So far, we've focused heavily on astronomy and some mathematics, but this might be the first example of pure mathematical theory for the purpose of practical astronomy. I'm not even sure whether Somerville cared for the practicalities of the heavens over the wonder of mathematical principles. "In mathematics, there is a necessity to be right; it is the only science where error is inexcusable because every calculation may be tested" (Somerville, 1874). We know how it feels to have a deep and underlying passion for something. Being able to apply ourselves to the problem enthusiastically is an almost trope by default, but at the time Mary was learning and being excited by maths, it was still so unusual. "Mathematics opened up a new world to me; I found it full of beauty and enchantment. I had a profound sense of the wonderful power of analysis, and of the application of abstract reasoning to the real phenomena of nature" (Somerville, 1874).

Somerville's work went beyond mere translation; she provided her own insights and clarifications, often expanding on Laplace's ideas to make them clearer. This not only made the text more accessible but also demonstrated Somerville's deep understanding of the subject matter. Her ability to connect abstract mathematical theories with real-world phenomena helped bridge the gap between theoretical mathematics and its practical applications. By doing so, she made it possible for others, including women who had been excluded from formal scientific education, to engage with these complex ideas (Osen, 1974).

The work became a foundational textbook for students of mathematics and physics, bridging the gap between the theoretical mathematics of the time and its applications to the real world. Somerville's skill lay in her ability to make complex mathematical ideas accessible and understandable, synthesising existing knowledge and pushing the boundaries of what could be achieved through analytical thinking. Her contributions to the understanding of electromagnetism and her insights into the connection between light and heat further underscored the real-world applications of abstract mathematics. Her work could be found and can still be found at the University of Cambridge and from James Clerk Maxwell, one of the most significant physicists of the 19th century, who would later develop the theory of electromagnetism; today her impact and legacy are well documented (Howell, 1981).

Mary played a pivotal role in making mathematics accessible during a time when the discipline was largely confined to the realms of academia and predominantly male scholars, as we've already learned. Her ability to simplify complex ideas and present them in a way that was understandable to a broader audience not only demystified mathematics but also paved the way for future generations of women in science, including Ada Lovelace, but please be under no illusion, Ada would not have been the only woman Mary Somerville inspired.

As a kid, I would watch a limited TV series on the BBC. It was called *The Royal Institution Christmas Lectures,* and it played host to Carl Sagan, Heinz Wolff, David Attenborough, and latterly Susan Greenfield (the first woman to present the Royal Institution Christmas Lectures broadcast). However, it was Leonard Maunder, a man we have so quickly forgotten, but who sadly taught me more in that lecture series about jet propulsion and quantum mechanics than my dad ever did in our whole time together. Maunder, who had that Mary Somerville swagger and who was able to cut through the Newtonian laws and get me directly to Frank Whittle.

The Royal Institution, established in 1799, is a prestigious scientific organisation in London, dedicated to promoting science through public lectures and research throughout the world. At the time, it was dominated by male scientists, and it was extremely rare for a woman to be invited to speak. Somerville's invitation to address the Royal Institution in 1826 was a significant milestone, as it marked one of the earliest instances of a woman being recognised for her scientific contributions in such a prominent and public forum. The fact that she was invited to lecture speaks volumes about the respect she had earned in the scientific community, despite the widespread gender biases of the time.

When Somerville stood before the members of the Royal Institution, she would have faced an audience that was not only predominantly male but also comprised of some of the leading scientific minds of the day. These were men who were not accustomed to hearing scientific discourse from a woman. Somerville, however, was no ordinary woman; she had already established herself as a formidable intellect through her work on *The Mechanism of the Heavens,* which had been highly praised for its clarity and depth.

Her presentation likely focused on the complex mathematical and astronomical concepts that she had mastered and translated in her works. She would have needed to present these ideas in a way that was not only accurate but also compelling to engage an audience that might have been sceptical of a woman's ability to contribute to such advanced fields. The social pressures on Somerville would have been immense. She was not only representing herself but also, in many ways, all women who aspired to participate in the scientific community. Any misstep could have been used to justify the exclusion of women from such intellectual pursuits. However, by all accounts, Somerville's lecture was well-received, further solidifying her reputation as a leading scientific thinker.

Addressing the Royal Institution would have been a moment of both personal triumph and broader social significance. Somerville's success in this setting helped to challenge the prevailing notions of women's intellectual capacities and paved the way for future generations of women in science. Her ability to communicate complex ideas effectively to a learned audience was a testament to her skill as both a mathematician and a teacher, and it underscored the importance of her contributions to the scientific community of her time. And I have so much FOMO that I was not only not there, but that I have never been intelligent enough to deliver a lecture on video game design.

Somerville's experience as a self-taught scholar who had to overcome societal barriers undoubtedly shaped her views on women's education and their role in intellectual life. Throughout her life, she advocated for women's access to education and supported other women in their scholarly pursuits. She was keenly aware of the challenges faced by women who wished to engage in intellectual activities and used her influence to encourage greater acceptance of women in science and mathematics. She mentored younger women scientists and corresponded with them, offering advice and encouragement. Her support extended beyond direct mentorship; she also championed the cause of women's education more broadly, arguing that women should have the same opportunities as men to study and contribute to scientific knowledge. Her advocacy helped pave the way for future generations of women in science, demonstrating that intellectual achievement was not limited by gender (Ogilvie, 1986).

REFERENCES

Bertrand, G. (2006) Le laboratoire montagnard de l'astronome Lalande. Du *Voyage en Italie* à ses comptes rendus dans le *Journal des savants* (1769-1789), dans Sophie Linon-Chipon et Daniela Vaj, dir., *Relations savantes, voyages et discours scientifiques*, Paris, Presses de l'Université de Paris-Sorbonne (PUPS), Collection Imago Mundi, pp. 299–325.

de Lalande, J.-J. (n.d.). *Bibliographie astronomique, avec l'histoire de l'astronomie depuis 1781 jusqu'à 1802*. L'Imprimerie de la République. [online] Available at: https://archive.org/stream/bibliographieast00lala#page/676/mode/2up [Accessed September 23, 2024]

Del Centina, A. (2008) 'Unpublished manuscripts of Sophie Germain and a revaluation of her work on Fermat's last theorem', *Archive for History of Exact Sciences*, 62(4), pp. 349–392.

Grier, D.A. (2005) *When computers were human*. Princeton University Press. [online] Available at: https://books.google.com/books?id=YTcDAQAAQBAJ&pg=PA82 [Accessed September 23, 2024]

Howell, K. (1981) *Mary Somerville and the cultivation of science, 1815–1840*. Dordrecht: Springer.

Kett, J.F. (1994) *Pursuit of knowledge under difficulties: From self-improvement to adult education in America, 1750-1990*. Redwood City: Stanford University Press.

Ko, D. (1994) *Teachers of the inner chambers: Women and culture in seventeenth-century China*. Stanford University Press.

Li, L. (1998) *Wang Zhenyi and the Cosmos: A life in Chinese astronomy*. Harvard East Asian Monographs.

Liu, L. (2011) 'Women in Chinese astronomy: Wang Zhenyi', *Journal of Chinese Studies*, 58(2), pp. 315–335.

Musielak, D. (2020) *Sophie Germain: Revolutionary mathematician*. Cham, Switzerland: Springer International Publishing.

Ogilvie, M. (1986) *Women in science: A historical perspective*. Cambridge, MA: The MIT Press.

Osen, L.M. (1974) *Women in mathematics*. Cambridge, MA: The MIT Press.

Sadd, M.H. (2005) *Elasticity: Theory, applications, and numerics*. San Diego, CA: Elsevier.

Sampson, J.H. (1990) 'Sophie Germain and the theory of numbers', *Archive for History of Exact Sciences*, 41(2), pp. 157–161.

Somerville, M. (1874) *Personal recollections, from early life to old age, of Mary Somerville*. London: John Murray.

CHAPTER 3

The Year Without a Summer

IN THE FINAL DECADE of the 18th century, as the streets of Paris buzzed with the fervour of revolution, another, quieter revolution was taking shape in the minds and hearts of women across Europe. This revolution wasn't about overthrowing kings or toppling empires; it was about dismantling the deeply entrenched societal norms that had, for centuries, confined women to the domestic sphere. At the forefront of this intellectual upheaval was Mary Wollstonecraft, a woman whose ideas were as radical as they were necessary. Born in 1759, into a world where a woman's worth was often measured by her ability to manage a household or secure a good marriage, Wollstonecraft refused to accept the limitations imposed upon her gender. Instead, she challenged these norms head-on, championing the revolutionary notion that women, too, had the right—and indeed the obligation—to engage with the world as intellectual equals to men (Gordon, 2005).

Wollstonecraft's seminal work, *A Vindication of the Rights of Woman* (1792), was nothing short of a clarion call for the education and intellectual empowerment of women. At a time when women were largely excluded from formal education and expected to focus on domestic duties, she argued that women should be taught to develop their reasoning and critical thinking skills, enabling them to contribute meaningfully to society. "Taught from their infancy that beauty is woman's sceptre," she wrote, "the mind shapes itself to the body, and, roaming round its gilt cage, only seeks to adorn its prison" (Wollstonecraft, 1792, p. 37). This metaphor of the mind as a caged bird perfectly captures the frustration and untapped potential of women who were denied the opportunity to cultivate their intellectual faculties. Her argument was revolutionary: she claimed that the perceived inferiority of women was not a natural condition, but rather the result of inadequate education and limited opportunities. This was a bold stance, and it provided a philosophical justification for the inclusion of women in intellectual pursuits, including science and mathematics (Taylor, 2003).

The echoes of Wollstonecraft's struggle are still heard in parts of our world where women continue to fight for equal education and rights, even as we fast forward to 2024. Her advocacy for women's education was more than just a plea for fairness; it was a strategic vision for the betterment of society. She believed that an educated woman could not only improve

DOI: 10.1201/9781003566465-3

her own life but also contribute to the moral and intellectual improvement of her children and her community (Todd, 2006). This idea—that the education of women was essential to the progress of society—would resonate through the centuries, influencing generations of women who sought to break free from the confines of their "gilt cages" and engage with the world of ideas.

As we reflect on the life and legacy of Wollstonecraft, it's impossible not to be inspired by her courage, her intellect, and her unwavering belief in the potential of women. She dared to imagine a world where women could be more than what society expected of them—a world where they could be thinkers, scientists, and leaders. And in doing so, she not only paved the way for her daughter, Mary Shelley, to become the "goddess of science fiction," but also for countless other women to step into roles that had long been denied to them. Wollstonecraft's revolution was one of the mind, and its impact continues to be felt in every woman who, today, refuses to be confined by society's expectations and instead chooses to engage with the world as an equal, with intellect and ambition as her guide (Gordon, 2005).

Wollstonecraft's legacy did not end with her own contributions: her work laid the foundation for the broader feminist movement, which would continue to fight for equality and inclusion in all aspects of life, including science and technology. She believed that society would benefit from the contributions of educated women, a belief that has been borne out as more women have entered and excelled in STEM fields (Taylor, 2003). Women like Mary Somerville and Sophie Germain—pioneers in their respective fields—were able to pursue their intellectual interests partly because the cultural attitudes towards women's education were slowly changing, influenced by thinkers like Wollstonecraft (Osen, 1974).

When researching this book, I have been keen to shine a light on everyday women doing extraordinary things in technology. We read about so many, and yet, the penny never really dropped for me until this era. So much had already happened for women in technology, and yet, just a short era gave me all my role models and my lust for learning and expression.

The impact of Wollstonecraft's ideas continued to ripple through time, influencing not just her daughter Mary Shelley but also future generations of women who would push the boundaries of what was possible. The year following the cataclysmic eruption of Mount Tambora in Indonesia (5 April 1815) plunged the world into an unexpected and severe climate crisis (Wood, 2014). Imagine waking up to a world where the sun is perpetually shrouded by thick, suffocating haze, and the once predictable rhythms of nature are thrown into disarray. This was the reality of 1816, a year that history would come to be remembered as The Year Without a Summer (Wood, 2014). Mount Tambora's explosive force was not an isolated event; it was the sixth major eruption among a series of volcanic activities along the Pacific Rim, along with the 1812 eruption of La Soufrière on Saint Vincent in the Caribbean. However, Tambora's eruption was particularly devastating, ejecting thousands of tons of sulphur dioxide and other aerosols into the stratosphere. These high-altitude gases acted like a giant sunshade, reflecting sunlight and causing a global temperature drop of approximately 1 degree Celsius (Wood, 2014).

This period of cooling exacerbated an already precarious situation, as the Earth had been gradually cooling since the 14th century, a trend known as the Little Ice Age (Fagan, 2000). The abrupt temperature drop in the North Atlantic disrupted weather patterns, leading to catastrophic agricultural failures. Crops that once thrived now withered, leading to widespread food shortages and famine across the northern hemisphere. The human cost was staggering, with an estimated 92,000 lives lost directly or indirectly due to the eruption and its aftermath. Communities that once relied on predictable harvests were now grappling with uncertainty and despair, as the natural world seemed to turn against them (Wood, 2014).

Amidst this global turmoil, the end of the Napoleonic Wars provided a temporary respite, allowing a unique convergence of minds. In the secluded Villa Diodati on the shores of Lake Geneva, a group of writers, poets, and intellectuals sought refuge from the relentless storms and eerie darkness that characterised the summer of 1816. This mansion, damp and foreboding, became the perfect setting for what would become one of the most significant literary gatherings in history (Hindle, 2006) Among the guests were the charismatic and often controversial Lord Byron, the brilliant and imaginative Percy Bysshe Shelley, Mary Wollstonecraft Godwin—who would later be known as Mary Shelley—and Claire Clairmont, Mary's stepsister and Lord Byron's lover (Hindle, 2006)

The scene at Villa Diodati was not just one of literary creation, but of intellectual exchange, driven by the same ideals of curiosity and exploration that Mary Wollstonecraft had championed decades earlier. Lord Byron's audacious challenge to pen a ghost story set the stage for a creative revolution, but it also set the stage for the exploration of themes that reached beyond mere fiction. The mansion, with its dark, stormy nights and the oppressive weight of impending famine outside, became a crucible for creativity, innovation, and surprisingly, technology (St. Clair, 2004). The darkness outside mirrored the depth of the stories being conceived within, as each writer delved into the unknown, exploring themes of creation, responsibility, and the ethical limits of human ambition.

Mary Shelley, still a young woman with a sharp intellect and a keen sense of curiosity, took up Lord Byron's challenge with fervour. Drawing inspiration from the scientific debates of her time, particularly the burgeoning field of galvanism—which explored the possibility of reanimating dead tissue through electrical currents—Shelley began to craft a story that would transcend the boundaries of traditional ghost tales. The result was *Frankenstein; or, The Modern Prometheus* (1818), a novel that not only pioneered the science fiction genre but also served as a profound commentary on the ethical implications of unchecked scientific advancement (Mellor, 1988).

The science of galvanism, as developed by Italian physician and physicist Luigi Galvani, was a key influence on Shelley's work. Galvani's experiments began in the 1780s when he noticed that the muscles of dead frogs twitched when struck by a spark from an electrostatic machine. He hypothesised that this reaction was due to what he called "animal electricity," a vital force inherent in the tissue of animals (Piccolino, 1998). This was a revolutionary idea at the time, suggesting that electricity was not just a physical phenomenon but also a fundamental part of biological life (Piccolino, 1998).

To test his hypothesis, Galvani conducted various experiments where he used different metals to connect the nerves and muscles of frogs. He observed that when the metals completed a circuit, the muscles contracted, even in the absence of an external electrical source. This led Galvani to believe that the tissues themselves were generating the electricity required for the contraction (Piccolino, 1998).

Galvani's work sparked interest across Europe and inspired other scientists to explore the relationship between electricity and biology. One of the most significant figures in this area was Alessandro Volta, an Italian physicist who disagreed with Galvani's concept. Volta argued that the electrical currents observed in Galvani's experiments were generated by the contact of different metals, rather than by the animal tissues themselves. This debate led Volta to develop the Voltaic Pile in 1800, the first chemical battery capable of producing a steady electrical current, which became the foundation for modern electrical batteries (Piccolino, 1998).

One of the most direct influences on Shelley's understanding of galvanism would have been the public demonstrations and experiments conducted by Giovanni Aldini, the nephew of Luigi Galvani. Aldini was known for his dramatic public demonstrations in which he applied galvanic currents to the corpses of animals and humans, causing the muscles to contract and creating the illusion of life (Bresadola, 1998). Aldini's experiments, particularly his attempts to reanimate the body of an executed criminal in 1803, were sensationalised in the press and captured the public's imagination. The idea that electricity could restore life—or at least mimic it—was a powerful and disturbing one, and it would have left a lasting impression on the minds of those who read about it or attended the demonstrations (Bresadola, 1998).

Humphry Davy, a prominent chemist and inventor, was another figure whose work may have influenced *Frankenstein*. Davy was a pioneer in the field of electrochemistry, and his lectures on chemistry were widely attended and discussed in intellectual circles (Knight, 1992). Davy's work on electricity and its effects on chemical reactions would have been known to Mary Shelley, especially through the influence of her husband and other contemporaries who admired Davy's work (Mellor, 1988). In Davy's published lectures and works, he often speculated on the nature of life and the possibility of using electricity to manipulate or even create life, ideas that directly resonate with the themes of *Frankenstein* (Knight, 1992). His speculations about the future of chemistry and the possibilities it might unlock would have been particularly intriguing to someone like Shelley, who was interested in the boundaries between life, death, and the ethical implications of scientific progress (Knight, 1992).

While Galvani's original theory has been refined and expanded upon, the foundational idea that electrical signals are crucial to biological processes remains central to modern science. Today, the principles of galvanism are applied in various medical technologies, including defibrillators (which use electric shocks to restore normal heart rhythm) and electrostimulation devices used in physical therapy to maintain muscle tone in paralysed patients (Bresadola, 1998). Additionally, the study of bioelectricity continues to be a vital field of research, with implications for understanding neural networks, cardiac function, and even the potential for regenerative medicine (Piccolino, 1998).

This exploration of life, electricity, and ethical responsibility was not merely a reflection of the era's fascination with technological progress; it was a deep, philosophical inquiry into the moral responsibilities of the creator. Shelley's *Frankenstein* delved into these questions with a narrative that questioned whether humanity was prepared to handle the consequences of its own ingenuity. The Monster, a being brought to life without regard for ethical considerations, symbolised the potential dangers of technological advancement when divorced from compassion and foresight (Mellor, 1988). This theme remains strikingly relevant today, as we navigate the complexities of artificial intelligence, genetic engineering, and other cutting-edge technologies (Chin-Yee, 2014).

The convergence at Villa Diodati was not just a moment of literary genesis; it was a testament to the resilience and creativity that can emerge from adversity. Wollstonecraft's legacy of advocating for women's education and intellectual empowerment found a powerful echo in Shelley's groundbreaking work. Despite the personal tragedies and societal constraints she faced, Shelley could harness her intellect and creativity to produce a work that continues to inspire and provoke thought (Gordon, 2005).

For today's women, the story of The Year Without a Summer and the creation of *Frankenstein* serves as a powerful reminder of the potential that lies within each of us to transform challenges into opportunities for innovation and expression. Just as Shelley used the oppressive darkness of 1816 to illuminate profound truths about humanity and technology, we can draw strength from historical figures like Wollstonecraft and Shelley to pursue their passions in science, technology, and beyond. The narrative of these pioneering women underscores the importance of perseverance, intellectual curiosity, and the relentless pursuit of knowledge—even in the face of seemingly insurmountable obstacles (Todd, 2006).

The environmental impact of that year not only influenced the literary masterpieces of its time but also set the stage for future advancements in technology and science. The intellectual ecosystem fostered by Wollstonecraft's advocacy and Shelley's literary genius created a fertile ground for future women like Ada Lovelace to emerge as pioneers (Gordon, 2005). Ada Lovelace was directly influenced by the intellectual legacy left by her predecessors (Toole, 1992). She was the product of the time. So, perhaps, the ability to see beyond immediate challenges and envision a future shaped by innovation is a thread that connects these remarkable women across generations (Essinger, 2013).

As we reflect on the events of 1816 and their enduring impact, it becomes clear that periods of crisis and uncertainty can serve as catalysts for profound creativity and progress. The collaboration and intellectual synergy that emerged at Villa Diodati demonstrate the power of collective effort and the importance of providing spaces where diverse voices can come together to challenge the status quo (Hindle, 2006). For women navigating a rapidly changing world, this historical insight offers valuable lessons on the importance of community, resilience, and the courage to push boundaries (Todd, 2006).

What might have begun as a simple contest of literary prowess became one of the most important moments in the history of literature. This dreary summer would give birth to two monumental works of gothic fiction. Polidori would write *The Vampyre,* and Mary Wollstonecraft Godwin—soon to be known as Mary Shelley—would pen what would become *Frankenstein; or, The Modern Prometheus*. In the cold, damp, and dark of that endless summer, Shelley crafted a story that transcended the genre of ghost tales, delving into themes of science, technology, and the hubris of creation (St. Clair, 2004).

In the dim, storm-laden atmosphere of the early 19th century, where the boundaries of science and nature were being tested in ways previously unimaginable, a young Shelley crafted a narrative that would echo through the ages—a story that not only reflected the technological advancements of her time but also delved into the deep ethical quandaries those advancements stirred. *Frankenstein; or, The Modern Prometheus* is not just a tale of horror but a profound exploration of the double-edged sword that is technological progress (Mellor, 1988). It is a story that resonates as powerfully today as it did when it was first penned, speaking to the very heart of what it means to wield the power of creation (Hustis, 2003).

The novel centres on Victor Frankenstein, a scientist driven by an insatiable thirst for knowledge, who dares to cross the ultimate boundary: the creation of life. Armed with the burgeoning science of galvanism, which suggested that life could be sparked by electrical currents, Victor uses advanced technological knowledge to animate a being from inanimate matter (Mellor, 1988). In doing so, he echoes the myth of Prometheus, the Titan who defied the gods to give fire—a symbol of knowledge and technology—to humanity. Like Prometheus, Victor's act of creation is both awe-inspiring and fraught with peril. He seeks to transcend the limits of human capability, to play God, but in doing so, he unleashes forces beyond his control (Morton, 2002).

Shelley drew from the scientific discoveries of her time, particularly those surrounding electricity and reanimation, to weave a narrative that is as much about the perils of unchecked scientific ambition as it is about the human condition. Her work explores the ethical responsibilities of creators—be they scientists, technologists, or innovators—towards their creations and the broader society. Victor's failure to foresee the consequences of his actions leads not only to his personal downfall but to a broader societal catastrophe (Mellor, 1988). The Monster, a being created without considering its potential impact, becomes a symbol of the unintended consequences of technological advancement. It is a force that, once unleashed, cannot be easily managed or undone, much like the rapidly advancing technologies of today (Landes, 1997).

In *Frankenstein*, Shelley anticipates many of the ethical debates that would later come to dominate discussions around technology in the 20th and 21st centuries—debates about artificial intelligence, genetic engineering, and the broader implications of scientific progress (Mellor, 1988). The novel is a meditation on the moral dilemmas that arise when humans push the boundaries of what is possible. Victor Frankenstein's obsession with his experiments and his eventual realisation of the horror he has unleashed serve as a cautionary tale about the dangers of overreaching ambition and the ethical void that can accompany technological progress (Landes, 1997).

Shelley's narrative is deeply intertwined with the context of the Industrial Revolution, a time when the world was beginning to grapple with the massive changes brought about by new technologies. The machines of the industrial age, much like Frankenstein's Monster, represented both the promise of progress and the fear of losing control (Hindle, 2006). These machines, which could perform tasks far beyond human capability, began to evoke a sense of dread and wonder—emotions she masterfully channels into her portrayal of the Monster. The cold, mechanical nature of the Monster, with its lifeless eyes, mirrors the fear of a future dominated by machines that could operate without human empathy or understanding—a fear that is eerily relevant in today's discussions of artificial intelligence and automation (Jager, 2014).

But *Frankenstein* is more than just a reflection of the anxieties of its time; it is a visionary work that continues to speak to the complexities of technological advancement. The story of Victor Frankenstein and his creation serves as a timeless reminder of the responsibilities that come with the power to create and innovate (Mellor, 1988). It challenges us to consider the ethical implications of our actions, especially in a world where technology continues to advance at an unprecedented pace.

For young women today, particularly those interested in technology, Shelley's *Frankenstein* offers both a cautionary tale and an inspiration. It is a reminder that with great power comes great responsibility, and that the pursuit of knowledge must always be tempered with a consideration of its ethical and societal impacts. Through her groundbreaking work, she invites us to question not just what we can do with technology, but what we should do, and how we must navigate the complex interplay between innovation and ethics (Rotman, 2013).

In the end, *Frankenstein* is not just a story about the dangers of technological overreach; it is a story about the potential for human greatness and the importance of approaching that potential with care and wisdom. Shelley's novel, with its rich exploration of the responsibilities of creation, continues to resonate in our modern world, where the lines between science fiction and reality are increasingly blurred (Mellor, 1988). As we stand on the brink of new technological revolutions, *Frankenstein* remains a vital touchstone, reminding us of the enduring relevance of the ethical questions Shelley so poignantly raised.

The world, gripped by fear and confusion in the face of natural calamity, served as a haunting parallel to Shelley's tale of Victor Frankenstein's monster. Just as the Earth had turned against its inhabitants with unpredictable force, so too did Frankenstein's creation rebel against its maker, embodying the dangers of unchecked scientific ambition. *Frankenstein* was more than a ghost story—it was a reflection of the anxieties of a world in flux, a tale of humanity's fraught relationship with the unknown forces it sought to control (Mellor, 1988).

The novel remains a seminal work in discussions about the ethical implications of technological advancement and a huge joy for nerds everywhere. So why did I choose it? Because of *Lord Byron*.

Mad, Bad, and Dangerous to Know—these were the words whispered about the infamous Lord Byron, the romantic poet whose name became synonymous with scandal, brilliance, and rebellion (St. Clair, 2004). His allure has transcended centuries, inspiring everything from the goth aesthetics of the 1980s to the fervent fandoms of today. If you've ever cosplayed as Yuki Cross from *Vampire Knight* or waited eagerly for the next *Final Fantasy* release, you're tapping into that same dark, magnetic energy that Byron embodied. He's the reason why some of us fell in love with Gary Numan's dystopian synths or binge-watched all 15 seasons of *Supernatural*. Byron was the original anti-hero, the one who made brooding, tortured genius irresistible. He was the template for Tomohisa Yamashita and Lee Dong Wook. Beyond his scandalous love affairs and the poetic genius, Byron's legacy carries something far more profound—something that would transcend his own life and echo into the birth of the digital age through his daughter, Ada Lovelace (St. Clair, 2004).

Byron's life was a tempestuous whirlwind of passion and intellect, yet it's often forgotten that he lived in ruin but is a history of practicality and innovation, far removed from the Byronic hero's moody allure. His ancestral home, Newstead Abbey in Nottinghamshire, was more than just a grand estate; it was a hub of technological advancement long before Byron's time. The Abbey, with its ancient fishponds and ingenious irrigation systems designed by mediaeval monks; the blending of nature and technology, a concept that would have seemed otherworldly in the age of swords and ploughs. These monks, with their knowledge of hydrodynamics, ensured that fresh water flowed continuously through the Abbey's systems, preventing the ponds from freezing over and securing a steady supply of fish for the community (St. Clair, 2004). Byron inherited this legacy of technological mindfulness, even if he didn't fully embrace it himself.

In fact, Byron's ambivalence toward technology was famously displayed during his maiden speech in the House of Lords in 1812. He passionately defended the frame breakers—workers who were smashing the new industrial machines that threatened their livelihoods. Byron argued that while these machines represented progress, they also heralded the displacement and dehumanisation of the working class. "Surely, my Lord, however we may rejoice in any improvements in the arts which may be beneficial to mankind, we must not allow mankind to be sacrificed to improvements in mechanism," he declared. His speech resonates eerily with today's concerns about automation and artificial intelligence—his words could easily be applied to the fears surrounding modern technology replacing human workers (St. Clair, 2004).

But perhaps the most poignant connection between Byron and the world of technology isn't found in his own work, but in the life of his daughter, Ada Lovelace. Born in 1815, just as the world was reeling from the global climatic chaos caused by the eruption of Mount Tambora, Lovelace was the product of two contrasting worlds. Her father's legacy of romantic poetry and rebellion was tempered by her mother Annabella's insistence on a rigorous, scientifically grounded education (Toole, 1992). Annabella, a formidable intellect in her own right, was determined that Lovelace would not inherit her father's "madness" and instead immersed her in the study of mathematics, logic, and science (Essinger, 2013).

As the 19th century unfurled its complex tapestry, the seeds of the digital age were being sown in ways that few could have anticipated. Among the most remarkable figures to emerge from this era of transformation was Augusta Ada Byron, better known as Ada Lovelace. Born in 1815, a year shadowed by the catastrophic eruption of Mount Tambora, Lovelace's life was one marked by the tension between her parents' contrasting legacies: the wild, untamed genius of her father, the famous poet Lord Byron, and the disciplined, intellectual rigour imposed by her mother, Anne Isabella Milbanke, commonly known as Annabella (Essinger, 2013).

Annabella, a woman of considerable intellect and education, was determined that Lovelace would not follow in her father's footsteps. Haunted by Byron's notorious reputation and his tumultuous lifestyle, Annabella sought to protect her daughter from what she perceived as the dangerous allure of her father's romanticism. To this end, she orchestrated a rigorous education for Lovelace, one that steeped in mathematics, science, and logic—subjects that were typically reserved for men of that era (Toole, 1992). Annabella's vision was clear: by immersing Ada in the precise and orderly world of numbers and equations, she hoped to safeguard her from the chaos and emotional volatility that had plagued Lord Byron's life (Essinger, 2013).

From an early age, Lovelace's education was meticulously structured, with a strong emphasis on mathematics and the sciences. This was highly unusual for a girl in the early 19th century, a time when women were generally expected to focus on more "feminine" pursuits such as music, art, and domestic skills (Toole, 1992). Yet, her mother was unrelenting in her quest to mould her daughter into a rational thinker, one who would be impervious to the supposed madness of poetic imagination. This upbringing instilled in Lovelace a profound intellectual curiosity and a passion for understanding the mechanisms that governed the natural world (Essinger, 2013).

Despite her mother's efforts to keep her away from the influence of Lord Byron, Lovelace was irresistibly drawn to the legacy of the father she never knew. Byron died when she was just eight years old, and she was only allowed to see a portrait of him when she turned 20. This moment had a deep impact on her, sparking a fascination with the man whose genius and flaws had shaped the course of her life (Wolfram, 2014). The tension between her mother's desire to fashion her as a model of rational thought and her own romantic inclinations would define much of her life and work (Essinger, 2013).

Ada's innate curiosity extended beyond the abstract world of mathematics to the tangible realm of machines and inventions. At the tender age of 12, while her mother was away for medical treatment, Ada designed a flying machine, drawing inspiration from her meticulous observations of birds. This early venture into mechanical design was a harbinger of her later work on the Analytical Engine, the first mechanical computer, which she would explore in collaboration with Charles Babbage (Essinger, 2013).

The turning point in Lovelace's life came in 1833 when she was introduced to Charles Babbage at a party. Babbage, a polymath known for his work on the Difference Engine—a mechanical calculator—was immediately struck by her sharp intellect and unbridled enthusiasm for his work (Toole, 1992). Their meeting sparked a deep intellectual partnership, one that would eventually lead her to study Babbage's designs in great detail and become one of his most trusted collaborators (Essinger, 2013).

In 1842, Lovelace was asked to translate an article written by Italian mathematician Luigi Menabrea about Babbage's latest invention, the Analytical Engine. As she translated the text from French to English, she began adding her own extensive notes and insights. These annotations, which ultimately exceeded the length of the original article, contained what many now consider to be the first algorithm designed specifically for implementation on a machine (Toole, 1992).

Lovelace's notes on the Analytical Engine are celebrated not just for their technical brilliance, but for their visionary scope. In these notes, she demonstrated a profound understanding of both mathematics and mechanical engineering (Essinger, 2013). One of the most famous of her annotations, labelled "Note G," describes an algorithm for calculating a sequence of Bernoulli numbers, a complex series of rational numbers deeply intertwined with number theory. This algorithm is widely regarded as the first computer program ever written, positioning Lovelace as a pioneering figure in the nascent field of computer science (Toole, 1992).

The significance of Lovelace's algorithm lies in several key aspects:

- **First Computer Program:** Lovelace's algorithm is widely recognised as the first computer program ever published. This establishes her as the first computer programmer in history, a title that is both historically important and symbolic of the early contributions of women in technology (Essinger, 2013).

- **Visionary Understanding of Computing:** In her notes, Lovelace went beyond the immediate application of the algorithm. She foresaw that the Analytical Engine could be used to manipulate symbols and data beyond numerical calculations, including creating music and graphics. This visionary understanding of computing as a general-purpose tool foreshadowed the modern concept of computers as versatile devices capable of handling a wide range of tasks (Essinger, 2013).

- **Bridging Mathematics and Machinery:** Lovelace's work on the algorithm exemplifies her ability to bridge abstract mathematical concepts with practical engineering. She understood the mathematical intricacies of Bernoulli numbers and the mechanical operation of Babbage's machine, showing how these two domains could be brought together in a single computational process (Toole, 1992).

What sets Lovelace apart is not just her technical skill, but her ability to see beyond the immediate applications of the Analytical Engine. She envisioned that the machine could do more than just perform arithmetic calculations; it could be used to manipulate symbols, generate music, and create art—essentially, to process and produce anything that could be represented in a symbolic form (Essinger, 2013). This foresight into the potential of computing machines far outstripped the technological capabilities of her time, and it is this visionary perspective that solidifies Ada Lovelace's place as the first computer programmer and a trailblazer in the field of computer science (Toole, 1992).

However, the collaboration between Babbage and Lovelace was fraught with challenges. Babbage, a perfectionist to a fault, struggled to bring his grand designs to fruition. Financial constraints and practical difficulties meant that the Analytical Engine was never completed during his lifetime. Lovelace, too, faced her own set of challenges—her health was often fragile, and the societal expectations placed on her as a wife and mother limited the time she could devote to her intellectual pursuits (Wolfram, 2014). Nevertheless, their work together laid the foundational principles that would guide the development of computing long after their deaths (Toole, 1992).

Lovelace's life was marked by a series of personal and professional struggles that, in many ways, mirrored the challenges faced by women in STEM fields today. After her work on the Analytical Engine, she continued to engage in intellectual pursuits, but her later years were marred by declining health, financial troubles, and societal pressures.

Despite her significant contributions to the early development of computing, her work was largely forgotten after her death (Wolfram, 2014). She passed away in 1852 at the age of 36, succumbing to uterine cancer after a prolonged and painful illness (Toole, 1992).

In her final months, Lovelace experienced a profound emotional and spiritual transformation. She grew increasingly religious and sought reconciliation with her estranged husband, William King, Earl of Lovelace. She also reflected deeply on her life, seeking atonement for what she saw as her past sins, including her struggles with gambling and the complexities of her personal relationships (Wolfram, 2014). Despite the turbulence of her final days, her legacy would eventually be recognised and celebrated—albeit posthumously (Essinger, 2013).

It wasn't until the 20th century that Lovelace was finally acknowledged as a pivotal figure in the history of computing (Essinger, 2013). Today, she is celebrated as a visionary who laid the intellectual groundwork for the digital age, a woman whose work bridged the worlds of mathematics and technology, and whose insights continue to inspire generations of scientists, engineers, and technologists (Wolfram, 2014).

Lovelace's story serves as a powerful reminder of the importance of perseverance, vision, and intellectual curiosity. Her life exemplifies the challenges and triumphs of being a woman in a field dominated by men, and her legacy is a testament to the enduring impact that one individual can have on the course of history (Essinger, 2013). Just as she stood at the dawn of the digital age, young women today stand at the forefront of new technological revolutions, with the power to shape the future in ways that even Ada could only have imagined (Wolfram, 2014).

So, why does Lovelace choose to be buried next to a father she never knew, in a modest grave in Hucknall Torkard, Nottinghamshire, far from the grand poetic legends of Byron's life? Perhaps it's because, despite the vast differences in their lives and work, they shared a common thread: a desire to transcend the limitations of their time and to explore the unknown, whether through poetry or mathematics, through the heart or the mind (Essinger, 2013). Her final resting place next to Byron is, to me at least, a symbol of the unity of art and science, the acknowledgement that both are driven by the same human need to understand and shape the world (Wolfram, 2014).

I got my first computer in 1982. It was a cold Christmas; we'd just moved to a new house, and I could see Newstead Abbey from a window on one side of the house and Rolls-Royce Trent Engine factory on the other side of the house. I remember wearing a thick woollen sweater watching the command line prompt flash repeatedly in bright white against a grey background. My parents couldn't afford to keep the place warm; they'd also borrowed a small black and white television for me to use until they could afford a colour television. I was an active insomniac, I used to read the telephone book in the light of the church's illuminated clock face in the next village. If that didn't work, I would listen to a crackly transistor radio playing short-wave languages or the shipping forecasts. And when all else failed I read my father's manuals on quantum chromodynamics, basic engineering and handbooks on how things worked: from his electric razor to a Haynes manual on his beloved Ford Cortina Mark II. However, it was *Childe Harold's Pilgrimage* that I never seemed to finish.

I didn't sleep the night I received that computer, and not because I was an insomniac, it was because the handbook that came with the computer opened a new world to me, more than the short-wave radio, more than quarks and gluons. It reached out to me in the darkness as the wonder of words evolved from being toys to the essence of programming. It was a deep conversation that I continue to have between me and my computer. Steven Vickers wrote the manual, but Lovelace wrote the code.

Out of DATA

You have tried to READ past the end of the DATA list (Vickers, 1982).

REFERENCES

Bresadola, M. (1998) 'Medicine and science in the life of Luigi Galvani', *Brain Research Bulletin*, 46(5), pp. 367–380.

Chin-Yee, B. (2014) 'In retrospect: Mary Shelley's Frankenstein and medical technology.' *University of Toronto Medical Journal*, 92(1). [online] Available at: http://utmj.org/index.php/utmj/article/view/1628/1354 [Accessed 23 September 2024]

Essinger, J. (2013) *Ada's algorithm: How Lord Byron's daughter Ada Lovelace launched the digital age*. Brooklyn, NY: Melville House.

Fagan, B.M. (2000) *The little ice age: How climate made history 1300-1850*. New York: Basic Books.

Gordon, L. (2005) *Vindication: A life of Mary Wollstonecraft*. New York: Harper Perennial.

Hindle, M. (2006). *Mary Shelley: Frankenstein*. London: Penguin Classics.

Hustis, H. (2003) 'Responsible creativity and the "Modernity" of Mary Shelley's Prometheus', *SEL: Studies in English Literature 1500-1900*, 43(4), pp. 845–858. [online] Available at: https://muse.jhu.edu/article/48650 [Accessed 23 September 2024]

Jager, B. (2014) 'Mary Shelley's Frankenstein and the fate of modern scientific psychology', *The Humanistic Psychologist*, 42(3), pp. 268–282. [online] Available at: https://tandfonline.com/doi/full/10.1080/08873267.2014.929900 [Accessed 23 September 2024]

Knight, D.M. (1992) *Humphry Davy: Science and power*. Cambridge, UK: Cambridge University Press.

Landes, D.S. (1997) *The unbound Prometheus: Technological change and industrial development in Western Europe from 1750 to the present*. Cambridge, UK: Press Syndicate of the University of Cambridge.

Mellor, A.K. (1988) *Mary Shelley: Her life, her fiction, her monsters*. London: Routledge.

Morton, T. (2002) *A Routledge literary sourcebook on Mary Shelley's Frankenstein*. London: Routledge.

Osen, L.M. (1974) *Women in mathematics: The addition of difference*. Cambridge, MA: MIT Press.

Piccolino, M. (1998) 'Luigi Galvani and animal electricity: Two centuries after the foundation of electrophysiology', *Brain Research Bulletin*, 46(5), pp. 381–407.

Rotman, D. (2013) *How Technology Is Destroying Jobs*. [online] Available at https://www.technologyreview.com/2013/06/12/178008/how-technology-is-destroying-jobs/ [Accessed 23 September 2024]

St. Clair, W. (2004) *The Reading nation in the romantic period*. Cambridge, UK: Cambridge University Press.

Taylor, B. (2003) *Mary Wollstonecraft and the feminist imagination*. Cambridge, UK: Cambridge University Press.

Todd, J. (2006) *Mary Wollstonecraft: A revolutionary life*. London: Weidenfeld & Nicolson.

Toole, B.A. (1992) *Ada, the enchantress of numbers: Poetical science*. Mill Valley: Strawberry Press.

Vickers, S. (1982) *The ZX spectrum instruction manual.* London: Sinclair Research Ltd. p. 53.

Wolfram, S. (2014) *Idea makers: Personal perspectives on the lives & ideas of some notable people.* Champaign, IL: Wolfram Media.

Wollstonecraft, M. (1792) *A vindication of the rights of woman: With strictures on political and moral subjects.* London: Joseph Johnson.

Wood, G. (2014) *Tambora: The eruption that changed the world.* Princeton, NJ: Princeton University Press.

CHAPTER 4

Thea Baumann and Hedy Lamarr

Designs for Realities

I LOVE IT WHEN I read that necessity is the mother of invention. For me, and in this context, it's the term *mother* which evokes a fostering of an outcome, or the birth of a different way. Technology has been bombarded by aggressive buzzwords that make the situation we find ourselves in so male-dominated and masculine. However, if necessity is the mother of invention, then surely this wipes the floor with buzz terms and jargon. This is about taking a problem and solving the problem by rounding the hard edges and developing in silence rather than in a loud LinkedIn silo. As women we shouldn't need to scream and shout about what we do or what we make; instead, we should be celebrated for what we deliver because we're amazing.

Thea Baumann and Hedy Lamarr are pillars of inspiration for me at either end of innovation or technology. These two remarkable women, separated by decades and immersed in vastly different computational landscapes, have left indelible marks on our technological world. In this chapter, we delve into the lives and contributions of Thea and Hedy, exploring their journeys as a viewpoint to the evolution of technology and the enduring power of human ingenuity.

THEA BAUMANN: THE GLAMOUR OF ALCHEMY

Thea Baumann's journey into the world of technology began with an unconventional yet deeply inspiring encounter with a bootleg Gameboy cartridge in her childhood. "I had a very close attachment to my Gameboy," she recalls. "I was a *Super Mario, Tetris* child. Essentially, I had this bootleg cartridge that my parents bought me from a market in Bangkok or something like that. It had like 50 games in one, but it was a bit of a pirated cartridge that had somehow landed in my hands. I was quite obsessed with it." This early fascination with technology wasn't just about playing games; it was about understanding

DOI: 10.1201/9781003566465-4

and manipulating them. "I wanted the technology to do things that it wasn't supposed to do." Baumann's curiosity led her to reverse engineering and circuit bending long before she knew these terms (Baumann, 2023).

Baumann's artistic journey is deeply influenced by a rich tapestry of visual and narrative mediums from anime to video games. These sources not only inspire her creative output but also challenge and shape her unique style, pushing her to explore new frontiers in art and technology. TV shows like *Sailor Moon*, along with superhero characters like Jem from *Jem and the Holograms* and She-Ra from *She-Ra: Princess of Power* played a significant role in her early development. These characters, often equipped with transformative gadgets and imbued with a sense of futuristic wonder, sparked her imagination. But anime and manga are also known for their complex narratives and detailed visual styles, which often explore themes of identity, technology, and transformation.

Baumann delved into the intricate relationship between the psychology of art and technology, providing a nuanced perspective on how these elements interplay in her work. Reflections on the psychological aspects of her art reveal her deep understanding of how technology can be used not just as a tool, but as a medium to evoke emotional and cognitive responses. She speaks about her early fascination with the emotive potential of machines, inspired by watching shows like Astroboy, and describes her childhood curiosity about how machines could be imbued with human-like qualities, such as love and passion. This fascination with the intersection of human emotions and technology became a central theme in her work. "As a child, (I wanted to know) how do I embed love and passion into technology or into the machine?" (Baumann, 2023). This early questioning laid the groundwork for her later explorations into how digital art can convey complex emotional narratives.

Baumann's approach to art is heavily influenced by her desire to create "beautiful, sparkly experiences" that resonate on a deep emotional level with her audience (Baumann, 2024). Her works often aim to create a sense of magic and wonder, challenging viewers to see technology not just as a functional tool but as a medium capable of evoking profound emotional responses.

Her formal education in fine arts was a blend of creative expression and technological experimentation. She attended art school in the early 2000s, a time when digital tools were beginning to appear in the artistic sphere. Access to emerging software versions like Final Cut Pro were great, but the tipping point was the Genesis 3D engine. "What I was doing was creating my own textures, which was like HTML poetry, this is very kind of like software as aesthetic. And then creating these textures, that would create these spaceships that were floating in black in computer game void space, which was what I call it. And then I would project that up on white cube gallery walls, in a kind of 360-degree experience, because I wanted to create this virtual reality experience. But I didn't have the tools. I made something which I think was pretty sophisticated" (Baumann, 2024).

The Genesis 3D engine was an early rendering engine developed by Eclipse Entertainment between 1996 and 1999 and later acquired by WildTangent in 2000. Genesis 3D was one of the pioneering open-source rendering engines and attracted a large community of aspiring game developers, many of whom transitioned into professional roles within the industry and continue to contribute today. Although Genesis 3D is no longer compatible with modern hardware, it remains a significant historical benchmark in the evolution of graphics engine development. Noteworthy games using Genesis 3D around this time include *Dragon's Lair 3D: Return to the* (2002), *Extreme Paintbrawl 2* (1999), and *F.D.N.Y. Firefighter: American Hero* (2002).

In the late 1990s and early 2000s, game engines such as Unreal Engine, and Unity emerged as powerful tools for artists and developers, providing unprecedented opportunities to create complex and visually rich digital environments. These engines introduced integrated development environments (IDEs) that combined rendering, physics, and scripting capabilities, allowing artists to create detailed and interactive 3D worlds without needing to code everything from scratch. Features like real-time rendering, complex lighting models, and physics simulations enabled more immersive and realistic experiences (Ceruzzi, 2003). Additionally, the development of powerful graphics processing units (GPUs) by companies like NVIDIA and ATI (now AMD) played a crucial role. Early GPUs like the NVIDIA *GeForce* series brought hardware acceleration for 3D graphics, allowing for higher polygon counts, advanced shading techniques, and faster rendering times. This made it possible for game engines to support richer and more detailed textures, complex visual effects, and smoother frame rates, enhancing both the development process and the final user experience (McCartney, 1999).

With the advent of more advanced graphics cards, artists could use higher-resolution textures and more sophisticated materials. This period saw the transition from simple, flat textures to more complex and realistic surface details through techniques such as bump mapping, normal mapping, and specular mapping. These advancements allowed for more lifelike and visually appealing environments and characters. Open-source projects like Genesis3D and the availability of affordable game engines democratised game development, making these technologies accessible to a broader audience, including indie developers and artists (Light, 1999). The open-source nature and extensive community support fostered an environment of collaboration and knowledge sharing, further driving innovation and creativity. Additionally, game engines began to integrate various multimedia elements, including audio, video, and interactive storytelling, allowing artists to explore new forms of digital expression and blend traditional art with interactive and dynamic media. This era marked the beginning of a new chapter in digital art, where the line between artist and developer blurred, leading to innovative works that combined technical proficiency with artistic vision (Abbate, 2012).

Baumann's journey into the world of extended reality (XR) and the metaverse is deeply rooted in her early experiments with technology and art. One of her early notable works, *Virtual Terrain Triptych* (2002), exemplifies her innovative approach. This installation featured three interconnected virtual landscapes that viewers could navigate, each representing different facets of digital and physical reality. By using early game engines and projection technology, she created an immersive environment that allowed viewers to experience a blend of the real and the virtual. It's easy to see the influence of anime's intricate storytelling and visual innovation. This work was a precursor to her later explorations in augmented reality, setting the stage for more complex interactions between users and digital art.

Ghost Virus Puppet Virus (2002) further showcased Baumann's ability to merge narrative and technology. In this installation, she used machinima—an artistic practice that involves creating films using real-time computer graphics engines from video games—to create a haunting narrative about digital infection and transformation. Characters created from game engines moved through eerie, virus-infected landscapes, embodying her early interest in how digital and biological viruses mirror each other in their capacity to spread and mutate. Her work often evokes a sense of unease and curiosity, encouraging viewers to question the implications of technological integration into daily life and the human body. This piece was not only a technical achievement but also a narrative one, using the digital medium to tell a compelling and visually striking story. The vibrant, otherworldly aesthetics and the exploration of virtual and real-world intersections are reminiscent of the narrative depth and visual richness found in many anime and manga series from *Akira* to *Paprika*.

Baumann's work *Face of the Metaverse* (2013) marked a significant development in her artistic journey, as she began to incorporate augmented reality into her installations. This project involved creating holographic representations that interacted with viewers in real time, effectively blending the physical and digital worlds. The installation featured a series of AR-enhanced sculptures that would change and respond to viewers' movements and gestures, creating a dynamic, interactive experience. The interactive, immersive experiences she creates are akin to the magical transformations and virtual adventures that define much of anime's appeal. The machinima practice continues to align with her broader goal of creating art that not only tells a story but also allows for active participation and engagement from the audience or avatar. By using game engines and digital tools, she can create rich, interactive experiences that challenge traditional notions of spectatorship and storytelling. This work highlighted her commitment to pushing the boundaries of technology to create new forms of artistic expression (Baumann, 2023).

Baumann's art has always been influenced by her involvement with fringe feminist art collectives like VNS Matrix. The VNS Matrix collective, known for their cyberfeminist manifesto *A Cyberfeminist Manifesto for the 21st Century* and their work *Daddy Mainframe*, played a crucial role in shaping her artistic vision. VNS Matrix's approach, which involved subverting the traditionally male-dominated tech industry through provocative art that challenged patriarchal structures, resonated deeply with Baumann. This influence is evident in her works that often explore themes of identity, gender, and the body in digital spaces ('Thea Baumann', 2021).

The influence of VNS Matrix's *Daddy Mainframe* approach is particularly visible in Baumann's commitment to creating spaces where marginalised voices can be heard and celebrated. Her projects often focus on providing platforms for underrepresented groups, particularly women and non-binary individuals, to engage with technology in empowering ways. Her work reflects a similar ethos to that of VNS Matrix, seeking to democratise technology and make it accessible to all, while also challenging the dominant narratives within the tech industry (Wikipedia contributors, 2021).

Baumann's dedication to exploring the intersections of art, technology, and social commentary has established her as a significant figure in the realm of AR and the metaverse.

Though, like many of her forebears and contemporaries, "I look at reality as my medium […] any medium that an artist might explore or experiment with (I start with) how do I experiment with reality? *And that's how I approached the creation of my artworks is what can I do to disrupt this perceptual reality forcefield that I'm in at the moment*" (Baumann, 2024). Her innovative use of technology to create immersive and interactive art challenges and pushes narratives to the point of visceral extrusion in digital art making her contribution this space both aesthetically and commercially advanced. I agree with Baumann when she talks about thinking differently and applying her own techniques "it's really about shredding reality and moulding it: I'm creating a new way of seeing" (Baumann, 2024).

Her company, Metaverse Makeovers, started in a nail store. She was experimenting with the idea that her own nail art should do something and that nail art clients, as she was at that time, should be able to experience something as part of the nail art experience. The owners of the store she was experimenting in said "you should do something with this idea"; and thanks to the community in her local town, she was able to take this experiment out of its experimental phase. Metaverse Makeovers was born from extending art and technology into a more commercial route, I would say, without ever losing its DNA of exemplifying the function of the metaverse in this case through the portal of augmented reality (AR) to create social mobile products for the digital generation. The idea for Metaverse Makeovers was deeply rooted in her fascination with cyberpunk narratives and the transformative potential of technology but more "glam tech."

These fashion accessories, worn on the nails, trigger virtual content when scanned with an app, creating a unique AR experience. Virtual content was designed to "fly" out of the wearer's nails via an AR app, which combined the content with the ability to share content to social media. For Baumann, AR is not just a technological tool but a medium for artistic expression and social interaction. "I thought there was a potential there for creating a new wearable content distribution platform. What would a wearable gaming platform look like? So, the fashion nails became the first conduit into (building) this hologram brand" (Baumann, 2023).

The development of Metaverse Nails involved significant technological and entrepreneurial challenges. Baumann's journey took her to China, where she navigated the complexities of manufacturing and app development. She used Unity to create AR experiences before and was actively involved in the process for how her factory would manufacture small micro-curved surfaces to interact individually with mobile apps (Baumann, 2023). Metaverse Makeovers extends the embodiment of cyberfeminist ethos by creating AR experiences that are both visually captivating and socially conscious. By focusing on fashion and beauty—areas traditionally associated with femininity—and integrating cutting-edge technology, she subverts traditional gender roles and asserts the importance of diverse perspectives in tech innovation (Baumann, 2023).

AR is a technology that superimposes digital content, such as images, sounds, and other sensory enhancements, onto the real world through devices like smartphones, tablets, and AR glasses. In practical terms, AR works by using a device's camera to capture the real world and then overlaying digital content onto the live video feed. This is achieved through sophisticated algorithms that recognise patterns and track objects in real time. Metaverse

Nails utilised this technology by embedding QR code-like decals on the nails, which, when scanned by the Metaverse Makeovers app, trigger a burst of digital content. This process involves:

1. **Scanning**: The app scans the nail decals using the device's camera.

2. **Recognition**: The app's algorithms recognise the specific pattern of the decal.

3. **Rendering**: The app overlays the pre-programmed digital content onto the real-world view.

4. **Interaction**: Users can interact with the digital content and share their experiences on social media.

Baumann's work with AR extends beyond just the aesthetic to explore the possibilities of wearable tech and interactive experiences. Her vision of integrating AR into everyday accessories like nails is a step towards making technology more personal and integrated into daily life.

Baumann's exploration of the metaverse is not confined to commercial applications. She envisions the metaverse as a platform for much more storytelling and cultural expression. She is working a lot with young and emerging artists who really are guiding her in terms of what they desire and how she might help to use hardware as a conduit for expression and experiment; she envisages a future where artists will play an important part in what that visual landscape looks like and what that immersive experience could be.

Baumann's current role as the Artistic Director at 4A Centre for Contemporary Asian Art marks a new chapter in her career, where she is focusing on supporting Asian artists and preserving cultural heritage through technology. At 4A, she is dedicated to platforming Asian and Asian-Australian artists, providing them with the resources and opportunities to showcase their work on both local and international stages. Her extensive background in art development and entrepreneurship positions her uniquely to guide emerging artists in navigating the complexities of the art world (Baumann, 2023).

Baumann's role at 4A includes curating exhibitions, organising artist residencies, and facilitating cross-cultural exchanges. By leveraging her network and experience, she can create programs that not only highlight the artistic talents of these individuals but also foster a deeper understanding and appreciation of Asian cultures. This is particularly significant in the context of the Australian art scene, which has historically marginalised non-Western perspectives (Baumann, 2023).

Her vision extends beyond traditional art spaces; I'm quite interested in the new trend of something I call art capitalism using tech companies such as Google or Adobe to buy. It's nothing new, but, if art really is for everyone, shouldn't everyone have access to it? Thea Baumann's perspective on tech capitalism critiques the commodification of art through corporate platforms, noting that while such platforms may democratise access to art, they often do so in ways that restrict how art is experienced, centralising control within the tech companies themselves. Baumann contrasts this with her role as an artistic director, emphasising the importance of working with culturally enriching art that promotes connectivity and humanity. She views this shift as a return to art's role in fostering community and preserving heritage, particularly through technology, after years of navigating what she calls the "machine of tech capitalism" (Baumann, 2024).

This critique resonates with broader discussions in the art world about how tech companies invest in and control access to art. Scholars have noted that tech firms often curate art under the guise of public accessibility but restrict it to their platforms, thus shaping cultural consumption through corporate-controlled ecosystems (McGuigan, 2016). This dynamic raises questions about who truly benefits from these investments in art and how they contribute to or undermine broader cultural and artistic engagement (Morozov, 2012).

She is actively working on creating a metaverse dedicated to Asian art experiences. "They use artificial intelligence technologies to digitise objects that are held in (other) collections and museums around the world. And then they (will) integrate them into *Fortnite*, so that you could literally run around like a *Tomb Raider* Lara Croft-esque character and run around these ancient objects" (Baumann, 2024). This virtual platform aims to be a dynamic and immersive space where users can explore digital recreations of traditional art forms, engage with contemporary works, and participate in interactive cultural events to invoke a "digital repatriation project, using games and AI technologies." By integrating AR and virtual reality (VR) technologies, she seeks to preserve and celebrate Asian cultural heritage in innovative ways, making it accessible to a global audience (Baumann, 2023).

Baumann collaborates with technologists, artists, and cultural institutions to develop a platform that not only showcases art but also serves as an educational resource. This initiative aims to provide a virtual space where users can learn about Asian art history, participate in virtual workshops, and interact with artists and curators. By doing so, she hopes to create a vibrant online community that bridges the gap between traditional and digital art forms (Baumann, 2023).

Baumann's current role at 4A Centre for Contemporary Asian Art allows her to explore the intersections of art, technology, and cultural heritage. She is building a platform called 4A Plus through her current position as CEO and Artistic Director of 4A. Essentially, it's a virtual destination for digital commissions from the Asia Pacific region: a Metaverse for Asian art. This initiative presents her continued commitment to using technology to preserve and promote cultural heritage. By creating digital spaces where artists can showcase their work, she is bridging the gap between traditional art forms and modern digital expression.

HEDY LAMARR: FRAU MASCHINE

Hedy Lamarr, whose original name is Hedwig Eva Maria Kiesler, was born on 9 November 1914, in Vienna, Austria, grew up in a household that both celebrated intellectual curiosity and cultivated an appreciation for the arts. Her upbringing was uncommon. "They lived [...] in a fashionable district. The 19th district was heavily Jewish, but also very artistically inclined" (*Bombshell: The Hedy Lamarr Story, 2017*). The only child of Emil and Gertrud Kiesler, "Hedy's parents were both assimilated Jews. That was very common in the Austro-Hungarian empire. They were wealthy. They were cultured. They took their daughter to the opera, to the theatre" (*Bombshell: The Hedy Lamarr Story*, 2017). This background encouraged her to pursue her passions freely, even in a society that expected women to prioritise domesticity over intellectual ambitions.

Lamarr's early life was largely shaped by her close relationship with her father. Emil Kiesler, a successful bank director, had a profound influence on his daughter's budding intellect, particularly in the areas of science and technology. From an early age, she was captivated by how things worked, and he fostered this curiosity by explaining the mechanics of the world around them. Anthony Loder (Lamarr's son) recalls how father and daughter would often take long walks together, with him explaining the workings of various machines, including the streetcars that traversed Vienna's busy streets. As Loder recounted, Kiesler pointed out how the streetcar wires connected to factories that generated electricity, teaching young Lamarr to associate invention with the technology surrounding her. "My father made sure that I understood how everything around me worked" (Lamarr, 1990).

Kiesler's tutelage went beyond the technical, cultivating in Lamarr a desire to think critically about the world. In the documentary, she reflects on her father's impact, stating that he "was a wonderful person" and that she missed him deeply after his untimely death. The bond between father and daughter was not only intellectual but emotional, with Lamarr attributing much of her success to the values her father instilled in her as a child.

Despite her mother's initial disappointment at not having a son, Lamarr's talents became undeniable as she excelled in school, particularly in chemistry, a subject she favoured. Her favourite class was chemistry, but her early ability to understand how things worked simply fuelled her passion for invention. The intellectual upbringing provided by her father created a strong foundation for her later achievements in both Hollywood and technology. However, it was the death of her father in 1935 that marked a turning point in her life. As Richard Rhodes notes, the loss of her father led Lamarr to reaffirm her desire for independence, reinforcing the values of self-reliance and innovation that he had instilled in her since childhood (Rhodes, 2011). It's exciting to see film historian Jeanine Basinger posit the idea that "in a different era, she might very well have become a scientist. At the very least, it's an option that was derailed by her beauty" (*Bombshell: The Hedy Lamarr Story*, 2017) and it's disappointing that we are so often judged by our appearances rather than our intelligence or aptitude.

Lamarr's beauty became a bane throughout her life. It was something she did not want to be defined by, and yet, as a self-proclaimed *enfant terrible* "there is a word for what I was" (Lamarr, 1990) Still known as Hedwig Kiesler, she caused a storm with her role in the 1933 film *Ecstasy* (*Ekstase*), directed by Gustav Machatý.

At just 18 years old, Lamarr portrayed a young bride in a troubled marriage who experiences sexual awakening and love outside of her marriage. The film was groundbreaking for its time, primarily because it featured one of the first non-pornographic depictions of female nudity and a simulated orgasm on screen. In an era of strict societal norms, these scenes caused a global scandal, earning the film both critical praise and severe condemnation (Rhodes, 2011).

Ecstasy not only launched Lamarr into the public eye but also set the stage for significant and tumultuous changes in her life. The film's notoriety attracted the attention of several prominent figures, including Friedrich 'Fritz' Mandl, an Austrian arms manufacturer and industrialist. Mandl, who was born into a wealthy Jewish family but converted to Catholicism, was a highly influential figure in European political and military circles. He was immediately captivated by Lamarr's beauty and allure, despite the controversy surrounding *Ecstasy*. He was obsessed with her, reportedly seeing her not only as a potential wife but as a trophy to display within his social and political circles. Their meeting led to a swift courtship, and despite her youth and his controlling nature, she married him in 1933. He was 14 years her senior, and quickly became overbearing in their marriage, attempting to control every aspect of her life, including her burgeoning film career (Horak, 2014). Mandl's obsession with *Ecstasy* went to extreme lengths. He reportedly attempted to buy up and destroy every existing copy of the film, wanting to erase any trace of what he saw as an embarrassing chapter in his wife's life (*Bombshell: The Hedy Lamarr Story*, 2017). Despite his efforts, the film continued to circulate internationally, and its legacy endured as a landmark in cinema history.

Mandl would later become one of the wealthiest men in Austria, supplying arms to various European powers, including Mussolini's Italy (*Bombshell: The Hedy Lamarr Story*, 2017; Rhodes, 2011). But in their marriage, Lamarr found herself ensnared in a gilded cage. He frequently hosted lavish parties attended by high-profile political figures, including figures such as Benito Mussolini. Mussolini, who was known for his extravagant lifestyle and keen interest in European culture, was a regular guest at Mandl's events. Lamarr was often placed on display at these gatherings, her beauty drawing admiration, but her personal freedom was becoming increasingly restricted (*Bombshell: The Hedy Lamarr Story*, 2017). What could she do whilst sitting through conveyor belts of social gatherings? Perhaps she absorbed every conversation through the boredom, perhaps she simply plotted her own later escape. "Hedy was Mandl's arm piece at the banquets that he served for admirals in the German Italian navy. She sat there, and it was her job to be beautiful, but she was bored out of her mind. Fritz Mandl was by German measures, Jewish, and therefore Hitler was concerned not to be seen with him. And I doubt very much if Hitler was a guest in one of their houses, but Mussolini was" (*Bombshell: The Hedy Lamarr Story*, 2017).

Mandl's connection to Mussolini and other fascist leaders, despite his Jewish heritage, positioned him as a key figure in European arms trading. This placed Lamarr near powerful and dangerous men. Although forbidden by her husband from continuing her acting career, she possibly absorbed the military and technical discussions that took place during these meetings, knowledge that would later inform her contributions to wartime innovations (Rhodes, 2011).

Lamarr's gilded cage became too much to bear, and her escape was more dramatic than any storyline of her future movies. "They had people watching her all the time. There was no way to break loose. So, one night, they were having a dinner party, and my mother helped choose the maids and caretakers. She found someone that looked like her a lot, because she had this in mind. She had this sleeping powder, and she made this tea, and she switched the cups with the maid, and the maid drank it kind of fell asleep, and my mother was ready. She [had taken] all her jewels, put them in the lining of her coats, she put on the maid's costume. She jumped on [the maid's] bicycle and rode off" (*Bombshell: The Hedy Lamarr Story*, 2017). Lamarr fled to Paris in 1937. It was there that she met Louis B. Mayer, head of MGM Studios, who was scouting for European talent, and her striking beauty and acting talent led to Mayer offering her a Hollywood contract, which she accepted, and she moved to the United States, changing her name to Hedy Lamarr to distance herself from her past.

The American film industry was booming in the 1930s and upon her arrival in Hollywood, she quickly became one of MGM's biggest stars, known for her stunning beauty and roles in films such as *Algiers* (1938), *Boom Town* (1940), *White Cargo* (1942) and *Samson and Delilah* (1949).

Lamarr's move to Hollywood in the late 1930s marked the beginning of her film career, but her inventive mind never ceased to explore technological possibilities. Her most significant contribution to technology came during World War II, when she co-invented a frequency-hopping spread spectrum technology with composer George Antheil.

Lamarr and George Antheil met at a dinner party in Hollywood in 1940, during a period when she had already begun showing a keen interest in inventing. He was a highly unconventional composer and pianist, known for his avant-garde works, including his notorious composition *Ballet Mécanique*, which featured synchronised player pianos and mechanical sounds. He had an unconventional creative approach that fascinated her. She, in turn, was drawn to his knowledge of synchronised machinery, music, and his experimental thinking, which aligned with her emerging desire to engage in technological invention.

Their meeting at that party sparked a friendship built on their shared unconventional intellects and their desire to move beyond their respective artistic disciplines. For Antheil, Lamarr's beauty and fame were less important than her sharp mind and engineering curiosity. For Lamarr, Antheil represented a brilliant and eccentric mind who, like her, was eager to apply his creative talents to more scientific and technical problems (*Bombshell: The Hedy Lamarr Story*, 2017).

Although their relationship was undeniably close and deeply collaborative, there is no credible evidence to suggest that Lamarr and Antheil were lovers. Both were focused on their invention work and seemed to have a mutual respect for each other's intellects rather than pursuing any romantic entanglement. Imagine how impossible it would be to be friends with someone who is not trying to hit on you? The Hollywood Set would have been riven with gossip. Not much has changed. Lamarr was known for having many romantic relationships, but with him, the relationship was built primarily on their shared goal of creating something to contribute to the Allied war effort. Their bond was platonic, creative, and technological. Moreover, it was completely healthy.

Lamarr and Antheil bonded over their mutual interest in contributing to wartime innovation. Her first marriage to the arms manufacturer Mandl had exposed her to technical discussions related to military technology, and she had retained a good deal of knowledge from overhearing these conversations. She had a genuine desire to contribute to the war effort against the Axis powers and was motivated by a sense of patriotism and moral obligation.

Antheil, on the other hand, had developed a fascination with synchronised devices through his musical experimentation, particularly his work with automated pianos. His experiences synchronising mechanical music systems, especially in his work *Ballet Mécanique*, gave him a unique perspective on systems that required coordinated timing. The Jacquard punched card system, controlled player pianos, determining which notes to play based on punched holes representing different commands. This mechanical sequencing informed Antheil's later collaboration with Hedy Lamarr on frequency-hopping technology (Lamarr and Antheil, 1942).

The Jacquard punch card system, developed by Joseph Marie Jacquard in 1804, was originally designed for textile looms. The punch cards controlled the loom's pattern by encoding instructions for which threads to lift, allowing for complex designs without manual intervention. This system was one of the earliest forms of programmable automation and later inspired computing and data processing systems, such as those by Charles Babbage. The punch card's logic has been adapted in various fields, including music and early computing technologies from Antheil's *Ballet Mécanique* to the ENIAC computer where the use of punched cards allowed computers to process large sets of data more efficiently than manual methods, forming an early interface between human operators and machine computation. This approach was a precursor to later developments in data storage and retrieval systems.

Their shared desire to aid the war effort, along with their complementary technical interests, provided the foundation for their collaboration. Lamarr's idea of developing a system for radio-controlled torpedoes that couldn't be jammed by the enemy combined with Antheil's knowledge of synchronisation and mechanical engineering led to their groundbreaking invention (Rhodes, 2011). The impetus for this collaboration came from Lamarr's frustration with the state of military technology during World War II. She was concerned about the vulnerability of Allied torpedoes to enemy interference. Radio-controlled torpedoes, while advanced for their time, were susceptible to jamming by enemy forces, which could block the signal and cause the torpedoes to veer off course or fail entirely.

Lamarr's mother, Gertrud Kiesler, was still in Vienna during this time, and Lamarr was deeply fearful for her safety. The Nazi regime was increasingly targeting Jews for persecution, and Lamarr was acutely aware of the risks her mother faced. Despite her growing fame in Hollywood and her financial resources and influential connections, she feared that she might not be able to bring her mother to safety in the United States due to the increasingly stringent immigration policies against Jewish refugees, as many countries, including the United States, had strict quotas on Jewish immigration at the time (*Bombshell: The Hedy Lamarr Story*, 2017).

Lamarr used every possible resource at her disposal to bring her mother to safety. She worked diligently through legal channels, securing visas and leveraging her Hollywood fame to pull strings. Eventually, her efforts were successful, and Gertrud Kiesler was able to emigrate to the United States, where she joined her daughter in Los Angeles during the war. She ensured that her mother was well taken care of and provided for her in every way possible, a reflection of her deep familial bond and sense of responsibility. This successful rescue became one of Lamarr's personal victories amid the backdrop of war and genocide in Europe (Rhodes, 2011).

Lamarr's determination to save her mother also underscored her profound connection to her Jewish heritage, despite her public distancing from it in Hollywood. The fear of losing her mother to the horrors of the Holocaust contributed to her sense of urgency in contributing to the war effort. This drive manifested in her co-invention of frequency-hopping spread spectrum technology, a method intended to help the Allied forces by securing radio-controlled torpedoes from Nazi interference (*Bombshell: The Hedy Lamarr Story*, 2017). The personal stakes for her during the war were extraordinarily high, with her inventive efforts providing a means to fight back against the fascist regimes that had upended her life and threatened her family.

The eureka moment came when Lamarr thought of a way to prevent these signals from being jammed by creating a system that would "hop" frequencies in a predetermined pattern, ensuring that the signals could not be easily intercepted or disrupted. The idea was to have both the transmitter and the receiver switch between frequencies simultaneously, making it nearly impossible for the enemy to lock onto a single frequency to jam it.

The invention of frequency-hopping spread spectrum was a significant breakthrough in secure communications. Lamarr and Antheil's system involved changing radio frequencies at irregular intervals between transmission and reception to avoid interception. The concept was patented in 1942 under US Patent 2,292,387 (Lamarr and Antheil, 1942). Frequency hopping works by switching the carrier frequency of a signal among many frequency channels using a pseudorandom sequence known to both transmitter and receiver. This method minimises the risk of interception and jamming because the signal hops to a different frequency at regular intervals, making it difficult for unauthorised users to follow the transmission. Frequency hopping involves several key steps:

1. **Initialisation**: Both the transmitter and receiver are initialised with the same pseudorandom sequence generator and starting frequency.

2. **Hopping**: The transmitter hops from one frequency to another at regular intervals according to the pseudorandom sequence.

3. **Synchronisation**: The receiver, knowing the pseudorandom sequence and the timing, hops frequencies in sync with the transmitter.

4. **Transmission**: Data is transmitted over these short bursts of frequencies, making it difficult to intercept or jam the entire transmission.

This technique forms the basis of modern wireless technologies such as Bluetooth, Wi-Fi, and GPS. In Bluetooth, for example, frequency hopping is used to reduce interference from other devices by rapidly switching frequencies, ensuring a more reliable connection.

The patent application for the frequency-hopping system detailed a method where a piano roll would control the frequency changes. This innovative approach was both practical and ahead of its time, blending Antheil's knowledge of mechanical synchronisation with Lamarr's vision of secure communication.

Lamarr's journey to receiving recognition for her groundbreaking invention, frequency-hopping spread spectrum technology, was fraught with obstacles, many of which stemmed from the challenges of patenting and the broader societal context of the time. One of the biggest challenges they faced was the military's lack of understanding and appreciation of their invention. Although they were granted the patent for their *Secret Communication System*, the Navy ultimately dismissed the idea as impractical. According to Richard Rhodes in *Bombshell: The Hedy Lamarr Story*, the Navy's rejection was rooted in their inability to see past the mechanism used to illustrate the concept—Antheil's background in synchronising player pianos. Navy officials reportedly asked, "What do you want to do, put a player piano in a torpedo?" before discarding the idea (*Bombshell: The Hedy Lamarr Story*, 2017). Their lack of technical vision and reluctance to embrace ideas from a Hollywood actress and a composer prevented the invention from being adopted during the war.

Lamarr's status as an immigrant also complicated the matter. Despite her efforts to aid the U.S. war effort, the government classified her as an "enemy alien" due to her Austrian origins and Jewish background. This classification led to her invention being seized under the Alien Property Act, further delaying any potential adoption of the technology. She reflects on this bitter irony: "I don't understand… they use me for selling bombs. Then I'm not an alien. And when I invent something for this country, I am an alien?" (*Bombshell: The Hedy Lamarr Story*, 2017). This classification undermined her ability to gain recognition or compensation for her patent during its active period.

Even if the military had adopted Lamarr and Antheil's technology immediately, they were never informed, and the patent expired in 1959—just before the proliferation of the modern communication systems that would benefit from their invention. At the time, the potential civilian applications of frequency-hopping technology, such as wireless communication, were not yet evident. As a result, the patent expired without being commercially exploited. Lamarr herself expressed frustration over this in her later years, as she saw her invention being used extensively without any personal recognition or financial compensation (*Bombshell: The Hedy Lamarr Story*, 2017).

The frequency-hopping concept from Lamarr and Antheil's patent became an ideal solution for the sonobuoy. Sonobuoys are used to detect submarines, actively or passively, but the data collected must be transmitted to the controlling vessel (such as ship or helicopter). By employing frequency-hopping, sonobuoys could transmit the collected data securely over multiple frequencies, reducing the risk of detection, jamming, or interception by the enemy. (Rosengren, 2022).

The challenges were like those faced by the early radio-controlled torpedo systems that Lamarr and Antheil sought to protect—enemy forces could potentially jam or intercept the radio communications between sonobuoys and their controlling vessels.

My long-suffering partner is ex-military and worked in the cold north of Scotland in the 1980s on radar technology. It is from his memory that I first got really interested about the practical application of frequency hopping. He explained to me, as I was gathering research for this chapter, that during the first Gulf War (1990–1991) "I was seconded to the Central Servicing Team for all the frequency agile radios. We had a base unit which was used by the forward air controllers to communicate with the close support aircraft. We thought, because we only tested in abstract, we didn't really have any experience with frequency hopping, so this was a good opportunity to try it. We synced the base unit to our airborne kit that we were testing in the bay with the same daily key. We got the other team to communicate through a resistance load, instead of an aerial, so the resistance load acts like an aerial. We actually tested frequency hopping and honestly, it was so interesting to see things that we'd never actually done before. You could hear the ever so slightly hopping of the frequency. It's just like a *tick, tick, tick, tick, tick*, in the background. I don't know how many times a second it could be heard on the NATO radios, but I've actually used it. And it was quite fun to us, because we all knew the theory, but we were able to set it up and use it in real life" (Crocker, 2024).

Lamarr's identity as a glamorous movie star further complicated her recognition as an inventor. She was often pigeonholed into the role of a beautiful actress, with little attention given to her intellect. Richard Rhodes notes that she felt she was never "seen for who she was" and that people underestimated her because of her looks (Rhodes, 2011). Her fame as an actress also contributed to the patent being overshadowed. The world was far more interested in her as a Hollywood icon than as an inventor. This bias, combined with the limited opportunities available to women in science and technology at the time, meant that her patent and its significance were largely ignored by the public and the military alike.

Lamarr's recognition as an inventor did not come until much later in her life. In 1997, the Electronic Frontier Foundation awarded her the Pioneer Award, acknowledging her contributions to the development of modern wireless communication. This recognition came more than 50 years after she and Antheil had filed their patent. It was not until after her death that she was posthumously inducted into the National Inventors Hall of Fame in 2014, cementing her place in history as a technological innovator (Rosengren, 2022).

Her son, Anthony Loder, reflects that Lamarr was finally recognised for her intellectual contributions later in life, though it was long overdue. In a conversation with her, he recalls telling her, "Mom, people are interested in what you [invented] of back in '42," to which she responded, "It's about time" (*Bombshell: The Hedy Lamarr Story*, 2017). This belated acknowledgement came after years of frustration and missed opportunities.

The challenges Lamarr faced in patenting her frequency-hopping technology were rooted in a combination of military short-sightedness, societal bias, and the timing of technological advancements. Her eventual recognition, while well-deserved, highlights the often-overlooked contributions of women in STEM, particularly those who had to overcome stereotypes and systemic barriers to gain acknowledgement for their work. She wasn't the first and she certainly will not be the last.

Lamarr's legacy also underscores the value of intellectual versatility. Her success in both the arts and sciences serves as a reminder that diverse interests and talents can intersect in meaningful and impactful ways. For women looking for role models who exemplify the fusion of creativity and technical prowess, Hedy Lamarr stands out as a shining example.

In conclusion, Lamarr's legacy is multifaceted and enduring. She is a symbol of resilience, creativity, and intellectual versatility. Her life story encourages women to pursue their passions, break through barriers, and contribute to the advancement of technology and society. She continues to inspire and empower women around the world, making her a timeless role model for generations to come.

Does Baumann, and did Lamarr, face significant barriers in their respective fields? Baumann's challenge was to educate a market that was not yet familiar with AR technology. Her success in raising investment and bringing her products to market reflects her ability to overcome these barriers through education and effective communication. "People didn't know what augmented reality was. So, I had to do a lot of educating not only the market but investors" (Baumann, 2023).

Lamarr, as a woman in a male-dominated field and a Hollywood actress, faced scepticism and dismissal of her technological contributions by virtue of being a pretty face. And the pretty sparkling glam effect was intrinsic to Baumann's core work. Demonstrating the importance of resilience in overcoming societal and generational barriers is vital to pushing the boundaries of innovation.

The stories of Thea Baumann and Hedy Lamarr are powerful reminders of the impact that visionary women can have on technology. Their journeys from study to action, their continuous development of skills, and their ability to build for an envisioned future despite significant barriers serve as inspirations for young women entering the fields of technology and innovation.

Baumann and Lamarr, though separated by time and the specifics of their technological environments, share a common thread of visionary thinking and grit either in a boardroom or the escaping of a controlling influence show other women that they can turn study into impactful action. Their contributions to AR, wireless communications, and the arts, respectively, highlight the diverse ways in which women can shape the future of technology. As we continue to advance in the digital age, their stories serve as guiding lights, inspiring new generations to dream big, embrace challenges, and create a future where technology enhances and enriches human life.

REFERENCES

Abbate, J. (2012) *Recoding gender: Women's changing participation in computing.* Cambridge, MA: MIT Press. pp. 45–56, 123–135.

Baumann, T. (2023) Personal communications. 12 November 2023.

Baumann, T. (2024) Interviewed by Kelly Vero. 1 August 2024.

Bombshell: The Hedy Lamarr Story. (2017) [Blu-ray]. Directed by Alexandra Dean. United States: Reframed Pictures.

Ceruzzi, P.E. (2003) *A history of modern computing.* Cambridge, MA: MIT Press. pp. 78–85, 201–210.

Crocker, S. (2024) Interviewed by Kelly Vero. 29 August 2024.

Dragonstone Software (2002) *Dragon's lair 3D: Return to the lair.* Montreuil: UbiSoft.

Hoplite Research (1999) *Extreme paintbrawl 2.* Minneapolis: Head Games Publishing.

Horak, J-.C. (2014) *High class whore: Hedy Lamarr's star image in Hollywood.* Los Angeles: UCLA Film and Television Archive.

Lamarr, H. (1990) *Ecstasy and me: My life as a woman.* New York: Bartholomew House.

Lamarr, H. and Antheil, G. (1942) Secret communication system. US Patent 2,292,387.

Light, J.S. (1999). *When computers were women*. Cambridge, MA: Harvard University Press. pp. 112–125.

McCartney, S. (1999) *ENIAC: The triumphs and tragedies of the world's first computer*. New York: Walker & Company.

McGuigan, J. (2016) *Neoliberal culture*. London: Palgrave Macmillan UK.

Mekada (2002) *F.D.N.Y. firefighter: American hero*. Houston: Activision Value Publishing.

Morozov, E. (2012) *The net delusion: The dark Side of internet freedom*. New York: PublicAffairs.

Rhodes, R. (2011) *Hedy's folly: The life and breakthrough inventions of Hedy Lamarr, the most beautiful woman in the world*. New York: Vintage.

Rosengren, P.L. (2022) *Famous women engineers in history - book 1: Hedy Lamarr*. New York: IEEE.

'Thea Baumann.' (2021) *Wikipedia, the free encyclopedia*. Available at: https://en.wikipedia.org/wiki/Thea_Baumann [Accessed 12 July 2023]

CHAPTER 5

Betty Snyder and Claire Blackshaw

Breakpoints and Bloom Effects

I N MY WORLD OF women in technology, it's hard to find pioneers. Technology is hugely male dominated, making it difficult for female voices to be heard. In this book, I'm celebrating women who, though not necessarily loud in voice or termed difficult (as I am), let their work speak for them. Betty Snyder and Claire Blackshaw are pillars of inspiration at either end of innovation and technology. These two remarkable women, separated by decades and immersed in vastly different technological landscapes, have left indelible marks on the world of computing and artificial intelligence. In this chapter, we delve into the lives and contributions of Betty and Claire, exploring their journeys as a viewpoint to the evolution of technology and the enduring power of human ingenuity.

BETTY SNYDER: PIONEERING THE PATH

Frances Elizabeth Snyder was born on 7 March 1917, in Philadelphia, Pennsylvania. (McCartney, 1999). As a young girl, she exhibited a keen interest in mathematics and problem-solving, defying the societal norms of the early-to-mid 20th century that denied women a technical education or occupation. Her father was a passioned supporter of education and encouraged her curiosity and ambition. She wanted to study mathematics, but the misogyny of the time pushed her towards studying journalism—a strategic choice in the 1940s that allowed her to take extensive courses in mathematics and logic, as these were part of the curriculum required for a journalism degree at the time. Her natural aptitude for numbers and problem-solving was both exceptional and unconventional (Abbate, 2012).

Snyder wasn't alone in her struggles against the barriers imposed on women in technical fields. Her colleague Betty Jean Jennings Bartik, one of the six original Electronic Numerical Integrator and Computer (ENIAC) programmers, had a similarly challenging

DOI: 10.1201/9781003566465-5

experience. Bartik recalled the constant pressure women faced to conform to traditional gender roles. Like Snyder, Bartik was steered away from mathematics and encouraged to become a teacher instead, a job seen as more appropriate for women during that era (Bartik, 2008). Bartik once shared that even though she excelled in mathematics from an early age, her professors and mentors tried to push her into a more "feminine" career path—teaching. She was even told that staying in a small town as a teacher would make her a "respected" member of the community (Bartik, 2008).

Snyder encountered a similar struggle when she applied to the University of Pennsylvania. Her dreams of studying mathematics were crushed by a professor who dismissed her ambitions and told her to pursue home economics or journalism instead (Beyer, 2009; Holberton, 2021). In a time when the intellectual potential of women was often underestimated, she had to navigate the entrenched biases of the academic world. The fact that women were expected to adhere to socially acceptable roles made it difficult for them to access the same opportunities as men. Both Snyder and Bartik defied expectations by finding ways to pursue their love of mathematics; Snyder cleverly took advantage of the logic and mathematics courses offered as part of her journalism curriculum at Penn, gaining the skills she needed despite institutional opposition (Abbate, 2012; Holberton, 2021).

During World War II, six women were recruited to serve as "computers"—people responsible for calculating complex ballistics trajectories for the U.S. military. Know their names: Fran Bilas, Betty Jean Jennings, Ruth Lichterman, Kay McNulty, Betty Snyder, and Marlyn Wescoff. The ENIAC was the world's first general-purpose electronic digital computer (IEEE, 1997)

The war created unprecedented opportunities for women in technical fields, as the absence of men opened doors that had previously been shut (Goldstine, 1993; Light, 1999) But even with this new opportunity, they were still not considered equals to men. The ENIAC women were referred to as "sub-professionals," a classification that further emphasised the hierarchy between them and their male counterparts (Bartik, 2008).

Bartik's experiences highlight the challenges that came with this role. Despite being one of the primary programmers for the ENIAC, Snyder and her colleagues were initially not allowed to touch the machine until they could prove themselves worthy through their calculations and understanding of the wiring diagrams (Bartik, 2008). When they were finally granted access, the work was gruelling. As Bartik recounted, the women had to invent their own methods to debug and program the machine, often without any formal guidance from the engineers who had built it (Bartik, 2008). Like Bartik, Snyder refused to be sidelined. Her analytical mind and creative problem-solving skills quickly earned her respect among her peers, even if the broader scientific community was slower to recognise the contributions of women (Holberton, 2021). Snyder's work on debugging ENIAC demonstrated the vital role women played in the machine's success. According to Bartik, Snyder was a meticulous problem solver who could figure out how to fix the machine's errors when others were stumped, often working with Bartik in a partnership that allowed them to test and correct ENIAC's programming (Bartik, 2008; Holberton, 2021).

ENIAC was a behemoth developed to calculate artillery firing tables for the U.S. Army's Ballistic Research Laboratory. Snyder's role was to breathe life into its digital circuits, learning the language, deciphering its blueprints, and programming it to perform complex calculations. Snyder's era was marked by an intimate relationship between humans and machines, where learning and teaching were inseparable. Weighing in at 30 tons and consuming 150 kilowatts of electricity, ENIAC consisted of nearly 18,000 vacuum tubes, 70,000 resistors, 10,000 capacitors, 1500 relays, and about 5 million hand-soldered joints (Goldstine, 1993).

In Snyder's time, computing was not a perfunctory series of machine tasks, but an extension of human intellect. Programming the ENIAC was no small feat (IEEE, 1997) Picture Snyder at work, amid the clatter of punched-card machines and the aroma of freshly brewed coffee. With her mix of intellect and charisma, she led a team of pioneers, deriving algorithms, solving equations, and forging the path for digital miracles. The ENIAC had no programming language as we understand it today. Instead, programs were manually set up using plugboards, switches and punch cards requiring an intricate understanding of both the machine's hardware and the problem at hand. Her pioneering work laid the foundation for the algorithms and programming languages that would follow (Ceruzzi, 2003).

Snyder's ability to break down complex problems into manageable tasks was instrumental in programming the ENIAC. She and her team developed methods to efficiently program the machine to perform ballistic calculations. This involved a deep understanding of numerical methods and the underlying physics of projectile motion.

The ENIAC "80 feet long, eight-foot tall, black metal machine drawing its power through a programming interface using dozens of wires and 3000 switches" (O'Bryon, 2008, cited in Bartik, 2008) was one of the earliest electronic general-purpose computers, developed during the 1940s. Unlike modern computers with integrated debugging tools and breakpoints, the ENIAC did not have a built-in mechanism for setting breakpoints during runtime as we understand it today. Debugging and monitoring of programs on the ENIAC were quite different from contemporary methods. Debugging involved manual inspection and verification of the wiring, output verification, and incremental testing. Snyder developed innovative methods to debug the machine, often through trial and error, making significant contributions to the field of software engineering. Her techniques for detecting and correcting errors laid the groundwork for modern debugging practices (Light, 1999). That's the human part of "human computer." The programming team had to manually trace wires, check connections, and verify that each plugboard was correctly configured. This process often involved running the machine for short periods, inspecting the results, and adjusting as necessary. Her meticulous approach to this task was crucial in ensuring that the ENIAC operated reliably. Bartik reflected on their success, emphasising that they thrived because of their dedication to finishing projects when others preferred only the "fun part of a design or a program." According to Bartik, they excelled at the "nasty little details" that were essential to making a system work, and while Bartik considered herself skilled, she said Snyder was "even better" at it (Bartik, 2008).

Here's a simplified overview of how debugging might have been done on the ENIAC:

1. **Manual Inspection.** Debugging often involved physically checking the wiring and connections on the plugboards. Engineers and programmers would inspect the setup to identify any mistakes or issues.

2. **Output Verification.** Since the ENIAC had a combination of electronic and electro-mechanical components, programmers would examine the output of the machine to ensure that it matched the expected results.

3. **Incremental Testing.** Programmers might run the machine for short segments of the program at a time, examining the intermediate results and ensuring that each part of the computation was functioning correctly.

4. **Trial and Error.** Debugging on the ENIAC often involved a fair amount of trial and error. If there was an issue, programmers would need to identify the source of the problem, correct the wiring or logic, and then rerun the program.

5. **Instrumentation and Printouts.** The ENIAC did have some instrumentation for monitoring the state of the machine during runtime. Engineers could use oscilloscopes and other tools to observe signals at various points in the system. Printouts and punched cards were also used to document and analyse the program's behaviour as well as to predict and track trajectory.

It's important to note that the concept of breakpoints as we know them today, where you can halt program execution at a specific point and inspect variables, did not exist in the same form on early machines like the ENIAC. Debugging was a more manual and hardware-oriented process. As computing technology advanced, the development of debugging tools, including breakpoints and interactive debugging environments, became integral to the programming process.

Barthik talks about Snyder's programmer prowess with a great deal of love. Women supporting women means that Snyder and Barthik (or Betty and Betty, as they were known), found that pairing up enabled them to design and test or deploy and fix errors as they appeared. Bartik recalled a critical moment when Snyder's leadership came through during the ENIAC trajectory program. Herman Goldstein asked whether the program was ready, and while Snyder confidently said yes, they encountered "a few little errors." Bartik vividly remembered their team scrambling to resolve these issues, even prompting John Mauchly to arrive with a bottle of apricot brandy to ease the tension. Bartik recalls that everyone including the Dean of Moor School in Philadelphia where ENIAC was based was very worried. The press would be coming to hear about this groundbreaking research and "the trajectory worked, except when the shell hit the ground, it kept right on going, so we could not figure out what was going on." But Snyder came to the rescue. "I came in the next morning, and she said, 'I just went over, flipped a switch and it worked!'" (Bartik, 2008) but that wasn't the real story here according to Bartik. The real story was about Snyder's innate gift of distance. She removed herself from the problem. She had a long journey back to where she was staying on the Philadelphia City Mainline. "I have always said that Betty does more logic in her sleep than most people do when they're awake! When we used to have problems, she would come in the next day and she would say, 'This occurred to me this morning,' and she would be right. And I would think, *what is she doing?* Is she going home at night, working all night? She was and she wasn't. She would go home and think about the problem before she went to sleep, and her brain kept working all night, and she would present a solution the next day" (Bartik, 2008).

Many may argue that Snyder's debugging "breakpoints" would have been discovered eventually by someone else as computers moved from the first mainframe to the PC I'm using right now to develop this book. Debugging is essential in software development as it serves to identify and rectify errors within the code, ensuring the reliability and stability of the software. Here's how:

1. **Machine Breakpoints on Early Mainframes.** Mainframes like the IBM/360 featured console switches/dials for setting breakpoints at specific instruction storage addresses. This allowed for a "single cycle" operation, enabling the observation of register and memory contents directly on console lights. However, the advent of multitasking limited the use of this option as it halted the entire machine.

2. **Non-Interactive Breakpoints with Core Dumps.** In the early days of computers, programmers used machine code patches to implement single destructive breakpoints. This deliberate "crash" would generate a core dump, providing the state of registers and memory at the moment of the intentional crash.

3. **Interactive Breakpoints with Teletypewriter Consoles.** Teletypewriter consoles in the 1960s introduced more interactive command-line debugging capabilities. By the early 1970s, video monitors connected to mainframes enabled fully interactive, full-screen debugging in multitasking environments. This allowed step-by-step program execution with optional register and memory alterations simultaneously displayed.

4. **Conditional Breakpoints.** Breakpoints are commonly used to interrupt a running program before the execution of a specified instruction (instruction breakpoint). Additionally, conditions such as reading, writing, or modifying specific memory locations (data breakpoint or watchpoint) can trigger breakpoints. Conditional breakpoints activate only if specific conditions are met, such as a variable having a certain value.

5. **Inspection Tools for Breakpoints.** When a breakpoint is hit, various tools are used to inspect or alter the program's state. This includes stack traces to view the chain of function calls, a list of watches to see variable values, and tools displaying the contents of registers, loaded program modules, and other relevant information.

After the success of ENIAC, Snyder played a crucial role in developing software for the UNIVAC I (Universal Automatic Computer I), the first commercial computer produced in the United States. Her work helped transition computers from military tools to essential business and government instruments, influencing the design and functionality of future computing systems.

UNIVAC I was developed by J. Presper Eckert and John Mauchly, the same team behind the ENIAC. Snyder joined their company, the Eckert-Mauchly Computer Corporation, and worked on the programming and development of UNIVAC I. This machine was revolutionary as it was designed for both numerical and alphabetical processing, making it suitable for a wide range of business applications.

Snyder's contributions to UNIVAC I included writing the operating instructions and developing key applications that demonstrated the machine's versatility. designing control panels that put the numeric keypad next to the keyboard and persuading engineers to replace the UNIVAC I's black exterior with the grey-beige tone that came to be the universal colour of computers. One of the notable applications she worked on was a program to predict the outcome of the 1952 U.S. presidential election, which successfully predicted Eisenhower's victory, showcasing the potential of computers in processing large datasets and performing complex analyses.

Another of Snyder's most significant contributions to early computing was her pioneering work on data sorting and merging algorithms. These tasks, essential for organising and processing large datasets, were critical to the functioning of early computers like ENIAC and UNIVAC I. Snyder's revolutionary SORT/MERGE algorithms laid the groundwork for efficient data processing, establishing core principles still used today in computing. By simplifying complex concepts with practical analogies, like comparing data sorting to a deck of cards, she made cutting-edge computational techniques accessible.

This foundational work continues to influence modern data management frameworks, from database systems to cloud computing. Snyder would shuffle a deck of cards and then sort them by suit or rank. This analogy demonstrated how sorting could be broken down into smaller, manageable steps that could be applied to data processing on computers like the UNIVAC I. Her method illustrated a divide-and-conquer approach, where smaller sorted subsets were combined to form a final sorted list (Beyer, 2009). After sorting the individual subsets, she would demonstrate how to merge them into a single sorted set. This process mirrored how the computer handled sorted datasets—by comparing elements from each subset and merging them in order. Her analogy not only simplified the technical aspects of sorting and merging but also helped her team develop efficient algorithms that could be implemented on early machines.

This practical approach to teaching programming enabled the early teams to develop more sophisticated methods for sorting and merging large datasets. Snyder's innovations were critical to the operation of early computers and the efficiency of data handling in fields like military computation, census management, and business applications.

Snyder's work on SORT/MERGE algorithms continues to have a lasting impact on modern computing. Sorting and merging algorithms remain integral to data processing, and many contemporary algorithms are direct descendants of the techniques she helped develop. For example: Merge Sort is a classical divide-and-conquer algorithm that recursively breaks down a list into smaller sub-lists, sorts them, and merges them back together. Merge sort is still widely used today for its efficiency, particularly with large datasets. Quick Sort is another popular sorting algorithm that selects a "pivot" element and partitions the other elements around it. Like merge sort, this algorithm is efficient for large datasets and widely used in modern applications. Heap Sort is a comparison-based algorithm that uses a binary heap data structure to sort elements. Its efficiency and reliability make it a mainstay in modern programming.

The merging of sorted data is equally important in today's large-scale data processing. External sorting, for instance, is a technique used when datasets are too large to fit into memory. The data is broken down into smaller chunks, sorted individually, and then merged—a direct extension of the principles Snyder first helped codify. In contemporary computing, frameworks like Apache Hadoop and Apache Spark rely heavily on sorting and merging operations when processing massive datasets across distributed systems. These frameworks reflect the evolution of Snyder's early innovations into powerful tools for the digital age.

Snyder's contributions in developing UNIVAC I, the first commercial computer, were revolutionary in transitioning computing from military and academic use to business and government applications. Her work in designing operating instructions and pioneering data sorting and merging algorithms allowed UNIVAC to handle large datasets, streamlining processes that would otherwise take days or weeks to complete manually. The SORT/MERGE algorithms she developed laid the groundwork for efficient data processing, and these principles are still integral to modern computing systems, from database management to large-scale cloud operations. Snyder's influence extends beyond the technical achievements of her time—she helped to shift the perception of computers from niche scientific tools to essential business machines, showing the world the power of automated computation. This pivotal contribution opened doors for future generations of women in tech to see themselves as creators and architects of software systems that power entire industries.

Betty was very active in the participation of Hopper's FORTRAN and COBOL (Common Business-Oriented Language), one of the earliest high-level programming languages designed for business data processing. After World War II and when working at the U.S. Bureau of Standards, Snyder's expertise would have been called up regularly. Barthik recalled "Grace Hopper had a compiler, and she could not find the error in it, so Grace asked to borrow Betty from the Bureau of Standards. She wanted to borrow her for a week, so Betty could find out what was wrong with the compiler. The problem was fixed in three days because what Betty found was that the UNIVAC used mag tape (about 1500 to 2000 feet of tape which ran back and forth). If one wrote a full tape and then read it back and then, did a merge or something like that, and wrote it back. It might not work, even though it's the same number of blocks of data and would not end up in exactly the same place. So, every time one writes on the tape, [it needed to be] relabelled. And what Grace had done was to not do that: she did not replace the labels. Even though this, [was the same label], [it still needed to be] redone. Grace said that Betty was the best programmer she ever saw in her life" (Barthik, 2008).

COBOL's readability and simplicity helped democratise programming, making it accessible to a broader audience. Snyder's contributions to symbolic programming languages paved the way for the development of modern programming languages (Beyer, 2009). The language was developed in the late 1950s and early 1960s as a part of an effort led by the U.S. Department of Defence to create a standard programming language that could be used across different types of computers. Her main work focused on ensuring that the language was easy to read and write, even for those who were not professional programmers. This accessibility was crucial in encouraging the widespread adoption of COBOL in business and government applications.

The women of ENIAC, like the early NASA 'Hidden Figures', were just that. *Hiding.* In plain sight, renamed "computer", a word that we associate with a non-sentient object. Linda O'Bryon in her interview with Betty Jean Jennings Barthik wonders why the women were not recognised. As the penultimate surviving member of six women, Bartik, explained why it was important that the future generations of females remember them. "Marlyn Westcoff had been hired when she graduated college. She didn't want to teach [at a] school either, so someone told her that John Mauchly was hiring people to do calculations for him. She went to work for John Mauchly, and she was fantastic. She had a reputation of never making a mistake. When John moved to build [and design] the ENIAC, he didn't have us then. We figured that Marlyn was selected as an ENIAC programmer, probably because she didn't make mistakes. And then, of course, Kay [Kathleen Rita McNulty] and Fran [Frances V Bilas] were selected because they ran the differential analyser, and the view was that, with all these switches and stuff and cables, they were sort of like the cranks (machinery) and the stuff you do with the differential analyzer. Betty [Snyder] had been assigned special projects like doing trajectories, where they fired the guns in very cold weather, up in Maine. And then Ruth [Lichtermann] [...] had gone to Hunter College, and she'd been recruited, to come to be a computer. The smartest thing we did was to have Marlyn and Ruth calculate a trajectory exactly the same way the ENIAC did it. You know, add time by add time. This was the document that made people respect us. Because of those 18,000 vacuum tubes, we could find the one that wasn't working in a very few minutes with that."

A group of women who contributed so much were almost erased from history were it not for the curiosity of computer science undergraduate Kathryn Kleiman who opposed the "refrigerator women" portrayal of these geniuses. Refrigerator women is a derogatory term to describe women of the 1940s, 1950s, and 1960s who modelled white goods to sell lifestyles. "I found myself wondering if women had much of a role in the history of computing at all," Kleiman said. "So, I turned to history to see if I could find any role models." (Sheppard, 2013).

This book is not about finding fault with how history is written, it's about finding our place in history as everyday women who make discoveries—in the case of Snyder, after a night's sleep or by wanting to use software that do not exist yet. Whilst we lament some of the great discoveries such as DNA being male dominated, we should remember that Lovelace worked on a theory that was never deployed to practice and that was more than enough for women like me to find other women in this vast network of the mundane.

How did the men of ENIAC decide that they would hide their human computers? "All I know is that [the men] all went out to dinner and at the announcement, we weren't invited. There we were, we were never people, never recognised. They never acted as though we knew what we were doing. I mean, we were in a lot of pictures, but they never asked us anything. Well, we did all the programming for it. I mean, it was, it was absurd" (Bartik, 2008).

Today, there is a growing recognition of the contributions of women to technology, and efforts are being made to increase their representation in STEM fields. This book is living proof of that! Snyder's legacy is a source of inspiration for these efforts, and her story serves as a reminder of the importance of diversity in driving innovation and progress. "Look like a girl, act like a lady, work like a dog and think like a man!" (Snyder, c.1946, cited in Bartik, 2008) Her famous quote might seem a little dated in these more gender-advanced years; but we can identify with it, can't we?

The pioneering work of Betty Snyder in the 1940s laid the essential groundwork for the technological advancements that innovators like Claire Blackshaw continue to push forward today. Snyder's early efforts in debugging and programming ENIAC, a machine that required intimate, hands-on interaction, established the foundational principles of human-machine collaboration. Her methods of breaking down complex problems into manageable tasks directly influenced the creation of modern programming languages and algorithms that underpin today's computing systems. Decades later, Blackshaw stands on this legacy, harnessing advanced artificial intelligence (AI) and extended reality (XR) technologies that build upon the logical structures Snyder helped define. While Snyder worked in an era where machines were tools for computation, Blackshaw operates in a time where machines are creative partners. Together, they represent a continuum of innovation, where the breakthroughs of the past empower the possibilities of the future. As we move into the contemporary era of technology, innovators like Claire Blackshaw take the baton passed down by Snyder, pushing the boundaries of what machines can achieve, not as mere tools but as creative partners in an increasingly immersive digital world.

CLAIRE BLACKSHAW: THE MODERN MAVERICK

Claire Blackshaw pushes boundaries where creativity and innovation form the modern technology, we use, but a bit *more*. An unprecedented bit more. From an AI enthusiast in the late 90s/early 00s to a creative programmer and visionary at Adobe, Claire's mission is to bridge the realms of art and technology using generative AI. Her canvas is the virtual world, where she sculpts immersive experiences that blur the lines between human and machine creativity.

Knowing Blackshaw as I do, she is a fierce advocate for accessibility and inclusivity in all that she creates. Born in South Africa, she was always fascinated by the relationship between humans and computers, and, like me, found it difficult to find role models that drive the narrative for her to build her best work upon. Like all good pragmatists, she became her own role model on her journey and embodied the collaborative spirit of the metaverse, where AI is a partner in human expression.

Blackshaw's academic journey began with her degrees in AI computer science and cognitive philosophy at the University of Pretoria. Driven by a disdain for dialogue trees in role-playing games, she sought a better way to handle human-computer interaction. She explored the intersection of human thought and computer thought, leading her to develop innovative solutions. It's no secret in our area of expertise and interest that if we can't find that widget or tool, we always create our own. During her time at Northumbria University, she continued her academic pursuits, despite complications in recognising her prior degrees. She set about conducting an independent study on semantic nets, a field considered dead at that time. However, her persistence paid off when her supervisor was hired by Google to work on the first natural language search, highlighting the significance of her early work. Ironically, though semantic webs have become irrelevant in many ways, by virtue of LLMs (Large Language Models); semantic webs are still very useful working *alongside* modern LLMs.

In the secret chambers of virtual reality (VR), Blackshaw pioneered communication applications, birthing patents and talks that would shape the digital narrative. Her partnership with YouTube, Twitch, and others paved the way for meta-gaming systems, esports integration, and the immersive social UX that defines today's digital ecosystems. Her early efforts at Sony aimed to improve lobbies and metaverse work. One of the most interesting public software patterns was developed for VR social, focusing on expression in social spaces between avatars. This work revealed that hand gestures driving the emotive state of avatars were powerful tools, a discovery now core to VR chat (Figure 5.1) and other social metaverses. This was patented in 2016 incorrectly and assigned to Sony Interactive Entertainment. "We did a talk at GDC 2015 and told everyone this is how you do it please steal it, and many early social games did. It has since spread. Funny, talking to the VRChat team, [I discovered] it was introduced as a community mod initially" (Blackshaw, 2023).

Blackshaw's hands have also shaped the network technology group at Sony and she has consulted on iconic titles like *Horizon*, *Uncharted*, and *Driveclub*. Her contributions in esports at Sony led to the development of PlayStation tournaments, and she still believes that play and competitive nature are central to social infrastructure, and providing tools for people to play and compete in persistent social spaces is crucial. Blackshaw's passion reignited when she championed *Dreams*, the cornerstone of what could have been an amazing metaverse. From UX to the Dreamiverse's social fabric, her touch is always

Figure number	Gesture	Facial expression triggered
Figure 16	Both hands open and forward	Enthusiastic face
Figure 17	One open hand against forehead	Stressed face
Figure 18A and B	Both hands pointing	Super concentrating face
Figure 19A and B	Two fists	Super angry
Figure 20A and B	Two thumbs down	Super sad
Figure 21A and B	One hand pointing	Slightly concentrating face
Figure 22A and B	Two open hands	Neutral
Figure 23A and B	One fist	Slightly angry
Figure 24A and B	One thumb down	Slightly sad
Figure 25A and B	Two thumbs up	Super happy
Figure 26A and B	One thumb up	Slightly happy
Figure 27A and B	Two open hands palm-up	Expression of distaste

FIGURE 5.1 Claire's VRChat style gesture patent (along with team) EP3427103B13B1.

transformative. When her expertise found a new home in the world of technical art specifics in deep aesthetic, it left an indelible mark on the ultimate creation tool of the virtual realm. Making *Dreams* at Media Molecule, a studio more famous for *Little Big Planet*, Claire's initial push was for better spatial representation of scene graphs. She and her team rewrote the entire network infrastructure in three months for the beta launch of Dreams. Blackshaw's role in the creation of *Dreams*, a revolutionary game creation system developed by Media Molecule, represents a profound leap in both technology and creative freedom. Because *Dreams* empowers its users to build complex virtual worlds, transforming game development into an accessible, user-driven process; Blackshaw's work on the recommendation engine and the social infrastructure of *Dreams* set new standards for how players interact with both the technology and each other, emphasising collaboration and creativity. The modular design and spatial representation systems she helped develop have since influenced other metaverse projects and interactive environments. By lowering the technical barriers to entry for game development, *Dreams* has inspired a new generation of women and creators to engage with technology not just as users, but as inventors. Blackshaw's influence on immersive experiences and user-generated content continues to shape the future of XR, VR, and AI-powered creativity.

More recently at Adobe, Blackshaw's work on the VR Sculpting app Modeller exemplifies a synergy of aesthetics and code; allowing individuals to tap into the power of generative algorithms to create art and experiences that were once unimaginable. VR sculpting is a transformative innovation in the world of digital art, design, and 3D modelling. Unlike traditional 2D interfaces, VR sculpting provides artists, designers, and engineers with an immersive, spatial environment in which they can manipulate and shape virtual objects as though they were tangible materials. This technology is revolutionising industries such as gaming, animation, industrial design, and even healthcare, by offering unprecedented creative freedom and precision.

VR sculpting empowers creators to interact with 3D objects in real time using intuitive tools, allowing for unprecedented creative freedom. By combining tactile precision with digital flexibility, this technology offers artists the ability to explore designs that would be impossible through traditional methods, shaping industries from gaming to healthcare.

The importance of VR sculpting lies in several key factors:

1. **Creative Freedom**: VR sculpting eliminates many of the physical limitations of traditional sculpting. Artists can create massive or intricate designs without the need for physical materials, space, or time constraints. VR sculpting software, like Adobe's *Modeller*, enables users to work on objects from multiple perspectives and manipulate them with the ease of hand gestures, providing a fluid creative process.

2. **Accessibility and Collaboration**: In a collaborative VR environment, multiple users from different locations can work on the same 3D model simultaneously. This real-time collaboration is essential for industries such as architecture and product design, where teams often work together to refine a prototype. VR sculpting also lowers the barrier of entry for beginners, allowing them to learn 3D design more intuitively compared to using complex desktop-based software.

3. **Precision and Realism**: For industries like healthcare, VR sculpting has practical applications in areas such as prosthetics and surgical planning. Medical professionals can use the technology to design highly detailed, personalised prosthetic limbs or simulate complex surgeries with greater accuracy. The precision and realism of VR sculpting also make it ideal for developing lifelike characters and environments in the gaming and film industries.

4. **Training and Simulation**: VR sculpting offers a powerful tool for training in fields where physical models are costly or impractical. From automotive design to fashion, professionals can practise and refine their skills in a virtual environment, saving resources and accelerating the design process. Moreover, for educational purposes, students in fields like engineering and art can gain hands-on experience without the need for expensive materials or tools. (Chalmers and Debattista, 2020).

Blackshaw's contributions to the development of VR sculpting tools, particularly at Adobe, have been pivotal in bridging the gap between aesthetics and code. By integrating generative algorithms and VR interfaces, Blackshaw has enabled users to explore complex, interactive art forms that were previously unimaginable. Her work demonstrates how VR sculpting can enhance both creative expression and technical precision, paving the way for innovations that will shape the future of digital art and design.

Driven by her hypothesis that language has poor spatial relationship tools and that most of our interactions with computers have been through abstract intermediaries lacking 3D spatial tools; she sees six-degree-of-freedom controllers and XR as providing the first native spatial interface when combined with language, a vital gap in the AI space. Blackshaw's contributions are etched into the annals of digital evolution. You may have watched her Twitch episodes where she is able to deconstruct and dissect the magic of technology guided by three things: curiosity, logic, and a cup of strong coffee.

In Blackshaw's era, AI is a tool that amplifies human potential, a bridge between imagination and realisation. Her futurist outlook envisions a metaverse where creativity knows no bounds, and generative AI is the paintbrush that brings dreams to life. In the grand tapestry of technological innovation, she emerges as a virtuoso, weaving threads of creativity and programming leaving an indelible mark on the digital landscape. She hasn't just made AI or created unfathomable programs for Adobe; her background is in video games, design, and storytelling.

I might not see her every day, but like her prolific output, I feel Blackshaw all around me. She's also one of the reasons why I wanted to write this book. Women need women to support and challenge them but also to be their guide and hopefully, we become each other's role models. In my career, it was very hard to find women who had the fortitude to withstand the changes and the politics of technology. Blackshaw is one of those people and she continues to inform and question technology's output and ethos as it evolves and flows through her experiments and papers.

Her passion for bridging technology and creativity in XR and everything else is truly inspiring to me, and hopefully, as you read this, you will feel inspired too! But where to begin? Well let's start with the world of tomorrow. That expansive realm of technology sits just moments away from us.

XR refers to a spectrum of technologies that encompass VR, AR, and mixed reality (MR). AI and Machine Learning (ML) can significantly enhance the capabilities and user experience of XR applications in various ways. Here are some ways in which AI and ML enhance XR:

Realistic Content Generation

- **AI-Generated Environments**: AI algorithms can be used to generate realistic and dynamic virtual environments, enhancing the quality of VR experiences. The Bloom Effect is a graphical enhancement technique used to simulate the appearance of bright light sources. It is commonly employed to enhance the visual aesthetics of XR applications, contributing to a more immersive and visually stunning experience for users. Programmers implement algorithms to achieve the bloom effect, adjusting parameters such as intensity and threshold to control the extent of blooming in the virtual or augmented scene.

- **Procedural Content Generation**: ML can aid in the creation of procedurally generated content, adapting virtual environments based on user interactions and preferences. This has been a constant in game development over the last 20 years and now finds itself as a companion to the development of experience in XR (Grier, 2005).

Natural Interaction

- **Gesture Recognition**: Computer vision algorithms play a crucial role in analysing the visual data captured by sensors. These algorithms identify and track key points or features on the user's hands, such as finger positions, hand orientation, and gestures. Depth information is particularly valuable for distinguishing between foreground and background elements.

- **Voice Recognition**: AI-driven speech recognition can enable hands-free control and communication in XR applications. A facet of the process is Natural Language Processing (NLP) and once the spoken words are transcribed into text, NLP techniques are applied to understand the meaning and context of the user's input. NLP allows XR applications to interpret not only individual commands but also more complex and context-aware interactions.

Personalised Experiences

- **User Behaviour Analysis**: ML algorithms can analyse user behaviour within XR environments to understand preferences and adapt content accordingly, providing personalised experiences. Adaptive learning (see below) is a key focus on any ML-driven XR application and vital to the overall understanding of the end user.

- **Content Recommendation**: AI can recommend personalised content or experiences based on user preferences. We've seen this in the past with the Genius Bar on our iTunes page or when we land in any marketplace. What this does is create a more engaging and relevant XR environment.

Improved Object Recognition

- **Object Detection and Tracking**: ML algorithms can enhance AR applications by improving object recognition and tracking, allowing virtual elements to interact seamlessly with the real world.

Dynamic Adaptation

- **Adaptive Learning**: It is possible to incorporate adaptive learning, allowing the system to adapt and improve its output accuracy over time based on user interactions from voice to gesture to choice!

Enhanced Realism and Immersion

- **AI-Driven Rendering**: AI techniques like deep learning can be used to enhance graphics rendering in XR, making virtual scenes more realistic and immersive.
- **Physics Simulation**: ML algorithms can improve the simulation of realistic physics in virtual environments, adding to the overall immersion.

Reduced Latency and Improved Performance

- **Predictive Rendering**: AI algorithms can predict user actions, allowing for pre-rendering of likely scenarios and reducing latency in VR applications.
- **Performance Optimisation**: ML can be used to optimise XR applications for various devices, ensuring smoother performance and better user experiences.

Enhanced Safety and Navigation

- **Obstacle Detection**: ML algorithms can be employed for real-time obstacle detection in AR and MR applications, improving safety and preventing collisions with physical objects.

Context Awareness

- **Environment Understanding**: AI can help XR devices understand and interpret the user's physical environment, allowing for more context-aware and responsive experiences.

User Assistance

- **AI-driven Guidance**: ML algorithms can provide users with assistance and guidance within XR environments, making navigation and interaction more user-friendly.

Integrating AI and ML into XR not only improves the technology's capabilities but also opens new possibilities for creating innovative and personalised experiences for users. The combination of these technologies has the potential to revolutionise the way we interact with virtual and augmented worlds.

I often lament the demise of Oculus Go. This is something Blackshaw and I debate upon with some frequency. The point is, there is nowhere for the Oculus to Go when refining technology for advanced use cases. I tend to live in a hopeful world where the digital skills and poverty gap are overcome at the point of crossing the chasm. Her argument is not about Oculus Go *per se*, though for her to continue her development it's important to acknowledge to let go of the past.

XR really does that, it extends reality to a place where our brains become receptive to change perhaps in the way that our hearts are not. In our debate which was really my lament of the end of Oculus Go, Blackshaw offered a solid reasoning that it held no promise for XR tomorrow. It didn't do anything but allow the user to wander from sofa to bathroom in an eternal quest for wirelessness. The joy for most users ended with Resolution Games' Bait! However, Blackshaw was much more focused on the Quest, Quest 2 and even the Steam VR. Having worked on various VR developments for Sony and Media Molecule, it makes sense that she is still way ahead of fishing games and wireless play.

Blackshaw was exploring the phenomenon of phantom touch in haptics for XR. Phantom touch refers to the perception of tactile sensations on a user's skin that are not physically present or initiated by an external source. In the context of XR, haptics technology is used to simulate the sense of touch or force feedback in virtual environments. It occurs when users experience the sensation of being touched, pressed, or contacted by virtual objects even though there is no corresponding physical interaction in the real world.

Several factors contribute to the occurrence of phantom touch in haptics for XR:

- **Illusory Sensations**: Haptic feedback in XR relies on the simulation of tactile sensations through devices such as haptic gloves or controllers. Illusory sensations can occur when the virtual stimuli provided by these devices create a convincing illusion of touch.

- **Brain's Sensory Interpretation**: The brain interprets sensory information from various sources to construct our perception of the environment. In the absence of real-world tactile stimuli, the brain may still generate sensations based on visual and auditory cues present in the virtual environment.

- **Crosstalk Between Senses**: The brain often integrates information from multiple senses to create a coherent perception of the world. In XR, visual and auditory cues can influence the perception of touch, leading to the illusion of tactile sensations that align with the virtual visual and auditory stimuli.

- **Expectation and Immersion**: Users' expectations and the level of immersion in a virtual environment can influence their perception of touch. If the virtual experience is highly immersive and users expect to feel certain tactile sensations, their brains may generate phantom touch sensations to align with those expectations.

- **Limited Fidelity of Haptic Devices**: Haptic devices in XR may not perfectly replicate the complexity and subtlety of real-world tactile sensations. The limited fidelity of these devices may contribute to the brain filling in the gaps and creating phantom touch sensations.

- **Sensory Substitution**: XR technologies often involve substituting or augmenting real-world sensory experiences with virtual ones. The brain's ability to adapt and interpret virtual stimuli as if they were real can contribute to the phenomenon of phantom touch.

Phantom touch will be important in designing more immersive and realistic haptic feedback systems for XR. Developers are already using this knowledge to enhance the user experience by optimising haptic feedback algorithms and considering how the brain processes and interprets multisensory information in virtual environments.

While Snyder's contributions are marked by her trailblazing work in the early days of computing, Blackshaw's expertise lies in the sculpting and crafting of code to create practical and impactful use cases in AI and ML for XR technologies and beyond, reflecting the evolution and sophistication of technology over time. Despite the time shift between these two and methodological pathways which differ depending on need, their contributions shape technology not just for women but for all of us.

Blackshaw and Snyder, though separated by time and technology, share a common thread—their unwavering commitment to innovation and the harmonious coexistence of humans and AI. Claire's work leverages the full potential of generative AI to amplify human creativity in the metaverse, while Betty's pioneering efforts paved the way for the digital era we inhabit today.

While Blackshaw operates in an era of advanced AI, where machines are increasingly autonomous, Snyder's work reflects the early days of computing when humans were the architects of AI's intelligence. From the punch card to the SORT/MERGE from a pack of cards and all the way to diagrams of gestures for VRChat (and PSVR!); both women exemplify the power of human ingenuity, adaptability, and the ability to harness technology to achieve remarkable feats.

Betty Snyder and Claire Blackshaw, though separated by decades and different technological landscapes, embody the resilience and innovation that have driven the evolution of computing. Snyder's groundbreaking work on ENIAC and UNIVAC laid the foundation for modern computing, shaping the algorithms and systems that power today's technology. Blackshaw, in turn, builds upon this legacy, pushing the boundaries of AI and XR to create immersive, user-driven experiences. Both women demonstrate that, while the tools may have changed, the spirit of invention and creativity remains timeless. Their contributions not only advanced technology but also paved the way for future generations of women to break barriers, proving that resilience, adaptability, and vision are the true driving forces behind technological progress.

REFERENCES

Abbate, J. (2012) *Recoding gender: Women's changing participation in computing*. Cambridge, MA: MIT Press, pp. 60–62, 110–112.

Bartik, J. (2008) Oral History Interview. Computer History Museum. Transcript.

Beyer, K.W. (2009) *Grace Hopper and the invention of the information age*. Cambridge, MA: MIT Press, pp. 48–50, 158–160.

Blackshaw, C. (2023–2024) Interview by Kelly Vero. 12 December 2023; 18 February 2024; 16 July 2024.

Ceruzzi, P.E. (2003) *A history of modern computing*. Cambridge, MA: MIT Press, pp. 34–35.

Chalmers, A. and Debattista, K. (2020) *Real-time rendering and VR for games*. Boca Raton, FL: CRC Press.

European Patent Office EP3427103B1 (2016) (https://patents.google.com/patent/EP3427103B1) Martin Shenton, Martin Echenique, Claire Blackshaw. Elisheva Shapiro.

Goldstine, H.H. (1993) *The computer from Pascal to von Neumann*. Princeton, NJ: Princeton University Press, pp. 154–159.

Grier, D.A. (2005) When computers were human. Princeton, NJ: Princeton University Press, pp. 245–246.

Holberton, P. (2021) Fireside Chat on Betty Holberton. Transcript.

IEEE Annals of the History of Computing. (1997) 'Betty Holberton Tribute.' *IEEE Computer Society,* pp. 27–32.

Light, J.S. (1999) 'When computers were women', *Technology and Culture*, 40(3), pp. 455–483.

McCartney, S. (1999) *ENIAC: The triumphs and tragedies of the World's first computer*. New York: Walker & Company, pp. 25–27, 88–91, 138–140.

Sheppard, A. (2013). 'Meet the "Refrigerator Ladies" Who Programmed the ENIAC', *Mental Floss*, 13 October. Available at: https://www.mentalfloss.com/article/53160/meet-refrigerator-ladies-who-programmed-eniac (Accessed: 9 October 2024)

CHAPTER 6

Kayleigh Oliver and Delia Derbyshire

Telling Truths

STORYTELLING IN TECHNOLOGY IS a fascinating topic, as it bridges the gap between creativity and technical proficiency. Storytelling helps humanise technology, making it more accessible, relatable, and impactful. Even for those who can't code, storytelling can be a powerful tool in shaping experiences and contributing to innovation.

Telling stories allows non-technical people to convey their vision and ideas effectively to developers and engineers. We can translate abstract concepts into tangible narratives that can drive innovation. Even without coding skills, someone with a strong sense of storytelling can define the *why* and *how* behind a product or experience.

Many great technological innovations start with a story—whether it's solving a real-world problem or creating a vision for the future. Designers and product managers often use storytelling to understand users' needs, then work with technical teams to bring those stories to life through code and design.

You don't need to be an artist to create beautiful experiences. Creative professionals like designers, artists, and writers work closely with developers to craft compelling narratives, visuals, and user experiences. Collaboration is key; developers can bring the technical aspect to life, while storytellers shape the direction and emotional resonance. Together we can create anything from nothing at all.

In this chapter, two amazing women tell stories in very different ways using hardware and using code. It's fantastic to be able to bring Delia Derbyshire and Kayleigh Oliver together because these are two women who exemplify what it means to break through bytes more than most.

DOI: 10.1201/9781003566465-6

KAYLEIGH OLIVER: CODING WITH PURPOSE

Women receive other women's respect and fealty for several reasons. They could have voices loud enough to be heard (that's mostly me) or they could be women who show their strength through skills (that's all the women in this book!). In the world of software development and technological innovation, Kayleigh Oliver is telling a story. This story is about progress and representation. She founded Figures of Black British Society (FOBBS) to reshape the educational landscape to encourage more diversity in the discussions we have about who we are and what things we might achieve. She has also pioneered new ways to ensure inclusivity in tech. Through her technical expertise and passion for diversity, Kayleigh has carved a path that empowers future generations to dream bigger, code smarter, and view technology as a tool for societal change.

I have been fortunate enough to work with Kayleigh; but even when I haven't, I have been quietly (and not always quietly) rooting for her. I am always drawn to people who reflect the work ethic I have, and often, it's a work ethic that is frowned upon, especially in the videogames industry these days. Hearing stories about crunch and long hours at the keyboard are not always horror stories, sometimes it's simply people like me, and maybe Oliver, who want to learn as much about our field of understanding as we can.

From being named one of the *50 Most Inspiring Women in Tech UK* to winning the *Precious Leadership Award*, Oliver's journey reflects the power of resilience, innovation, and a desire to impact her community. Whether creating mobile apps or pioneering software solutions, Oliver's commitment to problem-solving has made her a transformative figure in the tech world. But her contributions go far beyond just technical achievements—her work serves as a call to action for diversity and inclusion, ensuring that stories like hers are woven into the very fabric of our society.

For Oliver, the spark of technological curiosity was ignited in her childhood, surrounded by the hum of the family's Sega Mega Drive and the excitement of problem-solving games. It was her father's love for technology that set the foundation, making theirs one of the first families in her community to own a personal computer. While the games were fun, what truly captivated young Oliver was the challenge they presented—games like *Broken Sword: Shadow of the Templars* and *The Dig* demanded strategic thinking and creativity, and she revelled in it.

"I've always enjoyed fixing things," I agree that this tends to be the starting point for many women in technology "[…] I also love the satisfaction of repairing something that's broken. It's like a little challenge for me, and I win if I can fix it." This passion for solving puzzles would later evolve into a defining characteristic of her career as a software developer. But games weren't just a pastime; they became a family affair. Oliver and her sisters would spend hours immersed in both video and board games, reinforcing her belief in the power of play to bring people together. The early lessons she learned from these experiences— creativity, perseverance, and a love of problem-solving—would shape her path forward.

Oliver's journey into software development began with an ambition that was as bold as it was unconventional—she wanted to create video games that better represented the world she saw around her. As a young woman of Jamaican descent, she longed to see characters in games that looked like her, that reflected her experiences. Her early interest in games led her to pursue a degree in software engineering at Nottingham, where her curiosity about technology deepened.

However, even as Oliver honed her skills, the idea that she could make a career out of gaming seemed distant—until her placement year with a games company opened her eyes to new possibilities. "I wanted to become a games designer," she recalls. "I eventually got a role as a Senior Quality Assurance (QA) tester within a games company and began my path to be a games designer." As she navigated the gaming industry, she realised that its culture and operational outlook didn't fully align with her own vision. The lack of diverse representation, both on-screen and in the industry itself, left her yearning for something more impactful.

Representation of Black, Asian, and Minority Ethnic (BAME) characters in video games has seen improvements in recent years, but significant gaps remain, particularly when it comes to lead characters and creators in the industry. A study found that between 2017 and 2021, only 8.3% of protagonists in major video games were both female and non-white, demonstrating the underrepresentation of people of colour in leading roles. Many lead characters—79.2%—were male, and 54.2% of them were white (TheGrio, 2023).

Despite the diversity among gamers, with over half of Black and Hispanic individuals identifying as gamers, the gaming industry remains predominantly white and male. Only 2% of global game developers identify as Black, while 10% of those working in the UK gaming industry are from BAME backgrounds, with much lower percentages in senior roles (2Game, 2023). "Before the world of the internet, social media and amazing communities like Black Girl Gamers (we) felt isolated because (we) thought (we) were alone so I wanted to change that feeling" (Oliver, 2024).

Progress has been made with some notable Black characters taking central roles in games, such as Miles Morales in *Spider-Man: Miles Morales* and Saga Anderson in *Alan Wake 2*. These characters have been praised for their depth and representation of modern, diverse experiences (Culture Bay, 2023; TheGrio, 2023). Additionally, there are rising efforts, such as the *BAME in Games* initiative, to foster more ethnic diversity within the industry, focusing on nurturing talent from underrepresented backgrounds and addressing the lack of diversity in the workforce (BAME in Games, 2024). These statistics and initiatives highlight the need for ongoing efforts to improve representation, both in terms of game characters and the creators behind the scenes, ensuring that the gaming world reflects its diverse player base.

Oliver's pivot from games to software testing as a QA Engineer marked a significant turning point. In this role, she not only developed deeper technical skills but also found a way to merge her passion for problem-solving with her desire to make meaningful contributions to society. "I stayed in QA because I found a really good match with my natural abilities," But her desire to make a tangible difference didn't stop there. After working for two years as a QA Engineer, she transitioned to .NET development, diving into the world of C# programming, a field that fuelled her love for creating "digital things out of nothing."

C# (pronounced *C-sharp*) is a high-level, object-oriented programming language developed by Microsoft in the early 2000s. It was designed by Anders Hejlsberg as part of Microsoft's .NET initiative (Hejlsberg, 2000), which aimed to provide developers with a unified platform for building Windows applications. C# was first introduced in 2000, with its initial release alongside the .NET Framework in 2002. It was created to combine the simplicity of Java with the flexibility and power of C++. C# was particularly aimed at building Windows desktop applications and web services through the .NET Framework.

The first official version of C# was released with the .NET Framework 1.0. It featured object-oriented programming constructs such as classes, inheritance, and polymorphism. It supported garbage collection, type safety, and managed code execution within the Common Language Runtime (CLR). Other releases have improved the language through additional features from generics and nullable types to more recent introductions of records, which are immutable data structures ideal for functional programming. The language continues to evolve with new releases that include enhanced support for performance optimisation, functional programming, and developer productivity.

C# has become one of the most popular programming languages globally, particularly for enterprise-level applications, web development, and game development (with Unity using C# as its primary scripting language). It's widely used in backend services, desktop software, and mobile app development via Xamarin. C# is an integral part of Microsoft's ecosystem and remains highly relevant due to its integration with the .NET ecosystem, offering robust frameworks, libraries, and tools for developers.

It was this deeper dive into coding that illuminated a new revelation for Oliver—while designing games to entertain was rewarding, technology had the potential to do so much more. She wanted to use her skills to change lives, to build solutions that could make the world a better place. "I learned that while being able to create games to entertain people is great, technology has the power to change people's lives for the better," she explains. This realisation was the seed that eventually grew into her most ambitious project: the *Figures of Black British Society (FOBBS)* platform, an educational resource designed to shine a light on Black British achievements, inspire children, and provide educators with much-needed tools to diversify their teaching.

In March 2020, as the world grappled with the early stages of the COVID-19 pandemic, Oliver found herself on maternity leave, reflecting on how she could contribute to a more inclusive and equitable society. Balancing life as a mother and a software developer, her thoughts shifted towards her children and their future. She wanted them to grow up in a world where they could see themselves reflected in history, celebrated for their heritage, and empowered to dream big. This desire became the catalyst for her most significant project to date: the *Figures of Black British Society* app.

FOBBS was born out of a realisation that there was a glaring gap in the UK's educational curriculum—Black British history was largely absent. "In the 25 years since I had left school, not much had changed in the UK education system," Oliver observed. It was this frustrating void, compounded by the Black Lives Matter protests in 2020, that pushed her to act. She knew that her own children, along with thousands of others, needed to see stories of Black British achievements integrated into their education, not as an afterthought during Black History Month, but as part of a consistent and comprehensive narrative.

The FOBBS app was designed to address this gap by providing teachers and students with an accessible, engaging resource that celebrated Black British history. Oliver's objective was simple but powerful: to give every child the opportunity to learn about the achievements of Black Britons, not only during Black History Month but year-round. In doing so, she hoped to inspire a new generation to see themselves as future leaders, innovators, and creators.

"It's said that children as young as five already know what they want to be when they grow up. I'm lucky that my work with FOBBS is being shared with users as young as five to help them broaden their career options and help them dream bigger" (Oliver, 2024). Research suggests that children as young as five years old begin to form ideas about their future careers, influenced largely by their environment and social interactions. A study called *Drawing the Future* surveyed over 20,000 children aged 7 to 11 and found that many express aspirations aligned with familiar roles such as teachers, athletes, and entertainers (Education and Employers, 2018). Moreover, research from the University of Washington suggests that by age 5, children already possess a well-developed sense of self-esteem, which significantly influences their future career aspirations (University of Washington, 2015). These studies highlight the importance of early exposure to diverse career possibilities to broaden young children's aspirations. "By doing this, I hope it shows every child that a career in app development is a real option" (Oliver, 2024).

Despite the clear need for such a resource, the journey to develop FOBBS was not without its challenges. One of the first obstacles Oliver faced was determining the criteria for who to include in the app's content. The UK is home to many incredible Black Britons, but how could she ensure the selection was fair, inclusive, and representative? After extensive research and consultation, she established criteria that balanced historical significance with modern-day relevance, ensuring the app featured a diverse array of figures from across the spectrum of British history.

Another hurdle came when many schools began transitioning from tablets to Chromebooks, creating a technical challenge for Oliver's mobile-first app. But ever the problem-solver, she quickly adapted by using a no-code tool to build a web version of FOBBS. While it initially offered fewer features, the web version ensured that the essential content was still accessible, particularly in schools where budgets were tight.

In addition to these logistical and technical challenges, maintaining a team of volunteers for FOBBS proved difficult. As the founder, Oliver often had to deal with the natural ebb and flow of volunteer commitment, especially when balancing the demands of her own full-time job and family life. Over time, she learned how to set clear expectations for volunteers and create a structure that allowed everyone to contribute meaningfully, while managing the project's ongoing needs.

Despite these challenges, FOBBS has already begun to make an impact in schools across the UK. One primary school used the platform to celebrate *Refugee Week*, showcasing Black British refugees in a way that not only educated students but also helped to shift the negative narratives often associated with refugees. The app provided content that was both timely and accessible, empowering teachers to create engaging and informative displays for their students.

As Oliver continues to expand FOBBS, she regularly visits local schools to show students firsthand that app development—and a career in tech—is not only possible but achievable.

"I want these children to see that I, a Black British female of Jamaican descent who is also a mum, am the developer for an app that they can use" (Oliver, 2024). The journey to building FOBBS, much like Oliver's path in tech, and for so many women in this book have been a test of resilience and ingenuity. Every challenge she faced became an opportunity to innovate, problem-solve, and grow. As a Black British woman in the tech industry, Oliver was no stranger to overcoming hurdles, whether they were related to societal bias, technical constraints, or the inherent difficulties of leading a project from the ground up.

One of the earliest challenges Oliver encountered when developing FOBBS was determining who to include in the platform. Black British history is rich with figures whose contributions span generations and sectors, but not every story could be told at once. Establishing fair, realistic, and representative criteria for inclusion was essential to ensure the app delivered both breadth and depth in its content. After rigorous research, she and her team devised a framework that balanced historical significance with cultural impact. Yet, she remains committed to revisiting and evolving these criteria as more stories come to light, ensuring FOBBS continues to reflect a diverse array of achievements.

The next challenge came in a form no developer can fully predict—technological shifts in the educational environment. As schools began transitioning from tablet devices to Chromebooks, Oliver realised that FOBBS, originally designed as a mobile-first app, might no longer meet the technical needs of many schools. This shift could have derailed her project, but she saw it as another problem to solve. Instead of starting from scratch or halting the project, she quickly adapted by using no-code tools to create a web version of FOBBS. The new version provided the same essential content, ensuring schools could still access the resources they needed. "This was a real problem but the no-code tool allowed me to quickly create a web version, and although it had fewer features initially, it ensured schools still had access to the content." In typical Oliver fashion, she took a limitation and transformed it into an opportunity, pushing her to experiment with more no-code solutions and explore how these tools could benefit other projects in her portfolio.

No-code is a software development approach that allows users to build applications, websites, workflows, and automations without writing traditional code. Instead, no-code platforms use visual interfaces, drag-and-drop tools, and pre-built components to enable users, even those without technical backgrounds, to create functional solutions. These platforms abstract the complexity of coding, making software development accessible to a broader audience. But what are the benefits of no-code when we've spent so long building and understanding programming and coding languages?

1. **Visual Development**: Users interact with a graphical interface to design applications by dragging and dropping elements, configuring settings, and defining logic through visual workflows.

2. **Pre-Built Components**: No-code platforms come with a wide array of pre-built templates, APIs, and widgets that can be customised for specific needs.

3. **Integration-Friendly**: Many no-code platforms offer built-in integrations with external tools (e.g. CRMs, databases, or cloud services), allowing users to extend functionality.

Popular No-Code Platforms:

- **Airtable**: Combines spreadsheet functionality with database features for building workflows.

- **Bubble**: Used for building full-stack web applications.

- **Zapier**: Focuses on automating workflows by connecting different apps.

- **Webflow**: Enables users to design and build websites without writing code.

Ease of Building No-Code Solutions:

- **User-Friendly**: The drag-and-drop interface and intuitive setup make it easy for non-developers to build projects quickly. A task that might take weeks in traditional coding can often be accomplished in a matter of days or even hours with no-code tools.

- **Rapid Prototyping**: No-code platforms allow for quick prototyping and iteration, enabling users to test ideas and refine them without committing significant development resources.

Adapting No-Code into Workflows and Pipelines:

1. **Ease of Integration**: No-code platforms are designed with flexibility in mind. Many provide native integrations with popular tools like Slack, Google Sheets, Salesforce, or AWS (Amazon Web Services), making it easier to incorporate them into existing workflows and data pipelines. Tools like Zapier or Integromat allow users to create automations that connect different services and platforms without the need for custom API (Application Programming Interface) coding.

2. **Scalability**: While no-code tools excel at handling smaller, simpler workflows, scalability can sometimes be a limitation. For complex workflows or large-scale applications, integrating custom code might be necessary. Some platforms offer low-code options, where developers can add custom code for advanced functionalities.

3. **Customisation and Flexibility**: Although no-code tools are flexible for common use cases, advanced customisation can be restricted by the platform's limitations. If your needs go beyond what the platform offers, it can be more challenging to adapt compared to custom-built software. However, many platforms have add-on features, plug-ins, or allow for scripting to extend functionality.

Challenges and Considerations:

- **Vendor Lock-In**: Since no-code platforms are proprietary, migrating a no-code solution to a custom code environment can be difficult if the business needs to scale or move to a different platform.

- **Complex Logic Limitations**: No-code solutions can struggle with highly complex business logic, where traditional coding might be more efficient and scalable.

- **Security and Compliance**: For organisations with strict compliance or security needs, no-code platforms might not offer the level of control that custom development provides.

Another significant hurdle for FOBBS was maintaining a consistent team of volunteers. Enthusiastic as they were, many volunteers found it difficult to balance their work on FOBBS with their full-time jobs, personal responsibilities, and other commitments. This was a tough lesson for Oliver, especially in the early stages, but it taught her the importance of setting clear expectations. By introducing term-based volunteer commitments and regularly checking in with her team, she was able to ensure the project stayed on track without burning out her contributors. "I've learned to set expectations for both parties from the beginning […] it gives transparency and provides volunteers with something tangible at the end of their term" (Oliver, 2024).

Time management was another challenge that became particularly pressing as Oliver juggled her full-time role in tech, family life, and the development of FOBBS. The early stages of the app's creation often meant working late into the night after her children were asleep or carving out moments of focus during their naps. Over time, she discovered that splitting her time into themed weeks—dedicating some weeks to writing content, others to technical work, and still others to administrative tasks—helped her maintain progress on all fronts without feeling overwhelmed. "It keeps me focused and working towards my bigger goal, while also making progress in other areas" (Oliver, 2024).

Oliver's ability to balance her many roles—mother, developer, founder—while continuing to drive FOBBS forward demonstrates her resilience and her refusal to be defined by the limitations that others might place on her. Each challenge that surfaced along the way strengthened her resolve and sharpened her skills, further cementing her role as a trailblazer in tech. From defining the app's content to navigating technological changes and managing volunteer efforts, her ability to confront challenges head-on has resulted in a product that is more accessible, adaptable, and impactful than even she initially imagined. Through it all, her commitment to creating a tool that educates, empowers, and inspires young minds remains at the heart of everything she does.

The impact of Oliver's work with the FOBBS platform has already begun to ripple through schools and communities across the UK. What started as a personal mission to provide her children with a deeper understanding of their Black British heritage has blossomed into an educational tool that is making a real difference in classrooms, inspiring students, and equipping teachers with much-needed resources.

For Oliver, the most rewarding aspect of developing FOBBS is seeing it used in real-world settings. One of the early success stories came from a primary school that used the platform to celebrate *Refugee Week*. The school wanted to shine a light on Black British refugees, using FOBBS to build an engaging and informative display that helped shift the often-negative narratives surrounding refugees. Her research skills and the flexibility of the app allowed her to quickly create and deliver new content to the school within a day, demonstrating the platform's adaptability and value as a timely educational resource.

This is just one example of the platform's real-world impact, but for Oliver, the most powerful moments come from her visits to local schools. There, she stands in front of classrooms as a Black British woman, a mother, and an app developer, showing students that careers in tech are not only accessible but exciting and full of potential. Her presence alone breaks down stereotypes, and her story resonates deeply with students who might not otherwise see themselves reflected in the tech industry.

The feedback from both students and educators has been overwhelmingly positive. In a survey conducted by FOBBS with 141 children from Year 2 to Year 6, an impressive 76% said they would use FOBBS for their homework. Younger students noted how much they enjoyed the app's design, with its vibrant colours and user-friendly interface. Teachers have echoed this enthusiasm, praising FOBBS for filling a crucial gap in the curriculum and providing valuable, reliable content that is both relatable and easy to implement in the classroom.

"It is such a lovely resource," one teacher commented, noting that FOBBS helps make Black British history accessible in a way that had previously been missing from the UK's education system. Another teacher remarked, "The development of this app will provide everyone, but especially teachers and students, a reliable supplementary resource for their day-to-day learning. We need a resource that brings to life these forgotten figures of our British history and helps inspire the future leaders. FOBBS is a brilliant idea that will help provide this change" (Oliver, 2024).

Beyond the classroom, FOBBS has also started to spark conversations in the broader educational community. Oliver has been invited to speak on various platforms about Black people in tech, and her advocacy for incorporating more Black British history into the curriculum has caught the attention of companies and organisations looking to amplify her message. She recalls a memorable moment during a podcast interview where the host, who shared her Jamaican and British heritage, expressed deep gratitude for the work she was doing with FOBBS. "He told me how growing up in a majority-white town, there was almost no representation of Black British achievements in his education. He thanked me for creating a platform that fills this gap, saying it gave him and others a chance to feel seen and proud of their heritage," she reflects. This kind of feedback fuels Kayleigh's passion for continuing to expand the reach of FOBBS, knowing that it resonates so deeply with people from diverse backgrounds. It underscores the powerful potential of FOBBS to inspire pride, belonging, and ambition in children who may not see themselves in traditional history lessons. For Oliver, the impact of her work is just beginning, and she remains excited about the future possibilities for FOBBS to reach even more students, schools, and communities.

As the platform continues to grow, Oliver is focused on collecting more comprehensive feedback to ensure FOBBS meets the evolving needs of its users. Her ambition is to create an enduring resource that not only fills a gap in Black British history education but also encourages all children to dream bigger and consider careers in technology, knowing they can be part of shaping the future.

Oliver's work is rooted in her firm belief that technology, at its best, should be inclusive, diverse, and accessible to all. As both a developer and an advocate for representation, she has made it her mission to not only build innovative solutions but also to ensure that the process of creating these solutions reflects the diversity of the world around us. In every project she tackles, from software development to the creation of the FOBBS platform, Oliver integrates the principles of diversity, equity, and inclusion (DEI) into her work.

For Oliver, DEI isn't just a checkbox to tick—it's a fundamental part of how she approaches both her career and her role as a leader. "When interviewing candidates for my career and volunteers for FOBBS, I make a conscious effort to go beyond just reviewing their written applications" (Oliver, 2024). Her interview process is more than a mere formality; it's an opportunity to engage with candidates, understand their perspectives, and ensure they bring diverse voices to the team.

Oliver's personal commitment to DEI extends far beyond the hiring process. She actively works to identify and minimise biases, consistently challenging her assumptions and striving to ensure her decisions are equitable. This conscious effort helps her foster an inclusive work environment, where every member of her team feels heard, respected, and empowered to contribute.

At the heart of her work on FOBBS is the representation of Black British voices and stories that have long been overlooked. Oliver takes great care to ensure that the content within the app reflects a broad spectrum of experiences, from various cultural backgrounds to different gender identities and abilities. "With the FOBBS platform, I ensure the content we deliver represents diverse voices and experiences" (Oliver, 2024).

This approach has led her to continually reassess the content being produced, working closely with her team to ensure that it aligns with the broader goals of DEI. Oliver is mindful of showcasing Black British achievements from all walks of life—figures who inspire not just because of their success but because of the barriers they've overcome and the varied paths they've taken. Whether it's a story of an unsung historical figure or a modern-day trailblazer, her desire is to create content that resonates with students of all backgrounds and inspires them to see themselves as part of the narrative.

Beyond FOBBS, Oliver's advocacy for DEI is also reflected in her broader contributions to the tech industry. She frequently speaks about the importance of representation in technology, especially as the industry becomes increasingly reliant on artificial intelligence and other emerging technologies. Oliver understands that diversity is crucial, not just in terms of who is building the technology, but also in how that technology functions and serves the world.

"There's still so little representation of Black women in tech, and the products we make will eventually reflect this" (Oliver, 2024). The lack of diversity in AI development, for example, is particularly concerning, as algorithms created by a homogenous group may inadvertently perpetuate biases that harm underrepresented communities. "Only 22% of AI developers are women [...] we need to get behind the code of these tools that are building the future, so we can shape the future to benefit everyone" (Oliver, 2024).

The statistic that only 22% of AI professionals are women comes from a report by the World Economic Forum in collaboration with LinkedIn, highlighting the gender disparity in AI roles. This figure underscores the significant underrepresentation of women in the field, which poses challenges not just for gender equity but also for the development of fair and unbiased AI systems. In machine learning, a specific branch of AI, the gap is even starker, with women comprising just 12% of leading researchers (World Economic Forum, 2020).

Additionally, studies show that in the UK, the percentage of women in AI drops to 22%, compared to a global average of 26% in data and AI roles (Alan Turing Institute, 2023). These figures point to a persistent gender gap in AI and related fields, urging further efforts to close the gap through education, upskilling, and industry-wide changes.

Oliver's work on FOBBS, along with her broader advocacy in tech, speaks to her commitment to ensuring that technology is inclusive, equitable, and reflective of the diverse communities it serves. By championing DEI, both within her projects and in the industry at large, she is helping to pave the way for a future where technology is truly for everyone.

While Oliver's passion for social impact drives much of her work, her deep technical expertise is what enables her to turn ideas into reality. Over the years, she has developed an impressive range of skills, specialising in areas such as software testing, iOS and Android development, cloud applications, and mobile app development. Her ability to stay ahead of the curve in these ever-evolving fields has been key to her success—not only in her career but also in the development of the FOBBS platform.

In an industry that moves at lightning speed, Oliver knows that keeping her skills up to date is essential. Her strategy for staying current is a blend of continuous learning and hands-on experimentation. "I regularly rotate between different types of educational content—books, YouTube videos, podcasts—so I can gain deeper insights into my core focus areas," she explains. Whether diving into the complexities of clean coding principles or staying informed about the latest developments in cloud technology, she is committed to ensuring that her technical knowledge remains cutting-edge.

She is particularly focused on the areas of software architecture, microservices, and cloud technologies, which are becoming increasingly essential in today's tech landscape. This forward-thinking approach allows her to ensure that the products she works on are scalable, high-performing, and built to stand the test of time. "No-code tools have matured and become quite sophisticated [...] they are able to connect via API to the tools that natively coded mobile apps communicate with, at a fraction of the time spent in development" (Oliver, 2024).

Oliver's ability to pivot between traditional coding and no-code tools demonstrates her versatility as a developer. By embracing new technologies, she has been able to streamline development processes, build more efficient solutions, and ultimately create products that are both functional and accessible to a wide audience.

Her passion for design is another driving force behind her technical projects. While Oliver enjoys the nuts and bolts of coding, it's the user experience that excites her the most. "Using these no-code tools allows me to focus more on design, client satisfaction, and user enjoyment of a great product, rather than technical implementation" (Oliver, 2024) and her aim is to create technology that not only works seamlessly but also brings joy to its users which I think we can all attest to.

Beyond her work with FOBBS, Oliver continues to explore innovative projects that push the boundaries of what technology can achieve. Her hands-on approach, combined with her commitment to staying ahead of the curve, ensures that she remains at the forefront of technological advancement. Whether experimenting with new coding frameworks or leveraging cloud-based solutions, her technical mastery allows her to bring bold ideas to life in ways that are both creative and impactful.

For aspiring developers, Oliver's advice is simple: stay curious, stay adaptable, and never stop learning. Her approach to technical mastery is rooted in a desire to constantly improve—not just for the sake of keeping up with trends, but to create meaningful, user-focused solutions that have a lasting impact.

Oliver's achievements in the tech industry have not gone unnoticed. Over the course of her career, she has received numerous awards and recognitions, cementing her status as a trailblazer in the field. Being named one of the *50 Most Inspiring Women in Tech UK* and winning the *Precious Leadership Award* are just two highlights from a growing list of accolades that acknowledge her contributions to both technology and diversity.

For Oliver, these awards are more than just personal achievements—they're reminders of the barriers she has broken and the new pathways she is helping to carve for others. "These recognitions have validated the hard work and dedication I've put into my career and the teams I've worked within" (Oliver, 2024). More importantly, they have opened doors to new opportunities, giving her a platform to inspire and mentor others, particularly women and underrepresented groups in tech.

What makes Oliver's story so impactful is the way she uses her visibility to lift others up. As a Black British woman in an industry where diversity is still lacking, Oliver understands the importance of representation. She actively seeks out ways to serve as a role model and mentor for younger generations, showing them that careers in tech are not only possible but within their reach. Her leadership goes beyond the technical aspects of her work—she is committed to fostering a sense of belonging and empowerment for those who, like her, may have once felt they didn't belong in this space.

"I see my role as a leader and role model in the tech community, especially for young Black British women, as both a privilege and a responsibility […] it's crucial for me to be visible and active in this space, showing that it's possible to succeed in an industry where we are often underrepresented."

Through her mentoring efforts, Oliver encourages young women to think critically about their career paths, plan strategies, and confidently navigate the challenges they might face. She's especially passionate about supporting mothers returning to tech after maternity leave, as she knows firsthand the challenges of balancing motherhood and a demanding career. "Coming back into a tech role can be quite daunting because of the technology changes and just your lack of sleep" (Oliver, 2024). By offering support, direction, and mentorship, she helps women in similar positions re-enter the workforce with confidence.

But her leadership doesn't stop at mentorship. Oliver is also vocal about the need for diversity in tech, particularly in the development of new technologies like artificial intelligence. Oliver emphasises the importance of having diverse voices behind the code that will shape the future. Without representation, the very tools that are designed to serve society risk perpetuating bias and inequality.

"There's still so little representation of Black women in tech," she observes. "We need to get behind the code of these tools that are building the future, so we can shape the future to benefit everyone" (Oliver, 2024).

Oliver's leadership extends to her own children as well. Her awards and accomplishments are not just symbols of her success—they serve as visible reminders to her daughter and son that they too can excel in their chosen paths. "These award trophies are a visible reminder around my house to my children, especially my daughter, that these things are possible […] as well as being a mum, I can create a life around my children, and they see that mummy is awesome in all sorts of ways" (Oliver, 2024).

In every aspect of her career, Oliver leads by example. Whether she's building technology, mentoring young developers, or speaking out for greater diversity in the industry, she embodies what it means to be a true role model. Her influence is felt not only through the projects she's developed but also through the lives she's touched and the future leaders she's inspiring.

As Kayleigh Oliver looks to the future, her ambitions remain firmly rooted in her desire to build a more inclusive, innovative, and empowering tech landscape. Her work with the FOBBS platform has only just begun, and she envisions it becoming a vital resource for schools not only in the UK, but globally. Her purpose is for FOBBS to be the go-to tool for educators seeking to bring Black British history into the classroom all year round, ensuring that every child has access to stories that celebrate diversity, resilience, and achievement. "I want FOBBS to be the leading resource for schools to explore and understand Black British history […] the impact that Black Britons have made in the UK is profound, and it is only fitting that their contributions are celebrated alongside other historical icons" (Oliver, 2024).

Beyond FOBBS, Oliver has broader aspirations for her career. Oliver is committed to refining her technical skills and deepening her expertise in software architecture, cloud technologies, and microservices. While the idea of moving into management or mentorship is appealing, she remains passionate about hands-on development and innovation. She hopes to strike a balance between leadership and technical work, mentoring others while continuing to design and build solutions that push the boundaries of what technology can achieve. "I want to stay close to the code [..] But I also want to help others along their journey, sharing what I've learned and helping them find their own path in tech" (Oliver, 2024).

For Oliver, the legacy she hopes to leave is one of empowerment, inclusion, and lasting impact. Through FOBBS, she is already changing the way Black British history is taught, giving children the tools to see themselves in the narratives of the past and inspiring them to imagine themselves as leaders of the future. Her work in tech continues to challenge the status quo, advocating for greater representation and pushing the industry towards more inclusive practices.

Her vision for the future extends beyond her personal career or even FOBBS. Oliver dreams of a world where young Black British women, and all underrepresented groups, see themselves not just as consumers of technology but as its creators and leaders. She wants to leave behind a tech landscape that reflects the diversity of society, where every voice is heard, and every contribution valued. "We need to get more women, especially Black women, behind the code [...] If we're going to shape the future of technology, we need to make sure everyone is part of that process." Oliver's commitment to this vision is unwavering. Whether she is advocating for diversity in artificial intelligence, mentoring young developers, or continuing to develop FOBBS, her focus remains clear: to leave the world a better, more equitable place than she found it (Oliver, 2024).

As she moves forward, Oliver is excited about the possibilities. She is particularly focused on building out new features for FOBBS, such as gamification elements like quizzes and badges to increase user engagement. She's also exploring partnerships to expand the platform's reach and ensure it remains a vibrant, dynamic resource for educators and students alike.

"I want FOBBS to continue evolving with the needs of its users," she explains. "It's not just about creating a static resource; it's about building a community that values and celebrates Black British history all year round."

Ultimately, Oliver's legacy will be one of lasting impact—both in technology and education. She envisions a future where the contributions of Black Britons are not only acknowledged but integrated into the broader historical narrative, where young women are inspired to pursue careers in tech, and where the tools we use are designed by and for everyone. Through her leadership, vision, and relentless dedication, Kayleigh Oliver is paving the way for future generations to break through barriers and shape the world with technology that is inclusive, innovative, and transformative.

DELIA DERBYSHIRE: SINE OF THE TIMES

I'll come clean, the David Tennant years of *Doctor Who* passed me by. Stop reading this if this offends you in any way! By 2005, I was living my best neurodivergent life, not giving a thought about what I was doing in my downtime versus heavily thinking about what I was doing in my downtime. It was a heady mix of socialising and developing CSS files for my hobby projects. I was also into the early era of blogging and podcasting, so honestly, I had no time for David Tennant's flavour of *Doctor Who*. But *Doctor Who* is a leitmotif in most nerds' lives because it was never about the storyline or the subplots—it was mostly about the technology: ok, the technology *and* the theme tune.

Most children hid behind the sofa when the theme tune started, but I wanted to know how that theme tune was composed. It seemed much more integral to the show compared to *Sapphire and Steel* and *Blake's 7*. I could feel the story in the music. It meant something more than a signature. In the 1970s and 1980s, if I looked beyond the sartorial elegance of Tom Baker and Peter Davison, I felt something different about *Doctor Who*. I could see something I could identify with as the opening titles rolled and the TARDIS raced through hyperspace. That something I could identify with was a woman. Her name was Delia Derbyshire.

Derbyshire's legacy cannot be separated from the times she lived in a world in which women were not encouraged to enter the realms of mathematics, music, or technology. Yet, there she was, defying expectations and reshaping the world of electronic music from inside the BBC Radiophonic Workshop, a predominantly male environment. She never saw herself as fitting into any conventional boxes. Even before the feminist movement found its stride, she'd already declared herself a "post-feminist," working within the system and quietly infiltrating spaces women had traditionally been excluded from. She was part of a subculture of women who resisted limitations not through loud activism but by quietly becoming indispensable—by crafting work so compelling that it forced a reconsideration of women's roles in technological and creative industries.

Despite the challenges, Derbyshire's brilliance emerged through a unique blend of music and mathematics, technology, and artistry. Her groundbreaking work at the BBC Radiophonic Workshop would later influence generations of musicians, often without recognition. While her male counterparts were more readily acknowledged, alongside Daphne Oram, Derbyshire has become something of an integral cult figure, appreciated by those who recognised the genius behind the scenes but often hidden from the mainstream narrative. Outside of the BBC and the era that Oram and Derbyshire operated in, electronic music pioneers from Clara Rockmore to Laurie Spiegel have been consistently forgotten regardless of the regimen and in Laurie Spiegel's case, code, that brings us closer to the music.

Born in Coventry in 1937, Derbyshire excelled academically and won a scholarship to study mathematics at Girton College, Cambridge. Like her contemporary Daphne Oram, Derbyshire's world was soundtracked by the sounds of war. "Coventry born, bred and blitzed! (About air raid sirens) It's an abstract sound, because there's a source of it as a young child. And then the all clear (sound). That was electronic music in those days. After the Blitz, the worst of the Blitz, I was shifted off to Preston, which is where my parents came from. Well, I remember it myself, the sound of clogs on cobbles. You know, people going to the mill at six o'clock in the morning or something. That must have been such an influence on me. Even at school, I had this great interest in sound, a theory of sound. You know, the waves, the waves, the waves. I was quite a clever girl, and was accepted to read mathematics at Cambridge, which is quite something for a working-class girl in the 50s, where only one in 10 were female" (The Delian Mode, 2009).

It was mathematics that allowed her to break down the complexities of sound into its fundamental elements, understanding waves and frequencies in a way that very few could. At the time, few people understood the relationship between numbers and sound as deeply as Derbyshire, and fewer still could translate that knowledge into something as expressive and emotional as music.

For Derbyshire, mathematics was not merely about solving problems or running equations but about finding the harmony between abstract concepts and tangible outputs. She plotted her compositions with mathematical precision, using graph paper and a slide rule to visualise the music she was creating. While other composers might have approached sound with a more intuitive, performance-based method, she was meticulous and analytical. Her unique combination of creative flair and scientific rigour allowed her to manipulate sound in ways that were both innovative and emotionally resonant. In the documentary The Delian Mode by Kara Blake about Delia Derbyshire's life and work, Clive Blackburn notes "her approach to music was very mathematical. She used to plot out her tunes on pieces of graph paper and use a slide rule. […] other people just didn't work like that" (The Delian Mode, 2009).

Derbyshire was known for using graph paper to plan out her compositions. This method allowed her to visualise sound in a mathematical way. For example, she could plot the amplitude (volume) and frequency (pitch) of a sound over time, giving her a clear picture of how different elements would interact. Using tools like slide rules to make precise calculations would ensure that her compositions were mathematically sound. She would have used these tools to calculate the relationships between different frequencies, the lengths of tape required for specific pitches, and the timing needed for loops to synchronise.

Bringing music and maths at an intersection was necessary if Derbyshire wanted to move forward. The tools she worked with were rudimentary by today's standards—oscillators, tape loops, and early forms of synthesis—but her mathematical mind enabled her to unlock their full potential. In an era before digital workstations, she painstakingly spliced and layered tape, manipulating time and frequency with the precision of a surgeon. She could hear something others couldn't: the deeper potential hidden within the raw data of sound, the sine waves, and white noise. She did not directly employ the Fourier analysis to her work, her approach to sound was closely aligned with its principles. Fourier analysis is a mathematical method used to decompose complex sounds into their constituent frequencies. Her understanding of how to manipulate waveforms, harmonics, and overtones suggests that she intuitively grasped many of the concepts behind Fourier analysis, using them to create complex, evolving soundscapes from simple waveforms.

Before the advent of digital synthesisers and software instruments, musicians like Derbyshire had to work with physical hardware to create sound. The idea of "building" music was literal for her. In the 1960s, there were no off-the-shelf synthesisers like the Moog or Prophet; instead, there were tape recorders, oscillators, filters, and amplifiers. And it was with these crude tools that she sculpted her masterpieces. She also used phase shifts to create effects such as phasing and flanging. These effects rely on slight delays between two copies of the same sound, causing them to phase in and out of sync. The precise timing of these delays is a mathematical calculation, and she would have used her knowledge to adjust the phase shift for the desired effect.

At the BBC Radiophonic Workshop, Derbyshire and her colleagues were engaged in a form of music-making that was more akin to engineering than traditional composition. The *Doctor Who* theme, for example, was constructed entirely from manipulated tape and oscillator-generated tones. She meticulously recorded, spliced, and looped short snippets of sound, altering their pitch and timing by adjusting tape speed or reversing the tape entirely. Every note, every beat was physically constructed, cut, and reassembled by hand—a process that could take weeks or even months to complete. Mark Ayres observed "the final mix was done by playing all these pieces of tape together simultaneously off multiple tape machines and hoping they would stay in synchronisation from start to end" (The Delian Mode, 2009).

In this sense, Derbyshire was one of the earliest developers of what we would now call electronic music. Clara Rockmore's relationship to Leon Theremin's curious machine was a change of mindset, "I was a freak at the time, the public had to be won over into thinking of it as a real artistic medium played by an artist. And I won them over" (Sisters with Transistors, 2020). In this film documenting experimental female artists who use technology to express themselves, musician Laurie Anderson's paraphrasing of Rockmore describes Derbyshire's approach to music. "You cannot play air with hammers. Clara would say... you have to play it with butterfly wings" (Sisters with Transistors, 2020).

Derbyshire's use of hardware was groundbreaking because she was effectively building the tools she needed to create something that didn't exist before. Her work was a precursor to the digital revolution that would follow decades later, when computers would make these processes easier but with perhaps less intimacy. For her, the physicality of the process—the cutting, the splicing, the looping—was part of the art. She saw the potential in the hardware and used it to create software, albeit in an analogue form, that could tell stories and evoke emotions as powerfully as any traditional instrument.

Derbyshire's tools were as much a part of her identity as her ideas. The corridors of Maida Vale became her laboratory, where she would string tape across rooms to create enormous tape loops—*sonic maps*, as some have called them—that filled the air with strange, beautiful, otherworldly sounds. In a very real sense, she was making the invisible visible, creating soundscapes that transported listeners to places they could never physically go but could vividly imagine through her work. Here's how her workflow may have been:

1. **Generating the Basic Sound Waves**

   - **Oscillators**: Delia would begin by using oscillators to generate basic sound waves. Oscillators produce waveforms of different shapes such as sine waves, square waves, triangle waves, and sawtooth waves. Each waveform has its own unique sound characteristics.

      - **Sine Wave**: The purest sound, consisting of a single frequency with no overtones or harmonics. Delia often used sine waves as the foundation for her sounds.

      - **Square Wave**: A harsher sound due to its rich harmonic content, often used for more metallic or sharp textures.

   - These oscillators could be adjusted to produce tones at various frequencies (pitch) depending on the musical or atmospheric effect she wanted to create.

2. **Modifying and Shaping the Waves**

   - **Speed Adjustment (Time Manipulation)**: Delia would use tape machines to manipulate the pitch and speed of the recorded waveforms. For example:

      - **Slowing Down Tape**: Slowing down the tape would lower the pitch of the sound, creating deeper, more bass-heavy tones.

      - **Speeding Up Tape**: Conversely, speeding up the tape would raise the pitch, creating higher, more treble-focused sounds.

   - **Tape Looping**: She could create repeating patterns by cutting pieces of tape and splicing them together into loops. This technique was often used to create rhythms or repeated motifs.

3. Recording the Sound

- **Tape Recorders**: Once she had generated the basic waveforms and manipulated them, Delia would record the sounds onto magnetic tape. She used reel-to-reel tape recorders, which allowed her to capture and subsequently manipulate the sound.

- **Layering Tape**: Delia could layer multiple recordings on top of each other by playing them simultaneously on different machines. For example, she might record a low sine wave on one tape and a higher-pitched square wave on another, then mix them together.

4. Further Manipulation Using Effects

- **Filtering and Modulation**: To create more complex sounds, Delia would apply filters to the waveforms, which could remove or enhance certain frequencies. This allowed her to shape the timbre (or tone colour) of the sound.

  - **High-pass Filters**: These would remove lower frequencies, leaving only the high-frequency elements of a sound.

  - **Low-pass Filters**: These would do the opposite, cutting out the higher frequencies and emphasising the bass tones.

- **Reverb and Echo**: Reverb and echo effects were achieved by playing sounds into large echo chambers or using tape machines to create artificial reverberation. This added depth and a sense of space to the sound.

5. Splicing and Editing the Tape

- **Cutting and Splicing**: Delia physically cut the tape into segments using a razor blade and then spliced it back together in a different order. This method allowed her to rearrange sounds, create abrupt transitions, or produce specific rhythmic patterns.

  - **Precision**: This step required incredible precision, as each piece of tape had to be exactly the right length for the rhythm or note to work within the composition.

- **Creating Rhythm and Melody**: By assembling pieces of tape in different ways, Delia could create melodies or rhythms. For example, she could arrange short segments of tape in a sequence that repeats at regular intervals to create a rhythm, or she could assemble different pitch segments to form a melody.

6. Synchronising Multiple Tapes

- **Multiple Tape Machines**: For more complex compositions, Delia would play several tape loops simultaneously, each contributing a different element of the composition (e.g. rhythm, bass, melody).

- **Manual Synchronisation**: There were no digital tools for automatic synchronisation, so Delia had to manually ensure that all the tape machines stayed in sync. This required skilful timing and coordination to maintain the structure of the piece.

7. **Final Mixing**

- **Mixing the Layers**: The final step involved mixing the various elements together. She would adjust the volume and balance of each tape loop, layering sounds to achieve the desired texture and dynamics.

- **Live Performance-Like Assembly**: In many cases, the final mix would be performed live, with all the tape machines running simultaneously. Delia and her team would manually adjust the machines and controls to maintain the balance and timing throughout the performance.

8. **Playback and Refinement**

- **Listening Back**: Once the piece was assembled, Delia would listen back to the complete mix. If any parts sounded out of sync or needed adjustments, she would go back to the individual elements, re-cut the tape, or re-record segments as necessary.

- **Final Adjustments**: She might fine-tune the balance, volume, and timing to perfect the piece, often iterating multiple times until it meets her standards.

9. **Presentation**

- **Broadcast or Archival**: Once the final version was completed, the composition would be ready for broadcast or archival. Her works were often used in radio and television, notably in shows like *Doctor Who*.

- **Reusability**: Many of the sounds Delia created were saved and reused in other compositions, as each sound was unique and could be adapted for different contexts.

Derbyshire was a master storyteller, but she did not use words. Instead, she told her stories through sound, creating rich, immersive audio experiences that carried emotional weight and narrative complexity. Her sounds were not just abstract; they had a purpose, a direction, and a story to tell. Soundscapes created from the library; and Foley (which relates to the recording of or addition of sound effects to film) of people knocking on doors, ringing and pulling doorbells was almost documentarian in its construction but effortless in its aesthetic. It required record keeping, whilst at the same time it needed the artist's brush or a chef's kiss to present it as a format.

In *Doctor Who*, for example, Derbyshire's manipulation of sound was not merely about creating a theme but about setting a tone for the entire show. The otherworldly quality of her composition immediately transported audiences into the realm of science fiction, a universe where anything was possible. The theme wasn't just a piece of music; it was a story, a journey through time and space conveyed entirely through sound. She explains "the first stage in the realisation of a piece of music is to construct the individual sounds that we're going to use" (The Delian Mode, 2009).

Derbyshire's use of techniques like tape manipulation, reverb, and echo created a sense of movement and space that was both haunting and hypnotic. She could evoke a mood or suggest a narrative with just a few carefully constructed sounds. Whether she was creating the eerie, unsettling atmosphere of a science fiction drama or the playful, whimsical tones of a children's program, her sounds were always more than just background noise; they were integral to the storytelling.

Derbyshire's work extended beyond television and radio to more abstract compositions, such as her collaborations with Barry Burmange on the *Inventions for Radio* series. "Delia Derbyshire created some very, very beautiful things, and some things that had a kind of very strange and unearthly quality that couldn't quite be done, I think, by normal musical means, and yet didn't sound as if they were electronically manufactured" (Sisters with Transistors, 2020) where she used sound to explore themes of memory, time, and the subconscious. These pieces were not "music" in the traditional sense but immersive soundscapes that engaged listeners on an emotional and intellectual level. They were like audio films, with Derbyshire as the director, guiding the audience through a narrative made entirely of sound.

Derbyshire's most famous work remains her realisation of the *Doctor Who* theme, a piece of music that has become iconic not just for its association with the show but for its groundbreaking use of electronic sound. Ron Grainer composed the original melody, but it was Derbyshire who transformed it into the haunting, otherworldly piece that we all recognise today. Grainer himself was so impressed with her work that he asked, "Did I really write this?" to which she famously replied, "Most of it" (The Delian Mode, 2009).

This collaboration was a remix in the truest sense. Derbyshire took Grainer's composition and reimagined it using the tools at her disposal, and maths of course—oscillators, white noise generators, tape loops—she created something entirely new. Her version of the theme was not just a faithful rendition of Grainer's notes but a complete reinvention, a piece of music that felt like it had been plucked from another dimension. Peter Kember notes, "It must have been astounding, and now is easily recognised as one of the most famous, maybe best theme tunes. It certainly does its job incredibly well" (The Delian Mode, 2009). In many ways, her work on *Doctor Who* prefigured the remix culture that would come to dominate electronic music in the decades that followed. She was taking existing material and transforming it into something fresh, something that pushed the boundaries of what music could be.

Today, countless musicians cite Derbyshire's *Doctor Who* theme as an influence, and it's interesting to see how many female electronic artists influenced male ambient pioneers, so, artists as Éliane Radigue to Jean Michel Jarre, or Pauline Oliveros to Charles Amirkhanian from ambient pioneers like Derbyshire to Brian Eno and modern electronic artists from Add N To (X) and Boards of Canada who continue to experiment with sound in ways that echo her pioneering work. Her techniques—tape manipulation, layering, reverb—have become standard tools in the electronic musician's arsenal, but few have used them with the same level of creativity and artistry as Derbyshire.

Derbyshire was a genius, as most women working in this medium seem to be or have been. Anne Clark, Ann Shenton and Cosey Fanni Tutti will rarely receive the recognition they deserve during this lifetime. Their work has been often overshadowed by the fact that they are women in a male-dominated field, and their contributions, such as that of Suzanne Ciani, are frequently downplayed or credited to others. "The landscape that she must have walked into must have been like something from Mad Men. I remember Suzanne telling me stories like she'd turn up early to set up all the modular gear in studios, and the young engineer would come in and go, 'which mic you're gonna sing on, or what you're gonna sing for us?' Because those stereotypes were so commonplace in studios in those days" (Sisters with Transistors, 2020). The BBC refused to list Derbyshire as a composer, instead crediting her as a "technical assistant" or "realiser." *Sigh*.

This was not an uncommon experience for women in technology, whose work was often overlooked or attributed to their male colleagues. But despite these challenges, Derbyshire's genius shone through in everything she did. Her ability to combine technical skill with artistic vision was unparalleled, and her work has had a lasting impact on the fields of music and sound design. As Suzanne Ciani retorted to David Letterman on his show in 1980 "This is how I make a living" (Sisters with Transistors, 2020).

In many ways, Derbyshire's story parallels that of other women in technology, from Ada Lovelace to Hedy Lamarr. Like them, Derbyshire was ahead of her time, a visionary who saw the potential in technology long before others did. And like them, she faced resistance and marginalisation, but she never let it stop her from pursuing her work. Her legacy is one of quiet resilience, of pushing boundaries and breaking new ground even when the world was not yet ready to acknowledge her genius. As with most women working in this space, this was never not without its own personal struggles. "When she was enthusiastic, she was enthusiastic, she would really go over the top, just as when she was depressed, she would be really depressed and go really sink down or hardly speak to you for days" (The Delian Mode, 2009).

Mental health and personal well-being were replaced by the desire to create, complete, or achieve, not for anyone else but for themselves. Would such criticisms be launched at Frederic Chopin or Jim Morrison? Women of electronic music such as Maryann Amacher or Pauline Oliveros, like Derbyshire, were different. Either neurodivergent, avant-garde and eccentric or simply pushing the limits of their abilities. Maryann Amacher "wanted to develop an extremely rigorous approach to listening, […] She didn't want to push around dead white men's notes" (Sisters with Transistors, 2020).

But Derbyshire's influence can be felt across a wide range of musical genres and artistic disciplines. Her pioneering work in electronic music laid the foundation for everything from ambient music to techno, and her techniques continue to be used by musicians and sound designers today. Her legacy goes beyond the sounds she created; it lies in the way she approached her work, with a combination of scientific rigour and artistic intuition that allowed her to transcend the limitations of her time. The most significant tribute to her legacy is the way her influence continues to resonate in the work of contemporary artists.

Musicians like Aphex Twin, Boards of Canada, and many others have cited Derbyshire as a key influence, and her work has been sampled and remixed in countless tracks. Her approach to sound design, her use of technology, and her ability to tell stories through sound continue to inspire artists across genres. And while she may have been working in the shadows during her lifetime, today her light shines brightly, illuminating the path for future generations of women in technology and the arts.

Add N To (X)'s music is a particularly relevant example of the power of mathematics in oscillating musical forms with reverbs and all that magic to create something wonderful that you might want to hear in Barry 7's Contraption (Add N to (X), 1999). Ann Shenton of the band is an ardent Radiophonic Workshop fan and elements of Derbyshire can be heard in Add N To (X)'s work "They twisted, and they circuit bent stuff, and they did things that they weren't supposed to do, and that's how they got the brilliant sounds. It was like taking the back of the head off an object and doing a bit of, like, home DIY brain surgery" (The Delian Mode, 2009).

Stories find their way when we are ready to receive them. In technology, storytelling becomes an essential thread in the fabric of innovation. Every project starts with a set of requirements, and behind those requirements are stories—narratives shaped by user experiences, dreams, and unmet needs. Whether it's a software developer building an app or a sound designer composing an otherworldly theme, the process is rooted in storytelling. These stories, embedded in every line of code or melody, provide the direction, purpose, and meaning behind the technology. In the end, it's through these narratives that technology connects to humanity, shaping the future by understanding and addressing the experiences of today. The power of stories in technology reminds us that it's not just about what we create but the reasons behind it, the problems we solve, and the lives we touch.

REFERENCES

2Game. (2023) *The state of personal representation in gaming.* [online] Available at: https://2game.com/community/the-state-of-personal-representation-in-gaming-in-2023/?srsltid=AfmBOopkGVT3beaRC_DkmYImU6XEj0J5u2xpZ7TxVBFmO9hxx85uF3eP (Accessed: 7 September 2024).

Add N to (X). (1999) Barry 7's contraption. *Avant Hard.* UK: Mute Records.

Alan Turing Institute. (2023) Where are the women? Mapping the gender job gap in AI. [online] Available at: https://www.turing.ac.uk/news/publications/report-where-are-women-mapping-gender-job-gap-ai (Accessed: 7 September 2024).

BAME in Games. (2024) *BAME talent in games.* [online] Available at: https://bameingames.org/#about (Accessed: 7 September 2024).

Culture Bay. (2023) *The rise of Black lead characters in video games.* [online] Available at: https://culturebay.co/blogs/afrofuturism/the-rise-of-black-lead-characters-in-video-games (Accessed: 7 September 2024).

Education and Employers. (2018). *Drawing the Future.* [online] Available at: https://www.educationandemployers.org/wp-content/uploads/2018/01/DrawingTheFuture.pdf (Accessed: 23 September 2024).

Hejlsberg, A. (2000). Development of C#. Microsoft Docs: *History of C#* [online] Available at: https://learn.microsoft.com/en-us/dotnet/csharp/ (Accessed: 7 September 2024).

Oliver, K. (2024) Interview by Kelly Vero. 2 September 2024.

Sisters with Transistors. (2020) Directed by Lisa Rovner. YouTube, Feb 3, 2022, https://www.youtube.com/watch?v=lQPwPE567vI (Accessed: 7 September 2024).

The Delian Mode – Delia Derbyshire Documentary (2009). Directed by Kara Blake. YouTube, 15 May 2015, www.youtube.com/watch?v=nXnmSgaeGAI (Accessed: 7 September 2024).

TheGrio. (2023) *85% of Black gamers think video games lack accurate representation.* [online] Available at: https://thegrio.com/2023/11/17/85-of-black-gamers-think-video-games-lack-accurate-representation-dove-is-helping-to-change-that/ (Accessed: 7 September 2024).

University of Washington. (2015). *Children's self-esteem already established by age 5, new study finds.* [online] Available at: https://www.washington.edu/news/2015/11/02/childrens-self-esteem-already-established-by-age-5-new-study-finds/ (Accessed: 23 September 2024).

World Economic Forum. (2020) *Global gender gap report.* [online] Available at: https://reports.weforum.org/global-gender-gap-report-2020 (Accessed: 7 September 2024).

CHAPTER 7

Valerie Thomas and Rocio Evenett

Believing What We See

MANY OF THE WOMEN featured in this book are creators who transform abstract technology into tangible, meaningful forms. Whether in visual imagery or garment design, they make the invisible visible. They take unnatural constructs and naturalise them into understandable formats that we might see with our eyes or coordinates that we might use with our hands. What if magic can be caught in a jar? Is it something more existential than trapping lightning in a bottle? I think so. The magic of science is all around us waiting for us to create something else with it.

Valerie Thomas and Rocio Evenett embody this alchemy. Rocio is a pattern maker who has created a hub for emerging designers, tailors, and purists to explore the meticulous world of fashion by numbers. Valerie's work at NASA, especially the invention of the illusion transmitter, has revolutionised how we perceive and interact with visual information. They are both scientists whose innovative spirit and unyielding curiosity have led to groundbreaking advancements.

VALERIE THOMAS: LOOKING BEYOND THE MIRROR

Valerie Thomas saw a demonstration at a scientific exhibit where a light bulb appeared to be lit without being physically connected to a power source. And she was hooked. This display of science sparked her lifelong quest to explore the boundaries of technology and perception. Born in Maryland in 1943 her father encouraged her to embrace science by providing an abundance of technical books and equipment at home. "My father used to fix TVs. These big box TVs. And then [he] would open it up and I could see these mechanical things inside. And I was wondering how, how did those mechanical things end up with a picture on the screen?" (Thomas, 2020). That first experience with an illuminated light bulb, seemingly without a source, didn't just captivate Thomas—it defined her career.

DOI: 10.1201/9781003566465-7

From that moment on, she was drawn to the mysteries behind technology and perception, an obsession that led her to NASA and its cutting-edge work in data science and satellite imagery. But for Thomas, the heart of her work was always about transforming data into something tangible, something we could see and understand.

She later pursued her passion for science by earning a degree in physics from Morgan State University. Her education provided a solid foundation in the principles of physics and mathematics. She graduated in 1964. Physics and mathematics are no joke, and it's not for the faint of heart. But studying during the civil rights movement at a pivotal college in the United States of America would have enhanced the drive and desire that Valerie shows throughout her career both as a physicist and as a woman of colour.

Thomas joined NASA Goddard Space Flight Center in 1964, and straight out of college, at a time when the space agency was at the forefront of technological innovation. "I had to work on computers. I had not even seen a computer before in my life, except in science fiction movies" (Thomas, 2020). Her initial work involved developing real-time computer data systems to support satellite operations. She quickly established herself as a critical asset to NASA, known for her technical expertise and innovative thinking.

One of her significant contributions was in the development of image processing systems for the Landsat program. With her team, she ensured that the satellite data collected over decades remains one of the most valuable resources for studying the Earth and addressing some of the planet's most pressing challenges. Landsat satellites were designed to capture detailed images of the Earth's surface, Thomas played a pivotal role in creating algorithms and systems to enhance the quality and usability of these images, transforming raw satellite data into clear and informative visual representations. To fully appreciate Valerie's impact on satellite imagery, it's important to understand the tools she helped develop to process and interpret this data.

1. **Continuous Observation of Earth:** The Landsat program, initiated in 1972, marked the first time that Earth's surface was observed continuously through satellites dedicated specifically to this purpose. The program provided vital data for a wide range of scientific and practical applications, from monitoring natural resources to mapping human impacts on the environment. Its ability to offer "consistent, high-resolution imagery over several decades allows researchers to track long-term changes, such as deforestation, urban growth, desertification, and glacier melting." This continuity is crucial in studying the effects of climate change (NASA, 2021).

2. **Environmental Monitoring and Climate Science:** Landsat data plays a crucial role in monitoring climate change, enabling scientists to track phenomena like deforestation, ice loss, and desertification (Goward et al. 2015).

3. **Agriculture and Food Security:** The Landsat program has had a significant impact on agricultural practices, as satellite imagery allows for precise crop monitoring and management. By "analysing the data, farmers and agricultural agencies can improve irrigation techniques, predict crop yields, and manage pests more effectively." This has been particularly beneficial for improving food security in developing countries (USGS, 2019).

4. **Natural Disaster Management:** Landsat has been used extensively for managing and responding to natural disasters, such as floods, earthquakes, wildfires, and hurricanes. The satellite imagery provides "critical information for emergency services and governments to assess damage and coordinate relief efforts." For example, Landsat data was used to monitor the aftermath of Hurricane Katrina and track the spread of wildfires in California (Roy et al. 2014).

5. **Urban Planning and Land Use:** Landsat's high-resolution imagery allows urban planners and policymakers to better understand land-use patterns and the impacts of urbanisation. The data has been used to monitor urban sprawl, plan new infrastructure, and manage land resources more effectively. In addition, Landsat has "helped assess the environmental impacts of urban growth, such as the heat island effect in large cities" (Hansen et al. 2013).

By focusing on improving the quality and clarity of Landsat imagery, Thomas helped extend the program's impact in numerous fields, including agriculture, urban planning, and natural disaster management. But how? Valerie is very clear about her contribution not only to the program but also to her career, "I was a girl and a woman who wasn't afraid of challenges, that just got me to do what I needed to do to excel" (Thomas, 2020). This story, however, is not just about the early nature of the internet and its tectonic movements in the technology landscape. This is a story about visualising data. Because what we see at Landsat is data, lots and lots of data. And it's this data that puts Valerie Thomas in pole position for what she would achieve next.

For Thomas, each satellite image wasn't just a picture—it was a story, a piece of Earth's history unfolding in real time. These images revealed the secrets of the planet, from the shrinking polar ice caps to the spread of urbanisation. And in those stories, she saw the potential for change, for action. Her work wasn't simply about advancing technology; it was about giving the world the tools to better understand and protect itself.

As we evolve through data from this time to today, you'll notice the variability of volume as we try to digest it, and you might also understand why there are so many tools or methods for controlling it. Data drives everything we create, from complex environmental models to the clothes we wear. Whether we're mapping forests or designing the perfect garment, raw data is the invisible force that transforms ideas into reality.

Valerie Thomas entered NASA during an era when data processing was still in its infancy. Back then, the concept of raw data was almost as abstract as the images it would eventually produce. Data was collected in smaller, structured formats, often through basic sensors, punch cards, or magnetic tapes. But this raw information, while fragmented, held immense potential. Thomas saw beyond the limitations of early data systems, understanding that with the right tools, this raw data could be transformed into powerful visual representations of our world. NASA's early space missions and projects like Landsat captured data in relatively modest volumes by today's standards. Data storage was limited, and datasets often had to be carefully curated and optimised due to the expensive and constrained memory capacity of early computers (USGS, 2019).

She transformed raw, unprocessed data into meaningful, clear images that could be used by scientists worldwide. By developing advanced image processing systems, she made it possible to interpret the vast and complex data collected from satellite imagery, turning it into actionable insights for environmental monitoring, urban planning, and disaster response.

To Thomas, raw data was not just numbers and codes but a reservoir of untapped potential. She understood that these unprocessed data streams contained valuable information that could be revealed through meticulous analysis and innovative processing techniques. The characteristics of raw data—its unprocessed nature, lack of organisation, and sheer volume—presented both a challenge and an opportunity. Thomas' genius lay in her ability to see beyond the chaos of raw data and envision the structured, meaningful insights that could emerge from it.

Her process of extracting and understanding raw data began with data cleaning, where she would remove errors, duplicates, and irrelevant information. This step was crucial in ensuring that the data she worked with was accurate and reliable. For example, when handling satellite images, Thomas would need to eliminate any distortions or noise that could interfere with the clarity and usability of the images.

Characteristics of Raw Data

1. **Unprocessed**: Raw data has not been manipulated, cleaned, or transformed in any way. It is the direct output of data collection processes.

2. **Unorganised**: This data may lack structure and organisation, making it difficult to interpret without further processing.

3. **High Volume**: Raw data can exist in large volumes, especially in fields such as big data analytics, where vast amounts of data are collected from various sources.

4. **Variety**: It can come in multiple formats, such as text, numbers, images, audio, and video.

5. **Potential for Errors**: Since it is unfiltered, raw data can contain errors, duplicates, or irrelevant information that need to be addressed during processing.

Examples of Raw Data

- **Sensor Readings**: Data collected from environmental sensors, such as temperature, humidity, or pressure readings.

- **Survey Responses**: Raw responses from surveys or questionnaires, including individual answers and comments.

- **Transaction Logs**: Records of transactions in financial systems, including dates, amounts, and parties involved.

- **Social Media Feeds**: Unfiltered posts, comments, likes, and shares from social media platforms.

- **Web Server Logs**: Logs detailing requests made to a web server, including IP addresses, timestamps, and requested resources.

Processing Raw Data

To transform raw data into meaningful information, several steps are typically involved:

1. **Data Cleaning**: Removing errors, duplicates, and irrelevant information.

2. **Data Transformation**: Converting data into a consistent format or structure suitable for analysis.

3. **Data Organisation**: Structuring data in databases or data warehouses to facilitate easy access and analysis.

4. **Data Analysis**: Applying statistical methods, algorithms, or models to interpret and extract insights from the data.

5. **Data Visualisation**: Presenting the processed data in graphical formats like charts, graphs, and dashboards for easier understanding and interpretation.

Importance of Raw Data

- **Decision-Making**: Raw data serves as the primary input for data-driven decision-making processes in various fields, including business, healthcare, and scientific research.

- **Innovation**: Access to raw data allows researchers and developers to explore new ideas, identify patterns, and develop innovative solutions.

- **Accuracy**: Working with raw data ensures that analyses and conclusions are based on the most fundamental, unaltered facts, which helps maintain the accuracy and reliability of findings.

The tipping point for streamlined and faster data handling emerged from a combination of factors, including Moore's Law (1965), which increased computational power by doubling transistors on microchips every two years, and advances in storage technology such as hard disk drives (HDDs), solid-state drives (SSDs), and cloud storage, which improved speed and scalability. Distributed computing systems like Google's MapReduce and the Hadoop ecosystem revolutionised large-scale data processing by enabling parallel processing across multiple machines, while the rise of cloud computing platforms such as Amazon Web Services (AWS) and Google Cloud democratised access to scalable resources. Algorithmic advancements in machine learning, exemplified by deep learning and frameworks like TensorFlow, significantly enhanced data analysis, while network improvements (e.g. fibre optics and 5G) reduced latency, facilitating real-time data transfer. Advances in data analytics tools, such as SQL databases, data lakes, and modern visualisation platforms like Tableau, further streamlined data analysis. Collectively, these developments marked the turning point for efficient, large-scale data processing and real-time analysis.

In 1980, Valerie Thomas received a patent for her most famous invention, the illusion transmitter. This device creates the illusion of a three-dimensional image by using concave mirrors to produce optical illusions that can be viewed from multiple angles. The illusion transmitter works by transmitting an image from one location to another, where it is projected onto a concave mirror. The reflected image appears as a 3D hologram, giving the viewer the impression of depth and volume. This laid the foundation for modern 3D projection technology, influencing the development of augmented reality and holographic displays. Its applications in medical imaging and communications represent a leap forward in how we visualise complex data, making this invention a cornerstone of 3D technology.

The inspiration for this invention came from Thomas' observations of how concave mirrors could create optical illusions. She recognised the potential for this technology to revolutionise visual communication, leading to applications in fields ranging from medical imaging to telecommunications. The illusion transmitter represented a significant leap forward in our ability to create and interact with three-dimensional images, laying the groundwork for future advancements in virtual reality and augmented reality.

The images are gleaned from the raw data I explained above. However, these images are not raw images, but techniques or standards used in image development. We always assume that images or imaging is somehow visual. In this case, there is a greater volume of coordinates, algorithms, and early point cloud data being used to illustrate the process of visualisation. Valerie's innovations centred around making satellite data usable. Formats like TIFF and GeoTIFF were crucial in storing and georeferencing high-quality satellite imagery, allowing researchers to map and analyse Earth's surface more effectively. By standardising these formats, Thomas helped make complex, raw data accessible for scientists, environmentalists, and policymakers.

Image Processing Systems

1. **Pre-processing Systems:**

   - **Calibration and Correction**: Systems to correct atmospheric, radiometric, and geometric distortions in raw satellite data, ensuring the accuracy of the imagery.

   - **Cloud Detection and Removal**: Techniques to identify and remove cloud cover from images, enhancing the usability of satellite data for surface analysis.

2. **Data Compression and Storage:**

   - **Lossless and Lossy Compression Algorithms**: Techniques to reduce the file size of satellite images, balancing the need for data storage efficiency and image quality.

   - **Data Archival Systems**: Robust systems for long-term storage and retrieval of large volumes of satellite data, ensuring the preservation and accessibility of historical imagery.

3. **Data Enhancement and Visualisation**

   - **Image Enhancement Algorithms**: Methods to improve the visual quality of satellite images, such as contrast adjustment, edge enhancement, and noise reduction.

- **False Colour and Composite Imagery**: Techniques to create images that combine data from multiple spectral bands, revealing details not visible in natural colour images.

4. **Geospatial Analysis and Interpretation**

   - **Change Detection**: Systems to analyse temporal changes in satellite imagery, useful for monitoring environmental changes, urban development, and disaster impacts.

   - **Object Recognition and Classification**: Techniques to automatically identify and classify features in satellite images, such as vegetation, water bodies, and built-up areas.

Why is this important? For today's technology, this is the embodiment of XR applications that require reality to be the lightbox that we view everything. Developing standardised digital media formats was crucial in making satellite data accessible and usable for a wide range of users, from scientists to policymakers. High-quality image processing systems enabled the extraction of meaningful information from raw satellite data, thereby enhancing its value for various applications. This standardisation facilitated the sharing and accessibility of data, ensuring that users could efficiently utilise the information for their specific needs.

In environmental monitoring and management, the ability to process and analyse satellite imagery has been instrumental. It allowed for the monitoring of significant environmental changes, such as deforestation, urban sprawl, and climate change. Moreover, enhanced image processing systems provided more accurate and timely assessments of natural disasters, which was critical in aiding response and recovery efforts.

The advancements in digital media formats also revolutionised Geographic Information Systems (GIS). The integration of these formats with GIS allowed for more sophisticated spatial analysis, mapping, modelling, and decision-making. These improvements have had far-reaching impacts on fields such as agriculture, urban planning, resource management, and national security, enabling more effective and informed decision-making processes.

Finally, Valerie Thomas' illusion transmitter is a device designed to create 3D images that can be viewed without the need for special glasses. Here's what it typically looks like and how it functions:

1. **Basic Structure.** The illusion transmitter consists of two main components: a video camera and a concave mirror. The video camera captures images and transmits them to a distant location. The setup also includes a second concave mirror located at the receiving end. This mirror receives the transmitted images and creates the illusion of a three-dimensional image.

2. **Functionality.** The video camera captures an image of an object and sends this image to the concave mirror at the receiving end. The concave mirror reflects the transmitted image in a way that it appears as a three-dimensional object, creating an optical illusion.

3. **Appearance.** The device resembles a typical video transmission setup but with the distinct addition of concave mirrors. The mirrors are usually placed in a frame or a stand to maintain the correct orientation and distance necessary for the illusion to work. The overall apparatus might include a monitor or a display screen showing the transmitted images, with the concave mirrors positioned strategically to create the 3D effect.

4. **Design and Components.** The concave mirrors are typically made of reflective materials like polished metal or coated glass to ensure clear image reflection. The video camera and transmission system are like standard video equipment but configured to work seamlessly with the mirrors to produce the 3D illusion.

5. **Applications.** The illusion transmitter can be used in various fields, such as medical imaging, remote sensing, and entertainment, where visualising objects in three dimensions enhances understanding and interaction.

Without the need for special glasses? This sounds like AR! Thomas' invention of the illusion transmitter had far-reaching implications. In the medical field, 3D imaging technology improved the accuracy of diagnostics and surgical planning, allowing doctors to visualise internal structures with unprecedented clarity. In telecommunications, the ability to transmit 3D images opened new possibilities for remote communication and collaboration, paving the way for innovations such as holographic conferencing.

Moreover, Thomas' work in image processing and 3D projection technology contributed to the broader field of remote sensing. By enhancing our ability to capture and interpret visual data from satellites, her contributions helped advance our understanding of Earth's environment and supported efforts to monitor and mitigate the impacts of climate change.

Valerie's ability to understand and manipulate data has led to advancements in image processing, environmental monitoring, and scientific networking. To a younger version of me, she gave me a glimpse into physics from something I could relate to, and her achievements do not stop at the Illusion Transmitter. As the NSSDC Computer Facility manager in 1985, Thomas was responsible for a major consolidation and reconfiguration of two previously independent computer facilities. This role highlighted her ability to manage complex technological projects and improve operational efficiency. Her subsequent work as the Space Physics Analysis Network (SPAN) project manager from 1986 to 1990 further demonstrated her leadership skills. Under her guidance, SPAN underwent a significant reconfiguration, growing from a scientific network with approximately 100 computer nodes to one directly connecting approximately 2700 computer nodes worldwide. This expansion facilitated improved scientific collaboration and data sharing among researchers globally.

In 1990, SPAN became a major part of NASA's science networking and laid the groundwork for today's Internet. Thomas also participated in various projects related to Halley's Comet, ozone research, satellite technology, and the Voyager spacecraft. Her contributions to these projects underscore her versatility and ability to adapt to different scientific challenges.

Thomas' dedication to mentorship and community engagement is another cornerstone of her legacy. She mentored students in the Mathematics Aerospace Research and

Technology Inc. program and frequently spoke to groups of students from elementary school to university, as well as adult groups. As a role model for her community, she visited schools and national meetings, inspiring countless individuals to pursue careers in science and technology. Thomas also mentored students working in summer programs at Goddard Space Flight Center and judged at science fairs, collaborating with organisations such as the National Technical Association (NTA) and Women in Science and Engineering (WISE). At the end of August 1995, Thomas retired from NASA, concluding a remarkable career that spanned several decades. Her positions at the time of retirement included associate chief of the NASA Space Science Data Operations Office, manager of the NASA Automated Systems Incident Response Capability, and chair of the Space Science Data Operations Office Education Committee.

Visualising or crunching big numbers, such as those involved in satellite data or complex simulations, often requires sophisticated tools and technologies. The illusion transmitter, for example, showcases how 3D visualisations can help us understand intricate data in more tangible ways. This technology takes raw data and converts it into a three-dimensional form that can be visualised, making abstract concepts more accessible and easier to comprehend. Imagine trying to understand the vast amounts of data generated by satellite imagery? Each pixel of an image represents a data point that, when combined with millions of others, forms a comprehensive picture of an area. That's beyond exciting. By using tools like the illusion transmitter, this data can be visualised in three dimensions, allowing scientists to better understand the terrain, vegetation, and other features of a region. This form of visualisation transforms raw data into something more understandable and actionable.

This concept of transforming raw data into meaningful visual representations is also highly relevant in other fields, such as fashion design. Pattern makers, like the next interviewee in this book, use numbers and volumetric data to create clothing. They take measurements and other numerical data and transform them into patterns that can be used to cut fabric and assemble garments. This process involves a deep understanding of how to manipulate data and convert it into a physical form. By leveraging 3D visualisation tools and volumetric data, pattern makers can create more accurate and detailed patterns. They can visualise how a garment will look and fit before it is even made, allowing for adjustments to be made in the design phase. This not only improves the efficiency of the design process but also ensures a better fit and finish for the final product.

In both cases, whether visualising satellite data or creating clothing patterns, the ability to transform raw data into a tangible form is crucial. This process allows for better understanding, improved decision-making, and more innovative solutions. Valerie Thomas' work in developing tools for data visualisation has laid the groundwork for many of these advancements, demonstrating the power of technology to transform abstract concepts into something real and impactful.

ROCIO EVENETT: THE POETRY OF PATTERNS

The world of fashion is problematic. It's full of little pain points and head-scratchy moments, but for Rocio Evenett it's a place where innovation intersects with ancient crafts using modern technology. What sets her apart is her unique ability to bridge the gap between creativity and technology in a field not traditionally associated with high-tech innovations. Evenett's journey as a soft goods product engineer and founder of SewingIncubator.com reveals a woman constantly seeking to improve and streamline processes, ensuring that fashion meets function in the most efficient way possible.

Born in New York, Evenett was fascinated by science fiction and had an early interest in robotics. Her creative spirit was nurtured by her mother, who made clothes for Rocio and her sister, inspiring an early passion for sewing. By the age of 15, she had already started her first business, making and selling outfits. This entrepreneurial spirit, coupled with her love for design, would serve as the foundation for her future innovations in fashion technology.

Her journey took a transformative turn during high school when she was introduced to computers. Learning DOS on a Mac mainframe, this early experience with technology was pivotal in her decision to integrate digital tools into garment production. Encouraged by her boyfriend at that time, she realised the importance of these skills and how they would be crucial for her career.

When Evenett was 15 years old, she started her first business venture. She would make outfits to wear clubbing, and then sell the dresses on Monday through a magazine called *The Penny Saver*. Hand sewn, designed or fixed styles from pattern or upcycled, she didn't mind. This was entrepreneurship. She had a desire to make her own money, and she was able to use her skills (Evenett, 2024). This allowed her to earn money to buy new outfits to wear the following weekend when she went out with friends.

After high school, Rocio took advantage of a program that allowed her to start college courses in the evenings and on weekends. She crammed as many fashion-related classes as she could, including ones that gave her hands-on experience with CAD (Computer-Aided Design) systems. Her approach and how it contrasts with more traditional methods, as well as the impact it has on the broader fashion and garment industries is interesting to someone like me who tries to balance business with science.

Evenett's work goes beyond fabric and seams. Her early adoption of CAD technology wasn't just a career move; it was a revolution. CAD systems allowed her to digitise every step of the garment design process, from initial sketches to pattern grading. Her patterns represent people, culture, and creativity—each piece a testament to the art of making something meaningful from numbers and code. For her, technology is not only about efficiency but also about amplifying the voice of creators who otherwise might not have access to these powerful tools.

The Pattern Aided Design (PAD) system is a specialised CAD software created specifically for fashion and apparel design. Unlike more commonly used tools such as Adobe Illustrator or CorelDRAW, which are popular among fashion designers, the PAD system is explicitly designed to cater to the needs of pattern makers and garment technicians. It allows designers to create, manipulate, and grade patterns digitally, all while maintaining precise control over the garment's fit and design specifications.

Rocio's early adoption of PAD system in the 1990s set her apart from many of her contemporaries, who were still largely reliant on manual drafting methods or less specialised software. "I had already been doing patterns: I had formal training in pattern making, but I was determined to integrate technology to make the process faster and more efficient"

(Evenett, 2024). She not only learned the PAD system on her own but also mastered it to a level that allowed her to integrate it into her entire business model, making it a cornerstone of her workflow.

Evenett's innovations with CAD systems, revolutionised not only how patterns were made but also how they were produced at scale. By digitising the entire design and production process, she enabled real-time collaboration across global teams. Manufacturers in different countries could now access updated patterns instantly, reducing lead times and making it possible to adjust designs on the fly to meet shifting consumer demands. This seamless integration between design and production allowed for more sustainable practices, reducing waste and eliminating the need for excess materials.

In 1991, Evenett found herself working at Rampage Clothing Company, one of the few early adopters of CAD in garment manufacturing at that time. While the technology was far from what it is today, Evenett recognised its potential immediately. "We were one of the first companies that had gone all in on digitising patterns for production: we were one of the first places to have an automatic sample cutter." For Evenett, this was a revelation—one that showed her how fashion, design, and technology could be interconnected to reduce errors, streamline production, and ultimately lower costs. This experience shaped her understanding of how automation could revolutionise fashion manufacturing. By the time Evenett started her own company, she had already integrated these ideas into her business model (Evenett, 2024).

Most traditional pattern makers still rely on paper patterns or simple CAD programs that do not fully integrate with manufacturing systems. By contrast, Evenett's mastery of the PAD system allows her to digitise every step of the pattern-making process, from initial designs to final production-ready files. This enabled a seamless transition from concept to production and significantly reduced errors and time associated with manual pattern grading and revisions.

Garment manufacturers typically need to produce a variety of sizes (e.g. small, medium, large) from one original design. Pattern grading ensures that each size variation fits correctly without distorting the original design. It allows fashion brands to scale their designs to different body types and markets. How does it work?

1. **Master Pattern Creation:** The original design is created in a base size, which is typically a medium size or whatever size the designer considers the standard.

2. **Size Adjustments:** Using specific rules or "grading increments," the pattern is adjusted to create other sizes. These increments vary based on the sizing system (e.g. U.S. sizes, European sizes), garment type, and body measurements.

3. **Grading Techniques:** Manual grading was done by hand using rulers and special tools to increase or decrease the dimensions of each pattern piece. Each point of the pattern is shifted by specific measurements, such as increasing the waistline by an inch for larger sizes. In Digital grading modern pattern makers often use CAD software, like PAD System or Gerber, to grade patterns. This allows for more precise and quicker grading, reducing errors.

4. Grading rules are standard measurements that dictate how much to increase or decrease the pattern at different points, such as the waist, bust, or hips. For example:

   - Bust and hips might be increased by 1 inch per size.

   - Waist might be increased by 0.5 inches per size.

5. **Checking Proportions:** A critical part of grading is ensuring that the garment's proportions, design features, and fit remain consistent across all sizes. This can be tricky with elements like darts, seams, and curves, which need to be carefully adjusted without distorting the design.

There are several different grading methods, depending on the complexity and type of garment:

- Increase/Decrease by Shifting Points: This involves moving specific points on the pattern outward or inward to adjust the size.

- Proportional Grading: The amount of increase or decrease can be adjusted proportionally according to different parts of the body. For instance, the bust might increase more in a larger size than the shoulders or the length.

- Nest Grading: In this method, all sizes are laid on top of each other in one "nested" set to show how the pattern scales up or down.

The challenges of pattern grading mean that it has been impossible to innovate efficiently in this area of garment making. Certain design elements, such as darts, pockets, or collars, might not scale in a linear way. If not adjusted carefully, grading can distort the original design. Then, depending on the market (men's, women's, children's), body proportions may vary. For example, women's bodies typically have larger hips and busts relative to their waist than men's, so grading needs to take these proportions into account. Finally, while grading creates different sizes, the fit may need to be adjusted for different body types. What fits well in one size may require more complex adjustments in another.

Currently there are many tools available in manual pattern making, such as special rulers designed with graded increments that help adjust the size of specific pattern areas; marks or guides on the pattern to ensure the seams align correctly across all sizes. Digitally, tools like PAD System, Lectra, or Gerber can automate the grading process, making it more efficient and accurate. By replacing manual pattern grading with digital tools, Evenett significantly improved the precision of garment production. The CAD system allowed for exact measurements that minimised fabric waste, a major step towards sustainable manufacturing. In an industry notorious for overproduction and discarded materials, Evenett's system was a game-changer, helping brands meet their sustainability goals without sacrificing the quality of their designs (Fletcher, 2014).

Remember the Mac? Evenett does, fondly. So much so that she began creating a workflow to manage the efficiencies of pattern making, such as volume and scalability in what she can achieve by bringing in technology: she combined the PAD system with Information

Architecture (IA) through FileMaker Pro, a database software that is rarely used in fashion but is highly effective for organising and managing complex datasets. She still uses this system today, let's take a deeper dive.

In her workflow, Rocio uses FileMaker Pro to create databases that store and manage the vast amounts of information related to each garment she works on. This includes measurements, patterns, specifications, grading instructions, and even production timelines. The ability to export data from PAD and manage it within a customised IA system gives Rocio a distinct advantage.

Her use of IA creates a holistic digital ecosystem that connects every aspect of garment production, from the client's initial design brief to the final sewn product. This approach allows for:

- Instant updates and revisions to patterns across all team members and locations

- Seamless collaboration with manufacturers, designers, and clients

- Automated creation of technical packs and production guides, eliminating manual errors

- Streamlined management of multiple projects, ensuring no detail is overlooked

Rocio has explained how she tailors the IA to suit the specific needs of her clients, "I manage the information as I please, so I can create and adjust direction cards, tech packs, and specifications quickly. This cuts down on production delays and gives clients real-time visibility into their projects" (Evenett, 2024).

This workflow provides immense value to her clients and to the broader fashion industry, particularly for those who lack the technical knowledge or experience to streamline their processes. For many new designers, the technical aspects of pattern making, and production can be intimidating. By integrating the PAD system and IA, Evenett provides a framework that automates much of the complexity, allowing designers to focus on creativity rather than getting bogged down by technical details. Her use of technology significantly shortens production timelines. Designers and small businesses working with her can go from idea to market in just 90 days, thanks to her ability to quickly digitise and adjust patterns, create technical packs, and manage production through her IA. By digitising every step of the production process and using made-to-measure models, she minimises waste and overproduction. This sustainable approach is particularly appealing to ethical brands looking to reduce their environmental impact. She has embraced her role as a mentor and educator, teaching others how to integrate digital tools like the PAD system and FileMaker Pro into their own workflows. This opens new opportunities for designers who might otherwise be limited by traditional methods. Her online courses and consultancy offer emerging designers a chance to learn from one of the few experts who has mastered both the technical and creative sides of fashion production. With her global experience combined with her digital workflow makes it easier for teams spread across different countries to collaborate. Her workflow is scalable and adaptable, making it useful for brands that produce garments internationally.

Evenett's use of FileMaker Pro to integrate data management into her CAD process facilitated a global supply chain that connected designers, patternmakers, and manufacturers across continents. By enabling digital collaboration, her system allowed teams to work on the same designs simultaneously, no matter where they were located. This digital integration improved both the speed and accuracy of production, making cross-border manufacturing more efficient and reducing communication errors that traditionally plagued the fashion industry (Brun et al. 2008).

Evenett's early exposure to CAD systems wasn't just a tool she used; it became part of the foundation upon which she would build her career. When she later transitioned into her role as an entrepreneur, she didn't hesitate to adopt the latest technologies to improve her workflow. Armed with FileMaker Pro, Adobe Illustrator, and Adobe Photoshop, her natural inclination to solve problems led her to develop bespoke systems that transformed how she and her clients approached fashion production.

Evenett's rise in the corporate world was not without its hurdles. Early in her career, she faced sexual harassment, which ultimately pushed her to leave a job where her talents were being recognised but her well-being was not. "The production manager was asking me out on dates, because I turned him down, he started sexually harassing me," she explains. For many, this experience could have been the end of their aspirations. But for Evenett, it was the beginning of something new. Walking away from this toxic environment wasn't an easy decision. It meant leaving a promising role where she had learned valuable skills about tech packs, outsourcing, and the intricacies of production management. But she wasn't willing to sacrifice her dignity and well-being for the sake of a pay check. She chose to leave and carve out her own path, but she didn't have any role models (Evenett, 2024).

When women lack role models in industries such as fashion or technology, it can have significant effects on their career trajectories, workplace engagement, and overall success. Without role models, women may struggle to visualise themselves in leadership or highly technical roles, which can perpetuate gender disparities in these fields. Research from employment law, management consulting, and international statistics provides insight into these challenges.

Role models help individuals identify with specific career paths, increase self-efficacy, and provide critical mentorship. Women in male-dominated industries like fashion technology or IT often lack visible role models, leading to lower participation rates, slower career progression, and less representation in leadership roles. According to a 2019 McKinsey & Company report, women in leadership positions help reduce the confidence gap and can inspire other women to pursue similar paths. Companies with women in leadership positions are more likely to have robust pipelines for developing women at every level (McKinsey and Company, 2019). A lack of role models, however, can lead to imposter syndrome, where women feel inadequate or underqualified compared to their male counterparts.

Mentorship has been shown to be a crucial factor in retaining women in technology and fashion, something I have discovered since transitioning into this space. Without mentors or role models, women are more likely to exit the workforce or switch industries, particularly in environments where they feel isolated.

Legislation in many countries attempts to mitigate the lack of female representation in male-dominated industries through gender equality programs and affirmative action policies. In the European Union, the Gender Equality Directive (Directive 2006/54/EC) provides a legal framework for addressing gender imbalances, including in employment, but cultural barriers often make these policies less effective without role models (European Union, 2006) Employment laws in the United States, such as Title VII of the Civil Rights Act (United States Congress, 1964), also promote gender equality, yet persistent structural biases continue to limit the effectiveness of such laws, especially when there is a lack of senior women to mentor and guide younger employees.

The International Labour Organization (ILO) has identified the role of female mentors and role models as critical in closing gender gaps in leadership roles across industries. The ILO notes that in 2020, women made up only 25% of leadership positions in technology companies globally, a statistic partly attributed to a lack of visible female leaders (ILO, 2020).

In the fashion industry, a traditionally female-centric sector, women still face challenges in leadership. Although many garment workers are women, men dominate higher-paid roles, such as executives and designers. The Global Fashion Agenda (GFA) reported that less than 15% of fashion CEOs are women, despite women constituting the bulk of the workforce (GFA, 2020). Without role models, women in both the fashion and technology industries may find it difficult to envision themselves in leadership or technical positions, resulting in decreased engagement and slower career progression. Mentorship and legal frameworks help, but visible role models are essential for women to navigate these male-dominated sectors. Closing the gender gap requires intentional efforts to highlight and support women who can serve as role models for the next generation.

Then, Beverly Hills beckoned. Evenett would go on to do much more in fashion technology; but it feels like her experiences working for a tailor paid dividends to her abilities in innovation and problem-solving. The company specialised in providing custom-tailored garments for celebrities, politicians, and other high-profile clients in the Beverly Hills area. They had developed a unique system for taking client measurements and communicating those to their team of tailors located in Hong Kong. The margin for error was small; this was something she knew all too well from working with stage wear designers and managing pipelines at Rampage. She was hired as an assistant at this company, even though she didn't have prior experience in tailoring. However, her background in pattern making and her analytical mindset allowed her to quickly grasp and contribute to this unique measurement and communication system. The process she developed was way ahead of its time: it was to take Polaroid photos of the client wearing a jacket or garment they liked. Then she would then make any necessary modifications or notes on the Polaroid photos. She would then fax these Polaroid photos and measurement notes to the tailors in Hong Kong. As this was all happening before the widespread adoption of the internet, faxing the Polaroid photos was their way of efficiently transmitting the detailed measurement information to their overseas production team. This experience further developed her skills in problem-solving, leveraging technology, and finding innovative ways to streamline the design and production process—all of which would later benefit her when she started her own fashion business.

Starting the Sewing Incubator wasn't just about making clothes or launching another business venture; it was about offering support to those who, like her, might otherwise be left behind in the corporate world. Evenett has made it her mission to help creators and emerging brands bring their visions to life while navigating the complexities of the fashion and manufacturing industries. "I wanted to prevent people from being taken advantage of, like I was," she says. Her story of overcoming systemic challenges resonates with a generation of women who find themselves in similar situations—working in industries that, while reliant on their talents, often fail to offer them the support they deserve. Her resilience is not only in what she's overcome but in how she's reshaped her own path, turning adversity into an opportunity to lift others (Evenett, 2024).

After that, she worked at a company that had invested in a PAD (pattern design) system, which was new to the U.S. market at the time. Although she was hired as a pattern maker, the owner gave her just one day to figure out how to use the CAD software or she would be fired. She figured it out and was still fired so she took her employers to court for unfair dismissal and won. "I took my settlement, got myself a plotter, bought myself a used copy of the PAD system and I locked myself in my garage for two weeks," Evenett explains. It was this self-imposed crash course in technology that cemented her as an innovator—one who was unafraid to challenge the norms of an industry that often resists change. Her understanding of the PAD system combined with IA in her pattern-making process reflects a rare integration of digital tools and methodologies, making her an outlier in the traditional garment industry. Her workflow is not only innovative but also profoundly helpful to others, particularly those who are new to the field or seeking to streamline their design and production processes. In 1997, after a lawsuit settlement with her former employer, she finally launched her own business. This wasn't just a fresh start; it was a vindication.

Evenett's technical knowledge wasn't just about staying ahead of the curve—it was about solving real-world problems for her clients. She designed her systems to ensure that garments were produced on time, to spec, and with as little waste as possible. But perhaps what makes her work even more innovative is her commitment to using technology in a way that empowers creators, rather than replaces them. In an industry where AI and automation are often seen as threats to jobs, she views these tools as an opportunity to enhance creativity and streamline production. For her, the true potential of technology lies in its ability to help people, not displace them. She always looks for the path of least resistance (Evenett, 2024).

Today, Evenett has created a platform where technology is used to democratise fashion. Her business model is built around helping emerging brands take their ideas from concept to market in just 90 days—a feat made possible through the strategic use of SaaS and CAD technologies. Her vision for the future of fashion isn't just about selling clothes—it's about giving people the tools to build their own brands and enter the marketplace with confidence. Her approach is part of a larger disruption she sees happening in the fashion industry. "The disruption the industry is undergoing right now is going to evolve into a meritocracy, where talented creators make products, share their process, and consumers get to reward them for their talent," she predicts. For Evenett, the future of fashion is one where creativity, technology, and transparency work hand in hand (Evenett, 2024).

Evenett's early adoption of CAD and digital collaboration tools set a new standard in the fashion industry. What began as a tool for individual businesses soon became an essential part of the global fashion supply chain. Today, systems like the PAD and FileMaker Pro are widely used across the industry, ensuring that her contributions continue to shape how fashion is designed, produced, and consumed on a global scale.

The challenge for fashion integrating technology, especially AI, is that people fear it will optimise them out of a job. It can be assumed that this is true for many emergent technologies. Evenett expresses that this fear of job displacement due to AI integration is a significant challenge that needs to be overcome through education and understanding the operational requirements of new technologies (Evenett, 2024).

But what truly sets Evenett apart is her refusal to conform to outdated norms in the fashion world. In a traditionally elitist industry, she has created a space where technology meets creativity, and where anyone with a vision can access the tools they need to bring that vision to life. This mission became even more pressing after the passing of her mentor, a pattern-making expert who had once helped her navigate the complexities of garment technology. Her will to live as though everything will end tomorrow was also further compounded by her cancer diagnosis in 2017. "I realised that if I go tomorrow, all that knowledge is just going to disappear," she says. This sense of urgency has pushed her to share what she knows, making her platform not just a service for businesses but an educational hub. She regularly teaches courses on pattern making, garment technology, and fashion entrepreneurship, helping others avoid the pitfalls she encountered early in her career (Evenett, 2024).

Her ethos is simple yet profound: empower others through education and create opportunities where they don't exist. Evenett's platform goes beyond offering technological solutions—it provides a holistic approach to entrepreneurship, where creators can learn everything from manufacturing techniques to digital marketing and SEO, all while navigating the complexities of modern technology. Her job is to make things "more accessible, more understandable" (Evenett, 2024).

Her vision for the future isn't just focused on new technologies; it's about creating a balanced, ethical, and sustainable ecosystem. Evenett is committed to ethical garment production and believes that technology can help mitigate some of the wasteful practices that have long plagued the industry. She's already implementing made-to-measure models that minimise waste, and she sees digital innovation as the key to making the fashion industry more sustainable in the long run. "I hope I get to see a time when our clothes harness solar power to recharge our devices," Evenett muses, imagining a future where smart textiles will become an integral part of daily life (Evenett, 2024).

As she continues to grow her business and mentor the next generation of designers, Evenett remains grounded in her mission to make fashion accessible, ethical, and efficient. Her story isn't just about mastering technology—it's about using it to reshape an industry and empower individuals to realise their creative potential.

Her journey from a creative child with a toy sewing machine to a trailblazing technologist in the fashion industry is a story of resilience, innovation, and empowerment. Her ability to adapt to changing landscapes and incorporate cutting-edge technologies into her work has positioned her as a true pioneer in an industry that often resists change. But what sets her apart isn't just her technical prowess—it's her commitment to helping others and making sure that technology serves people, not the other way around. For Evenett, the future is bright—and it's one where creativity, technology, and ethics are in perfect balance.

Valerie Thomas and Rocio Evenett, though operating in vastly different fields, exemplify the transformative power of technology. They belong at that special intersection of creativity and science, where raw data becomes images that deepen our understanding of the world, and numbers become patterns that clothe the body. Both women have turned abstract concepts into tangible innovations—Thomas with her illusion transmitter and image processing systems, Evenett with her innovative approach to digital pattern making and fashion design.

Their stories underscore a powerful truth: technology is not just about machines, numbers, or code. It is about seeing beyond the obvious and believing in what is possible, even when the path forward is unclear. Both women have harnessed their unique visions to break through barriers, combining knowledge and curiosity to shape industries in ways that have a lasting impact. Their work turns data into stories, ideas into realities, and imagines a world where technology becomes a tool for creative expression and problem-solving.

Like the alchemists of old, Thomas and Evenett took the raw elements of their respective crafts and refined them, creating something new and unexpected. They remind us that the magic of technology lies not just in its functionality, but in its ability to inspire us to see the world differently—to look beyond the mirror, as Thomas did, or to make meaning from the patterns, as Evenett does. Ultimately, they show us that believing in what we can't yet see is the first step to making the impossible *possible.*

REFERENCES

Brun, A., Caniato, F., Caridi, M., Castelli, C., Miragliotta, G., Ronchi, S., Sianesi, A. and Spina, G. (2008) 'Logistics and supply chain management in the fashion industry', *International Journal of Production Economics*, 114(2), pp. 571–593.

European Union (2006). Directive 2006/54/EC of the European Parliament and of the Council of 5 July 2006 on the implementation of the principle of equal opportunities and equal treatment of men and women in matters of employment and occupation (recast). *Official Journal of the European Union*, L 204, pp. 23–36.

Evenett, R. (2024) Interview by Kelly Vero. 6 September 2024.

Fletcher, K. (2014) *Sustainable fashion and textiles: Design journeys.* 2nd edn. London: Earthscan.

Global Fashion Agenda (GFA). (2020) *CEO Agenda 2020: Closing the Gender Gap in Fashion Leadership.* [pdf] Available at: https://www.globalfashionagenda.com/publications/ceo-agenda-2020 (Accessed: 7 September 2024).

Goward, S.N., et al. (2015) 'Landsat's Role in Sustaining the Long-Term Record of Global Land Cover.' *Remote Sensing of Environment.*

Hansen, M.C. et al. (2013) 'High-Resolution global maps of 21st-century forest cover change,' *Science*, 342, pp 850–853. DOI:10.1126/science.1244693

International Labour Organization (ILO) (2020) *Women in Business and Management: The Business Case for Change.* [online] Available at: https://www.ilo.org/global/publications/books/WCMS_702002/lang–en/index.htm (Accessed: 7 September 2024).

McKinsey & Company. (2019) *Women in the Workplace 2019*. [pdf] Available at: https://www.mckinsey.com/featured-insights/gender-equality/women-in-the-workplace-2019 (Accessed: 7 September 2024).

NASA. (2021) 'Landsat Overview.' *NASA Goddard Space Flight Center.*

Roy, D.P., et al. (2014) 'The Landsat Data Continuity Mission: Terrestrial Imaging and Applications from Space.' *Remote Sensing of Environment.*

Thomas, V. (2020). Interviewed by Keisha Butts for CTV. *YouTube.* Available at: https://www.youtube.com/watch?v=Ipiireemmig (Accessed: 9 September 2024).

United States Congress (1964). Civil Rights Act of 1964. Public Law 88-352, 88th Congress, H.R. 7152. Approved July 2, 1964.

U.S. Geological Survey (USGS). (2019) 'Landsat and Agriculture.' *USGS.*

CHAPTER 8

Kate Edwards and Joan Clarke

Seek and Hide

M Y PARENTS WOULD REGULARLY boot me out of my room. When the computer found its way up into my inner sanctum, the teenager's bedroom, it was a recipe for more insomnia. So, they'd pack me off into the woods with my brother for the day. He would quickly tire of my nerdiness and chew his leg off to find his friends leaving me walking alone down an old disused railway track towards a deep mediaeval woodland. It was here that I would build a den. Find some sticks and with a can of chicken soup and a box of matches I have purloined from my father I would set about making a fire. I was free. Although no longer in front of my computer, I was able to sit alone and think. I had a notepad and a pen in my supermarket tote, and I could write all the things I wanted to do later when I was back at my beloved machine. I would sketch birds, write words and remind myself of things that the ZX Spectrum would only allow me to write when the monitor was blinking. The secrets contained in the den were stored in my head or on the page only to be burned by the fire before the day fizzled out. And then, in the faded light of the church tower in the next village and the heat of the black and white television would I remember.

Whether navigating unknown territories or deciphering complex codes, female trailblazers have left an indelible mark on the world. In our modern era, the realms of exploration and cryptography continue to be shaped by extraordinary women who break barriers and unravel mysteries. Their stories remind us that discovery—whether of new lands or hidden messages—is not just about curiosity, but also about the courage to challenge the unknown sometimes within ourselves. These women inspire the next generation to venture boldly into new frontiers, both digital and beyond.

KATE EDWARDS—A JOURNEY TO THE CENTRE OF THE MACHINE

Kate Edwards' story begins with summer. Taking annual road trips with her family invoked a curiosity and discovery which conjured in my mind at least, excitement and adventure. She has built a career out of stepping into the unknown, not with a ship or compass, but

DOI: 10.1201/9781003566465-8

with an insatiable curiosity, a love of maps, and a deep understanding of the geopolitical forces shaping our world. Just as Béláné Mocsáry mapped foreign landscapes with a quill or Gudrid Thorbjarnardóttir sailed across the unforgiving North Atlantic, Kate navigates the machine—an ever-evolving, intangible realm of digital content, ethics, and culture.

At the intersection of geography, gaming, and ethical design, Edwards has created a unique path that challenges conventional career expectations. Her journey illustrates the importance of combining different disciplines and thinking critically about the social impact of technology. In this digital age, the unknown isn't distant lands but the inner workings of technology, where the intersections of code, culture, and ethics present challenges that are no less daunting than the seas Gudrid crossed. Her quest is to explore these new territories, charting a course through virtual landscapes and global markets, always aware of the hidden dangers—misrepresentation, bias, and exclusion—that could wreck a project on the jagged rocks of cultural insensitivity. For young people, her journey offers a map to follow, one that invites them to embark on their own adventure inside the machine, where discovery awaits those willing to think beyond borders and disciplines. Whenever I speak with Edwards, and everyone should spend some time with her at least once in their lives, I am carried into a realm of possibility, exploration and quiet understanding.

Edwards' fascination with maps began early, driven by a love for J.R.R. Tolkien's Middle-Earth. The intricate maps of imaginary lands enchanted her, setting the stage for her future career. "The narrative of cartography, whether in fantasy or the real world, is built on historical, political, and cultural systems that dictate how we divide up the Earth" (Edwards, 2024). These early influences combined with the experiences from her family's travels inspired her to explore the world through maps—both real and imagined. Her love for fantasy world-building, combined with a passion for understanding why the lines on real maps exist, foreshadowed her career in digital world-building and culturalization.

Edwards always wanted to understand why borders existed and what stories they told. "Maps are political documents," as cartographer Monmonier (1996) famously noted, "shaped by power and ideology, not just tools for navigation." This insight became central to her approach, informing her work in understanding how digital content reflects and shapes cultural perceptions. From a young age, she knew that maps weren't just about geography; they were about history, power, and identity.

Edwards pursued her undergraduate studies in Geography at California State University (CSU), Long Beach. "Geopolitics and cross-cultural communication really became an interest when I started to explore the reasoning behind the lines on the map" (Edwards, 2024). She delved deeply into human geography, cartography, and cultural systems, equipping herself with the tools to understand the world from multiple perspectives. Her master's degree in Geography from the University of Washington, combined with a Postgraduate Certificate in Cartography from the CSU Long Beach, provided the technical foundation for her later career in culturalization and digital content strategy.

Cartography and Geographic Information Systems (GIS) became key tools in Edwards' professional journey, particularly in the realm of video game development. Geography and cartography are more than a technical skill set; for her, it is a means to navigate the digital and cultural complexities of world-building in games. Her studies in GIS and cartography certainly helped, but to create virtual environments where she infuses cultural and historical authenticity, she regularly draws upon her other knowledge areas.

Reflecting on her career, Edwards recalls how studying maps taught her to think beyond the physical space. Geopolitics and cultural communication drove her interest in how the lines on a map reflect historical and political forces (Edwards, 2024). This deeper understanding of maps and how layers of geographic phenomena are organised - much like in a GIS - helped her transition into world-building in the gaming industry.

One of her most notable contributions was in the *Age of Empires* franchise, where GIS played a critical role in shaping the game's content. Utilising her geography background, she could help the team create maps and scenarios that weren't just playable but historically coherent. Her attention to detail allowed players to engage deeply with the game's environments, enhancing their immersion and connection to the historical contexts they were exploring. "Players could feel like they were really walking through those times and places" (Edwards, 2024).

In games like *Mass Effect* and *Halo*, while not grounded in historical reality, Edwards' use of geographic principles helped create futuristic worlds that felt grounded. Her work ensured that the relationships between environments and characters made sense, helping developers design cohesive worlds that drew players in. Through her understanding of geography and spatial relationships, she helped pioneer new approaches to world-building, where digital landscapes are not only visually stunning but also culturally sensitive and historically accurate.

Studies such as geography and cartography are highly relevant to video games, especially in areas like world-building, environment design, and cultural representation. Spatial data science involves collecting, analysing, and interpreting data related to the Earth's surface, including terrain, geography, and human-made boundaries. This knowledge is directly applicable to video game development in several key ways:

1. **World-Building and Terrain Creation**
   In video games, especially open-world and strategy games, creating realistic environments is essential for immersion. A GIS-like approach to world building might create a type of blueprint within the experience that game developers could use to apply to a variety of spatial immersion. This methodology or system can be used to layer and later organise in similar ways to how architects use detailed plans to construct buildings. Developers could create GIS-like tools to craft towering mountains or winding rivers, making virtual worlds feel as rich and real as the landscapes we walk through in games like *The Witcher 3* or *Red Dead Redemption 2*.

2. **Geopolitical Strategy and Realism**
   Cultural geography can help developers understand how political boundaries, human settlements, and resources are distributed across real-world landscapes. This is particularly important in games that involve geopolitical strategy, such as *Age of Empires* or *Civilization*, where the placement of cities, resources, and political borders must make sense within the game's world and core-game mechanics.

In these games, this knowledge of geocultural and geopolitical systems can assist developers in creating maps that are not only fun to play but also reflect realistic historical or contemporary geopolitical situations. For example, a game set during the Roman Empire will use historical spatial data along with world-building tools to accurately place cities, trade routes, and natural resources in a way that reflects the historical context.

3. **Culturalization and Cross-Cultural Sensitivity**
   Culturalization, a concept that Edwards has pioneered, involves adapting digital content to different cultural and geopolitical contexts. Her experience in cartography, geoculture, and geopolitics allows her to be able to offer feedback to development teams who are making maps and creating land lore.

   For instance, a game set in a fictional country might draw on real-world geographic and cultural data to ensure that its environment feels authentic and respectful of real-world cultures. A geography-minded approach can help developers map out how people interact with their landscapes, from urban planning to the distribution of religious or cultural landmarks, allowing them to create worlds that reflect diverse cultural perspectives.

4. **Spatial Awareness and Movement Mechanics**
   Cartography and GIS studies teach spatial awareness—understanding how distances, elevations, and obstacles affect movement and interactions. This is crucial for game developers who design mechanics like character movement, pathfinding, and navigation in 3D environments.

   For example, in a game like *The Legend of Zelda: Breath of the Wild*, where players must traverse vast landscapes, GIS principles can help developers model realistic distances, slopes, and terrain types that affect how characters move through the game world. Elevation data, for instance, can be used to determine where it makes sense to place cliffs, valleys, or steep inclines that affect gameplay.

5. **Historical and Thematic Accuracy**
   Many video games are set in real historical periods or are inspired by real-world cultures. A knowledge of cultural and geographic patterns, along with historical data, allows developers to create maps and environments that are historically accurate. For example, in a game like *Assassin's Creed*, which takes players to historical settings, culturization will can help recreate the geographic layout of ancient cities, ensuring that the game world feels authentic.

   This is also important for games that require detailed reconstructions of real places, such as simulation games or games based on real-world locations like *Microsoft Flight Simulator*. Accurate geographic data from GIS ensures that players are navigating environments that resemble their real-world counterparts.

Edwards' role is critical in the gaming industry, where cultural missteps can lead to alienation or even boycotts in certain regions. For instance, a controversial level in *Call of Duty: Modern Warfare 2* titled "No Russian," (Stuart, 2009) which depicted violence against civilians, sparked significant public outrage upon its release. This incident highlights the need for cultural sensitivity in game development, as the level's graphic content led to heavy criticism and was censored in some international versions. The controversy surrounding the level underscores the complex ethical considerations developers face when addressing sensitive topics in games. Her work ensures that game developers take cultural differences into account from the start, creating content that resonates with players around the world without causing offence.

Culturalization, as pioneered by experts like Edwards, plays a pivotal role in shaping the future of digital media, especially as globalised digital content becomes increasingly prevalent. As digital products—whether video games, applications, or multimedia platforms—are consumed worldwide, ensuring they are culturally appropriate, inclusive, and relevant to diverse audiences is critical for both ethical and practical reasons. The process of culturalization extends beyond mere language translation (localisation) to encompass the adaptation of digital content to align with cultural, political, and social contexts of various global regions. This practice ensures that digital experiences are inclusive, reducing the risk of cultural misrepresentation or offence.

One of the most practical benefits of culturalization is its ability to expand the global reach of digital products. By tailoring content to fit the cultural sensitivities of different regions, companies can maximise their products' market potential. This is especially important for video games and apps, which often target diverse, global audiences. Studies show that culturally adapted content performs better in local markets, with users more likely to engage with and trust products that reflect their own cultural norms and values (Singh, 2011).

For example, video games like *Assassin's Creed* use culturalization to ensure that historical and cultural elements are portrayed accurately, fostering a deeper connection with players from various regions (Edwards, 2014). Games that fail to properly address cultural sensitivities, on the other hand, risk alienating users or even facing bans in certain countries. The game *Call of Duty: Modern Warfare 2*, faced backlash due to its portrayal of violence against civilians, highlighting the necessity of cultural awareness in digital design (Stuart, 2009).

Culturalization also plays a critical role in promoting inclusivity and ensuring that digital products represent a broad spectrum of human experiences. As the digital world continues to evolve, there is increasing awareness of the need to move beyond stereotypes and provide meaningful representation of different cultures, genders, and identities. Without culturalization, digital content risks perpetuating harmful stereotypes or omitting entire communities, which can reinforce social exclusion (Gray, 2014).

Incorporating cultural elements thoughtfully and respectfully into digital products helps to create more inclusive and diverse environments. This is especially true in video games, where narratives and character designs can significantly influence how different cultures are perceived. Research has shown that users are more engaged with content when they feel seen and represented in it (Nakamura and Chow-White, 2012), something already discussed in other chapters of this book but deeply relevant to creating a realistic canvas for expression or gameplay. Therefore, culturalization is not only a matter of ethics but also of engagement and immersion for global audiences and since we eat with our eyes, that's where we should begin.

Deploying a user interface (UI) design for digital applications such as video games is not just about aesthetics and functionality—it is also deeply intertwined with cultural and geopolitical considerations. Even seemingly simple design elements, like icons or characters, can carry cultural, political, or historical significance, which can influence how digital content is perceived in different regions (Edwards, 2024). A toolkit to address these complexities must go beyond the technical aspects of design and incorporate an understanding of cultural sensitivity, geopolitical awareness, and historical context.

Icons and symbols are fundamental components of UI design, serving as visual shortcuts that communicate actions, ideas, and functions quickly. However, the meanings of these icons are not universal. In some cultures, symbols that are innocuous in one context can carry offensive or problematic connotations in another. For example, the use of hand gestures (such as a thumbs-up or OK sign), colours (red symbolising good luck in some Asian cultures but danger in others), or religious symbols can vary significantly across regions (Singh, 2011).

A toolkit addressing these sensitivities would need to include:

- **Cultural Research Guidelines**: A structured approach to researching the cultural implications of specific UI elements for different regions. This research would involve understanding local customs, historical connotations of symbols, and current political sensitivities.

- **Icon and Symbol Database**: A repository of culturally vetted icons that designers can use, ensuring that common symbols like flags, religious imagery, or hand gestures are culturally appropriate for each target market.

- **User Testing Protocols**: Tools for conducting localised user testing to ensure that UI elements resonate well with local audiences and do not inadvertently offend or confuse users.

For example, in video games like *Civilization* or *Age of Empires*, the design of historical and cultural icons such as national flags, religious symbols, or even architectural styles must be carefully curated. Such details are often tied to regional pride or political identity, and missteps in these areas can provoke controversy (Edwards, 2014).

Geopolitical considerations are crucial in both UI design and marketing strategies. In some regions, political boundaries or even country names can be contentious. For example, including Taiwan as a separate country on a UI map can be deeply offensive to China, where it is seen as a violation of their "One China" policy (Schiller, 2011). Similarly, using certain flags, colours, or language in marketing campaigns can evoke unintended geopolitical tensions.

A toolkit to manage these concerns might include:

- **Geopolitical Mapping Tools**: GIS-based tools allow designers to visualise political boundaries and tensions. These tools could also provide historical context on how certain regions are contested, helping avoid potentially sensitive geopolitical errors.

- **Flag and National Symbol Guidelines**: Detailed guidelines on the use of national symbols in UIs or marketing campaigns, explaining which symbols should be avoided or used with caution in different regions. For example, guidelines could outline how the use of maps or certain symbols could provoke controversy in places like Crimea, Tibet, or Northern Ireland.

- **Localised Marketing Strategies**: Templates for crafting region-specific marketing strategies consider local political and social norms. For instance, a toolkit could provide guidelines on how to adapt a product launch in China versus one in India, where the social and political climates are vastly different.

Edwards' example of adjusting marketing and UI design for different locales speaks to this issue. When developing products for global markets, understanding the geopolitical landscape can help avoid mistakes that could result in boycotts, media backlash, or government sanctions (Edwards, 2014).

Games and their UIs often draw from real-world history, geography, and culture. However, using historical references in a game's UI or narrative design can be fraught with challenges. A game set in World War II, for example, must be careful about the use of Nazi symbols or references to colonialism, which can provoke strong reactions depending on the target audience. The historical portrayal of real-world events or characters in a game can carry ethical implications, influencing how audiences interpret history; because before being appropriated by the Nazi party, the symbol was (and for some people still is) an ancient religious and cultural symbol, predominantly found in various East and South Asian cultures.

A toolkit for managing historical sensitivity might include:

- **Historical Reference Checklists**: A guide to verifying the historical accuracy of UI elements like maps, flags, or architectural styles, ensuring they reflect the time and cultural context accurately. This could also include tools for fact-checking the portrayal of historical events, so they are not oversimplified or misrepresented.

- **Cultural Consultation Services**: Access to cultural and historical experts who can provide feedback on the use of historical references in a game's UI or storyline. These experts could ensure that the narrative and design choices do not unintentionally trivialise important historical events.

- **Ethical Storytelling Frameworks**: A framework for ensuring that games that draw on real-world history do so with ethical consideration. This might include rules for the portrayal of controversial figures or events, as well as guidelines for avoiding stereotyping or historical revisionism.

In Edwards' own work, she has referenced how characters or stories in games can carry unintended messages if not handled with care. For example, the portrayal of historical events in games like *Call of Duty* or *Battlefield* can affect how players interpret these events, and any inaccuracies or oversights in UI design (such as the use of flags or uniforms) can spark controversy (Edwards, 2014).

Often the creators of UI elements are not aware of the hidden messages that their designs may communicate. Cultural assumptions made during the design process can lead to unintended consequences. For instance, a character's clothing style, facial features, or gestures can evoke stereotypes that may be harmful or offensive to certain groups. A game or app interface that does not consider the local preferences for colours, symbols, or even user interactions can lead to poor reception in certain markets.

To prevent such missteps, the toolkit might focus on:

- **Inclusive Design Guidelines**: Principles of inclusive design that help developers build UI elements with diverse cultural perspectives in mind. This could include best practices for character creation, icon design, and the overall aesthetic of the game's interface, ensuring that no group feels excluded or misrepresented.

- **Cross-Cultural Empathy Training**: Resources for designers to learn about cultural differences, bias in design, and how their work can be perceived in different regions. Training modules or workshops could help designers develop the empathy needed to create UIs that resonate globally.

- **Bias Detection Tools**: Automated tools that analyse design elements for potential biases or cultural blind spots, flagging areas where additional cultural research may be necessary. These tools could scan character models, icons, or text for features that might unintentionally reinforce stereotypes or offend certain groups.

Creators are often unaware that their designs might include hidden messages, and by adopting a toolkit that emphasises empathy and inclusivity, designers can avoid many of these issues (Edwards, 2014). Building a UI that respects different cultural values and political sensitivities requires not only technical skill but also an understanding of the human context in which the digital product will be used.

Global digital products must account for the political and historical contexts of the regions in which they are released. Failure to do so can lead to significant issues, including government censorship or consumer backlash. When Edwards helped guide Microsoft's geopolitical strategy, it was akin to charting a course through unfamiliar waters. Like an explorer facing new terrain, she had to navigate the shifting boundaries of global politics, ensuring that digital content avoided the cultural pitfalls that could have derailed Microsoft's global ambitions. Her work in geopolitical strategy at Microsoft was groundbreaking but necessary and a prime example of how culturalization can help companies avoid these pitfalls (Edwards, 2014). It illustrates the real-world ethical challenges that companies face when launching products in international markets.

The *Encarta* encyclopaedia incident in Turkey, where the government jailed a Microsoft executive over a political map label, exemplifies the high stakes involved in corporate geopolitics. Edwards' role was to ensure that Microsoft's products were geopolitically sound, meaning that they did not unintentionally cause political unrest or violate cultural norms.

This work is crucial in a world where technology companies are global players, often influencing political and social dynamics in the regions they serve (Schiller, 2011). Her contribution to getting a "geopolitical and cultural accountability" item added to Microsoft's product checklist underscores her lasting impact on how tech companies approach global markets (Edwards, 2024).

This not only affects market success and inclusivity but also enhances user experience by making digital products more relatable and immersive. When users interact with content that reflects their language, cultural symbols, and values, they are more likely to engage deeply with it (Singh, 2011). In the context of video games, for instance, environments that are culturally coherent—whether real or fictional—heighten players' emotional engagement and suspension of disbelief.

Narrative design is enriched greatly by infusing it with culturally specific mythologies, histories, and narratives. Games like *Ghost of Tsushima*, which draws heavily from Japanese history and culture, provide players with a sense of authenticity and connection that transcends traditional game design (Kuchera, 2020). Such culturally rich experiences are increasingly becoming a hallmark of successful digital products, particularly in an era where users expect immersive and meaningful interactions.

As the digital world continues to globalise, critical ethical considerations are the metrics for success. The idea that digital products must be inclusive, respectful, and culturally sensitive is gaining momentum, especially in fields like artificial intelligence, where biases can easily be coded into algorithms. Culturalization ensures that digital technologies do not reinforce existing inequalities or perpetuate stereotypes. A well-known example is the use of facial recognition software, which has been found to be biased against women and people of colour (Buolamwini and Gebru, 2018). These ethical concerns highlight the importance of ensuring that technology serves the public good rather than amplifying inequality. For young people entering the tech industry, Edwards' focus on ethical responsibility offers a powerful reminder that technology is not neutral—it reflects the values of its creators.

In this sense, it is a moral obligation for creators of digital content. As Edwards argues, developers and designers hold the responsibility to ensure that their creations reflect a diverse and inclusive worldview, shaping how people interact with technology across different regions (Edwards, 2014). This ethical approach to digital content creation aligns with broader discussions about responsible innovation in technology, where inclusivity and fairness are prioritised (Binns, 2018).

Today, data breaches, misinformation, and bias in algorithms are ubiquitous so the question of ethics is more urgent than ever. Edwards' stance on ethical programming reflects a growing awareness in the tech industry that programmers and designers must have a strong ethical framework guiding their work. While she is not a programmer in the traditional sense, her work in content creation and world-building places her at the forefront of ethical dilemmas like those faced by coders. One of the key issues she has addressed is how different groups are represented in digital content, particularly in video games (Edwards, 2024). Representation is not just about visibility; it is about ensuring that diverse groups are portrayed accurately and respectfully.

Ethical programming means having a moral compass codified into a clear set of principles. How else might we feel respected and therefore safe in our digital travails? This approach aligns with broader discussions in the tech world about the need for ethical guidelines in AI, coding, and content creation. Companies like Google and Microsoft have created their own ethical AI guidelines, recognising the power they wield and the need for accountability (Binns, 2018).

The video game industry has been criticised for its lack of diversity and stereotypical portrayals of race, gender, and culture (Gray, 2014). Edwards' work helps combat this by ensuring that games represent a broader spectrum of humanity. Her focus on inclusion and exclusion echoes the broader conversations in the tech industry about the importance of diversity in programming and design. Studies have shown that diverse teams are more innovative and better able to design products that appeal to a wide range of consumers (Page, 2007).

Critical thinking and problem-solving is at the core of her approach to culturalization and ethics in this space. In her work on the *Age of Empires* franchise, Edwards helped ensure that historical accuracy was maintained while being sensitive to the cultural narratives of different regions. Similarly, her work on *Halo* and *Mass Effect* involved making sure that the futuristic worlds depicted were inclusive and diverse, without perpetuating harmful stereotypes. This has always been in the eye of its beholder. However, in the case of *Halo 3*, the inclusivity, though clunky, was attendant to the player. Edwards' practice of culturalization is not about diluting creative freedom. Rather, it is about expanding a game's potential by making it accessible and enjoyable for players from all over the world.

One of Edwards' core beliefs is that while creative freedom is essential in video games, it must be balanced with ethical responsibility. She argues that game developers have a duty to consider the impact their games may have on players, especially when dealing with sensitive topics like violence, gender, and race. This perspective aligns with recent discussions in the gaming industry about how games influence behaviour and social norms (Ferguson, 2013). While games are often seen as harmless entertainment, they can shape attitudes and reinforce stereotypes. Her work ensures that developers take these issues into account, making games that challenge rather than perpetuate harmful societal norms.

Cross-cultural competence is not just a buzzword in today's global tech industry—it's a necessity. I agree that while we live in an interdependent world, where technology crosses borders and cultures every day (Edwards, 2024); for those working in tech, this means understanding how people from different backgrounds will experience and interpret the products they create. Research supports this view, showing that cross-cultural competence leads to better problem-solving and more innovative solutions in diverse teams (Maznevski and DiStefano, 2000). By fostering empathy and understanding, companies can create products that resonate with a wider audience and avoid cultural missteps.

Might digital cartography in this all-encompassing sense become even more important as companies seek to expand their global reach? As more people from diverse social science backgrounds enter the field, this understanding of cross-cultural competence will continue to evolve, incorporating new insights into how digital content can be adapted for different cultures. That includes the role that AI will ultimately play. While AI is not yet fully sophisticated enough to understand culturalization, geopolitics, and historical conventions of geography, ongoing advancements in AI, particularly in natural language processing (NLP) and deep learning, may improve its capabilities. AI models trained on larger, more diverse datasets and equipped with better contextual understanding could assist human experts by offering preliminary analysis, identifying patterns, and automating aspects of content adaptation.

Edwards cautions that human empathy and judgement will always be crucial (Edwards, 2024). This reflects broader discussions about the role of AI in creative industries. While AI can assist in tasks like translation or data analysis, it cannot replace the human understanding of culture and emotion (Colman, 2020). The future of AI in culturalization and geopolitics will likely involve a hybrid model, where AI can assist human experts by processing vast datasets, identifying trends, and performing predictive analyses. However, the complex interpretative work—understanding the deeper meaning behind cultural symbols, political decisions, and historical contexts—will continue to rely on human experts for the foreseeable future (Schiller, 2011). Human-AI collaboration can ensure that digital content remains culturally sensitive, geopolitically informed, and historically accurate.

Edward's advice for aspiring professionals is grounded in her own journey: follow your curiosity, don't compare yourself to others, and embrace mentorship. She quotes Mark Twain's famous line "comparison is the death of joy" but feels this is particularly relevant in a world dominated by social media (Edwards, 2024), where constant comparison can lead to anxiety and self-doubt (Diener and Seligman, 2004).

The line between creative media, technology, and geopolitics and culture is becoming increasingly small especially in the video games industry where the once one-size-fits-all approach has been refined to a more agile workflow of linguistic and cultural lived experiences and ideas. Lean(ing) into it heavily and exploring all the different dimensions of what these fields offer means that there are more pathways to explore in this space (Edwards, 2024). How individuals approach the world will ultimately dictate which cultural lens they look through. Edwards' approach was to go "with the flow of things that interest me and now when I look back on it that's exactly what led me to do essentially what I love doing, i.e., effectively being able to create the most perfect job for myself." So, it doesn't matter that we might never get to Lorien; because instead we might create somewhere that lives in the consciousness of others, considerately, of course.

JOAN CLARKE—THE ART OF KEEPING A SECRET

Joan Clarke was born on 24 June 1917 in West Norwood, London, England, as the youngest of four siblings. Her family was intellectually inclined; her father, William Kemp Lowther Clarke, was a clergyman and a scholar, while her mother, Dorothy Fulford Clarke, was a devoted homemaker. Growing up in such a household, Clarke developed a strong intellectual curiosity early on, particularly in mathematics (Hodges, 1983).

Clarke attended Dulwich High School for Girls, where she quickly distinguished herself as an exceptional student. Her mathematical abilities caught the attention of her teachers, who encouraged her to pursue higher studies in the subject. The opportunity to develop her talent for mathematics was rare, particularly for a woman at that time when gender roles often limited educational opportunities for women. Mathematicians during this time were mostly men, but Shakuntala Devi, whose almost other-worldly approach to mathematics which seemed to entertain more than provide the basis for science is certainly noteworthy. For Clarke, despite societal expectations, her family supported her academic ambitions (Hodges, 1983).

In 1936, Clarke won a scholarship to Newnham College, Cambridge, one of the few women's colleges at the university. Alice Ambrose, Pat Ambler, Letitia Chitty, and Gillian Lovegrove are a few among many who have attended this most prestigious of colleges at Cambridge. There, she studied mathematics under the tutelage of renowned mathematicians, including G. H. Hardy and E. H. Neville. She excelled in her studies, earning a top First in the Mathematical Tripos, a prestigious academic achievement (Hodges, 1983).

Although Clarke achieved academic success comparable to her male peers, Cambridge University at that time did not award full degrees to women. Instead, she received a "titular degree," meaning she earned all the qualifications but was denied an official degree because of her gender. This discrimination, a reflection of the broader societal limitations on women, underscores the challenges she faced in her pursuit of a career in mathematics and cryptography.

Clarke's work at Bletchley Park during World War II was a pivotal contribution to the Allied war effort, specifically in breaking the German Naval Enigma code. Bletchley Park was a top-secret facility where the British Government Code and Cypher School (GC&CS) sought to decrypt German communications encrypted by the Enigma machine. The German military used the machine to encode messages that were nearly impossible to decipher without knowing the precise settings of the machine for a particular day. Her role as a cryptanalyst, despite her initial clerical posting, became integral to the success of the team at Bletchley, particularly in Hut 8, where she worked with Alan Turing and others.

Think of cryptography as creating a secret code to send messages. If you lock your message in a safe, only the person with the right key can open it and read it. Cryptography works in the same way by encrypting data, turning it into unreadable "ciphertext" that can only be deciphered by the person with the right key. It involves encoding (encrypting) data into an unreadable format to protect its confidentiality, integrity, and authenticity. Cryptography is essential in many modern applications, including online banking, digital communications, and secure government or military communications.

There are two primary components in cryptography:

1. **Encryption**: The process of converting plaintext (readable data) into ciphertext (an encoded format) using an algorithm and a key. The ciphertext can only be decrypted back into plaintext by someone who possesses the correct decryption key.

2. **Decryption**: The reverse process, where the ciphertext is converted back into plaintext using the decryption key.

Cryptography typically relies on mathematical algorithms to ensure security. Modern cryptography often uses complex methods such as symmetric-key encryption (e.g. AES: Advanced Encryption Standard/Rijndael algorithm) or public-key cryptography (e.g. RSA: Rivest Shamir Adleman algorithm), where different keys are used for encryption and decryption.

Cryptanalysis is the practice of studying and breaking cryptographic systems, with the aim of deciphering encrypted messages without knowing the encryption key. In essence, it's the art of codebreaking. Cryptanalysts attempt to find weaknesses in cryptographic algorithms, exploit vulnerabilities in encryption protocols, or use mathematical and computational techniques to reverse the encryption process and recover the original plaintext.

During World War II, cryptanalysis was crucial in breaking the encryption systems used by the Axis powers, such as the German Enigma machine, which encrypted military communications. Clarke, for example, played a key role in the cryptanalysis work done at Bletchley Park, where the British cracked Enigma-encrypted messages, giving the Allies a significant advantage (McKay, 2010).

The primary objectives of cryptanalysis are:

1. **Breaking the encryption**: This involves finding the key used in the encryption process to reveal the original plaintext.

2. **Discovering weaknesses**: Identifying flaws in the encryption algorithm or the implementation of the cryptographic system.

3. **Analysing patterns**: Using statistical and logical methods to detect patterns in ciphertexts, which could reveal information about the encryption method.

Cryptography and cryptanalysis are two sides of the same coin. While cryptography aims to secure information, cryptanalysis attempts to uncover the hidden content, often leading to improvements in cryptographic techniques as weaknesses are exposed and fixed.

Clarke began working at Bletchley Park in June 1940. Initially recruited for a low-level clerical position under the Civil Service Clerical Scheme, she was quickly identified by her former Cambridge tutor, Gordon Welchman, who was already at Bletchley Park, as someone with exceptional mathematical abilities. Welchman recommended Clarke for a cryptanalytic role (Hodges, 1983). Shortly thereafter, she joined Hut 8, the section dedicated to breaking German Naval Enigma codes, under the leadership of Alan Turing (Smith, 2011).

Clarke's initial work involved performing routine tasks, but her mathematical prowess soon became apparent. She rapidly advanced to more complex cryptanalytic work, particularly focusing on the German Naval Enigma, which was considered more challenging than other Enigma versions used by the German Army and Air Force. The naval version had additional complexity because of the high stakes: it encrypted communications used by U-Boats, which posed a significant threat to the Allied convoys in the Atlantic (Smith, 2011).

One of Clarke's most significant achievements was her work on *Banburismus*, a technique developed by Turing to reduce the number of possible settings for the Enigma machine. Imagine you're solving a complex puzzle, narrowing down possible answers with each clue. Banburismus worked like that—Clarke and her team compared patterns in the encrypted messages to eliminate wrong answers and get closer to the right settings of the Enigma machine. She excelled in this method, which required careful mathematical reasoning and significant intellectual rigour (Hodges, 1983).

Banburismus was crucial in breaking Naval Enigma because it allowed the team to significantly reduce the number of possible keys that needed to be tested, thereby saving time and allowing Bletchley Park to decipher messages more quickly. Clarke was a key player in performing Banburismus calculations, demonstrating not only her mathematical ability but also her deep understanding of the complex cryptographic processes involved. Her work in this area made her one of the few female cryptanalysts at Bletchley Park who had such a direct and impactful role in breaking codes (McKay, 2010).

Clarke's position in Hut 8 was notable because women were typically excluded from high-level cryptanalytic work. Most women at Bletchley were involved in clerical or operational roles, such as managing the Bombe machines or intercepting and transcribing enemy communications. Her promotion to cryptanalyst status was highly unusual at the time, as the field was overwhelmingly dominated by men (McKay, 2010).

However, despite her growing responsibilities and accomplishments, Clarke was often paid less than her male counterparts, a reflection of the institutionalised gender discrimination that pervaded the era. We don't have to wonder about this because this is one of the most common occurrences in any workforce. In 2022, women in the U.S. tech industry earned approximately 82 cents for every dollar earned by men, driven by factors such as occupational segregation, gender bias in hiring and promotion, and a tendency for women to negotiate salaries less aggressively due to fear of backlash (Institute for Women's Policy Research, 2022). The persistence of these inequalities is often accepted because of entrenched societal norms that devalue women's labour and the perception that tech is a *male* field.

Clarke's modest personality and reluctance to seek the limelight meant that her achievements often went unrecognised by the broader public, even though her peers at Bletchley, including Turing, held her in high esteem. Turing is reported to have valued her insights highly and viewed her as one of his most capable colleagues (Hodges, 1983). Fewer women pursue STEM degrees, and women are often discouraged from entering technical roles due to stereotypes, lack of role models, and hostile work environments. A survey revealed that 44% of women in tech experienced workplace harassment, compared to only 14% of men (Women Who Tech, 2020). Moreover, the educational pipeline plays a significant role, with women earning only 21% of computer science degrees in the U.S. (National Science Foundation, 2023). The perception that technology is a meritocratic field masks these systemic issues, allowing the pay gap and gender disparities to persist, with male-dominated leadership teams often overlooking the need for equity (Bowles et al. 2007; McKinsey & Company, 2019).

In 1944, Clarke was promoted to Deputy Head of Hut 8, serving directly under Turing and later Hugh Alexander, another key figure in the decryption of Naval Enigma. This role was significant as it placed her in a leadership position where she was responsible for overseeing the cryptanalysis efforts of others in the team. Her contributions were vital in helping to break key U-Boat communications, allowing the Allies to avoid deadly ambushes in the Atlantic and safeguarding vital supply convoys from the United States to Britain (Smith, 2011). This promotion is particularly notable given the resistance many women faced in advancing to leadership roles within the cryptographic community. Clarke, despite being an introverted figure, managed to earn the respect of her peers through her exceptional skills and the quiet tenacity with which she approached her work. Her leadership in Hut 8 was instrumental during the latter years of the war when German U-Boat tactics intensified.

Like many others at Bletchley Park, Clarke was bound by the Official Secrets Act, which prevented her from discussing her work, even with family members, for many years after the war. This secrecy contributed to her being an unsung figure for much of her life, with much of the public credit for Bletchley's work going to male figures such as Turing (Hodges, 1983).

After the war, Clarke continued her work with the Government Communications Headquarters (GCHQ), the post-war successor to Bletchley Park. Though much of her post-war work remains classified, it is known that she continued to make important contributions to cryptography and intelligence. However, because of the secret nature of her work, she lived much of her life out of the public eye, her contributions known only to a select few (McKay, 2010).

In addition to her intellectual pursuits, Clarke was described by her contemporaries as modest and reserved, with a deep passion for puzzles and intellectual challenges. She was known to have an interest in botany, classical music, and numismatics (the study of coins), which further underscored her well-rounded intellectual capabilities (Hodges, 1983).

Clarke's work at Bletchley Park was crucial in the Allied victory in the Battle of the Atlantic and in securing the encryption techniques used by German forces. Despite the challenges she faced as a woman in a male-dominated field, she rose to become one of the most important cryptanalysts working on the Naval Enigma. Clarke's contributions helped shorten the war and save thousands of lives, and her legacy as a pioneering cryptanalyst has since become more widely recognised, especially in the last few decades.

Cryptography and cryptanalysis play a foundational role in emerging technologies such as blockchain and Web3, driving the development of decentralised systems that are secure, private, and tamper-resistant. In these fields, cryptography is primarily used to secure data, authenticate users, and verify transactions. Blockchain, for instance, relies heavily on cryptographic techniques like hash functions, public-key cryptography, and digital signatures to ensure data integrity and the security of transactions. In Web3, cryptography is vital for enabling decentralised identities and trustless interactions, where participants can engage without needing a central authority.

Data integrity and security can be enhanced by cryptography that ensures that data remains unaltered during transactions and communication. Hash functions, like SHA-256 used in Bitcoin, guarantee that any modification to the data is easily detectable. This concept is vital in distributed ledgers where data transparency and immutability are critical.

Cryptographic techniques like zero-knowledge proofs and homomorphic encryption allow users to prove the validity of certain information without revealing sensitive data. This is increasingly important in Web3 applications where privacy is a priority for users interacting in decentralised environments. Public-key cryptography is like sending a message in a locked box. You send the box with an open lock to someone, and they can put their message inside and lock it with the padlock. Only you have the key to open it. This system makes sure that only the right person can access the message, ensuring security without needing a central authority like a bank. Smart contracts work like a vending machine—once you insert the right amount of money and choose an item, the machine automatically delivers your snack. In the same way, smart contracts automatically carry out an agreement when certain conditions are met, without needing a middleman.

I have been fortunate to work in the field of blockchain and web3 through my work in NFTs and the metaverse. Professions, especially cryptology and cryptanalysis are open to everyone. This requires a strong mathematical and technical foundation. Mathematical proficiency is one of the core skills for this space. Cryptography is heavily based on number theory, algebra, and discrete mathematics. A solid understanding of algorithms, finite fields, and elliptic curve cryptography is essential for anyone seeking to enter the field. Proficiency in programming languages like Python, C++, and Rust, as well as experience with blockchain development environments such as Solidity (for Ethereum), is necessary. Many roles in this space require the ability to implement cryptographic algorithms and build secure, decentralised applications.

An in-depth understanding of cryptographic protocols (e.g. RSA, Diffie-Hellman, elliptic curve cryptography) is required for those designing systems in blockchain and Web3. Although there are online courses and certification programs that provide a foundation in cryptography (e.g. Coursera's Cryptography I by Stanford University), entering a professional role often requires a degree in computer science, cybersecurity, or a related field. Advanced positions may require experience with applied cryptography, such as working with blockchain or privacy-focused applications.

However, barriers to entry are decreasing due to the increasing availability of educational resources and open-source tools. Communities in the Web3 space, such as Ethereum and Polkadot, actively support developers through grants, open-source code, and detailed documentation, allowing self-taught developers to contribute to projects without formal degrees. The demand for skilled cryptographers has also risen sharply, with roles available in sectors ranging from finance (for securing blockchain transactions) to cybersecurity.

The groundbreaking work of Joan Clarke and the Bletchley Park team during World War II laid the foundation for many modern cybersecurity practices. Their success in breaking the German Enigma code, which was believed to be unbreakable, represents a pivotal moment in the history of cryptography. Clarke's role in developing cryptanalytic techniques, such as Banburismus, introduced methods of reducing complex encryption settings—approaches that still underpin the optimisation and testing of encryption systems today. The team's ability to decrypt secure communications not only contributed to the Allied victory but also set the stage for the evolution of cybersecurity. The principles established at Bletchley Park, including the use of mathematical and probabilistic methods to analyse and break codes, remain central to modern encryption and the safeguarding of digital communications. In many ways, the success of Clarke and her colleagues marked the beginning of a new era of cryptography that continues to influence how we secure information in today's digital age.

Today, securing information relies on a range of cryptographic methods and cybersecurity protocols designed to protect data from unauthorised access, manipulation, or theft. Encryption is one of the primary tools used to secure data, transforming it into an unreadable format that can only be accessed with a decryption key. This is used in various applications, from securing online transactions with protocols like SSL/TLS to protecting sensitive information stored in databases. Additionally, multi-factor authentication has become increasingly important, requiring users to provide two or more verification methods to access systems, thus reducing the risk of unauthorised entry. Firewalls, intrusion detection systems (IDS), and secure access protocols further ensure that data within networks is protected from external threats. Beyond these technical measures, robust data governance policies and compliance with standards like GDPR (General Data Protection Regulation) also play a critical role in securing digital information by establishing clear rules for data handling and storage (Stallings, 2017). As cyber threats evolve, the continuous advancement of encryption techniques and cybersecurity frameworks remains essential to safeguarding information in the modern era.

These women ooze stories filled with the tension of discovery—the pursuit of hidden truths within maps, cultures, and encrypted messages. Kate Edwards sought to uncover and map the complexities of global cultures through technology, constantly seeking to understand the intersections of geopolitical borders and the virtual worlds she helped create. On the other hand, Joan Clarke's work was the quiet art of hiding and seeking within cryptography, unveiling hidden messages and breaking the codes that could change the course of history.

What unites them is a profound understanding of the hidden forces shaping our world—whether digital landscapes or encrypted wartime communications—and a steadfast commitment to deciphering what lies beneath the surface. Edwards's work in Culturalization is about illuminating the unseen biases and cultural dynamics that permeate digital content, seeking to make the invisible visible. Clarke's cryptanalysis at Bletchley Park was about decrypting the hidden messages encoded in military transmissions, seeking to unveil the secrets buried within the complexity of Enigma. Both women engaged in a form of intellectual hide and seek, revealing the concealed truths that others might overlook.

Their legacies teach us that the act of seeking is as important as the discovery itself. It is in the process—the journey through data, codes, and cultures—that we learn the most. For both women, the act of seeking was not just about solving immediate problems but about paving the way for future explorers in their fields. They serve as reminders that the pursuit of knowledge, whether in cryptography or Culturalization, is a perpetual game of seeking what is hidden, uncovering what is unknown, and navigating the complexities of both the digital and physical worlds.

The challenges faced by women in male-dominated fields are like a big game of hide and seek. Both Edwards and Clarke succeeded in disciplines where their contributions were often overlooked or undervalued, yet they persevered, seeking recognition in a world that, at times, sought to hide their achievements but they found their voices through their technology. Their stories encourage future generations to keep seeking, to persist in the face of invisibility, and to continue revealing the unseen possibilities in the realms of technology and beyond.

REFERENCES

Binns, R. (2018) 'Fairness in machine learning: Lessons from political philosophy', *Proceedings of the 2018 Conference on Fairness, Accountability, and Transparency*, pp. 149–159.

Bowles, H. R., Babcock, L., & Lai, L. (2007). 'Social incentives for gender differences in the propensity to initiate negotiations: Sometimes it does hurt to ask'. *Organizational Behavior and Human Decision Processes*, 103(1), pp. 84–103.

Buolamwini, J. and Gebru, T. (2018) 'Gender shades: Intersectional accuracy disparities in commercial gender classification', *Proceedings of Machine Learning Research*, 81, pp. 77–91.

Colman, A.M. (2020) *A dictionary of psychology.* Oxford: Oxford University Press.

Diener, E. and Seligman, M.E. (2004) 'Beyond money: Toward an economy of well-being', *Psychological Science in the Public Interest*, 5(1), pp. 1–31.

Edwards, K. (2014) 'Culturalization in games: How to avoid a social and political minefield', *Game Developers Conference*.

Edwards, K. (2024) Interview by Kelly Vero. August 31 2024.

Ferguson, C.J. (2013) 'Violent video games and the supreme court: Lessons for the scientific community in the wake of Brown v. Entertainment merchants association', *American Psychologist*, 68(2), pp. 57–74.

Gray, K.L. (2014) *Race, gender, and deviance in Xbox Live: Theoretical perspectives from the virtual margins.* London: Routledge.

Hodges, A. (1983) *Alan Turing: The enigma.* London: Burnett Books.

Institute for Women's Policy Research. (2022). *Gender and Racial Wage Gaps Marginally Improve in 2022 but Pay Equity Still Decades Away.* Retrieved from https://iwpr.org/gender-and-racial-wage-gaps-marginally-improve-in-2022-but-pay-equity-still-decades-away/

Kuchera, B. (2020). *Ghost of Tsushima: The revenge of the samurai.* Polygon. Available at: https://www.polygon.com/reviews/2020/7/14/21321836/ghost-of-tsushima-review-ps4-sucker-punch-samurai-open-world

Maznevski, M.L. and DiStefano, J.J. (2000) 'Global leaders are team players: Developing global leaders through multi-cultural teams', *Human Resource Management*, 39(2–3), pp. 195–208.

McKay, S. (2010) *The secret lives of codebreakers: The men and women who cracked the enigma code at Bletchley Park.* London: Aurum Press.

McKinsey & Company. (2019). *Women in the Workplace 2019.* [online] Available at: https://www.mckinsey.com/featured-insights/gender-equality/women-in-the-workplace-2019 [Accessed 9 December 2024].

Monmonier, M. (1996) *How to lie with maps.* Chicago, IL: University of Chicago Press.

Nakamura, L. and Chow-White, P.A. (2012). *Race after the internet.* Routledge.

National Science Foundation (2023) 'Science and Engineering Degrees Earned', *Diversity and STEM: Women, Minorities, and Persons with Disabilities 2023*. Available at: https://ncses.nsf.gov/pubs/nsf23315/report/science-and-engineering-degrees-earned (Accessed: 9 December 2024).

Page, S.E. (2007) *The difference: How the power of diversity creates better groups, firms, schools, and societies*. Princeton, NJ: Princeton University Press.

Schiller, H.I. (2011). *The mind managers*. Boston, MA: Beacon Press.

Singh, N. (2011) 'Localization versus standardization of global marketing and advertising strategies: Insights from the literature', *International Journal of Management Reviews*, 13(2), pp. 164–183.

Smith, M. (2011) *The Bletchley park codebreakers*. Oxford: Oxford University Press.

Stallings, W. (2017) *Cryptography and network security: Principles and practice*. 7th edn. Upper Saddle River, NJ: Pearson.

Stuart, K. (2009). *Should Modern Warfare 2 allow us to play at terrorism?* The Guardian. ISSN 0261-3077. [online] Available at: https://www.theguardian.com/technology/2009/oct/29/games-gameculture (Accessed: 1 August 2024).

Women Who Tech. (2020). *State of Women in Tech Report 2020*. [online] Available at: https://women-whotech.org/data-and-resources/state-women-tech-and-startups [Accessed 9 December 2024].

CHAPTER 9

Dani Bunten Berry and Marion Mulder

Beyond Binaries

I'VE BEEN PLAYING VIDEO games since I was 10. In a previous book, I detailed an arcade machine at the end of a quiet street and a pocket full of pesetas. The sights and sounds of Pole Position will stay with me forever. It was around that time I started to look for strong female role models who would nourish me with code and fortitude in what would become a very male world. As time passed so too did the balance of gender inside those studios. All the way through computer science labs to Gamergate, we can plot a timeline of how marginalised women have become.

In this narrative of everyday women in technology I leaned into all the women who use their abilities and their passions to speak for them. Not everyone is a scientist breaking new ground; heck, not everyone in this book is a *scientist*—but the understanding of systems and technologies and how they work together is their love language.

MARION MULDER: THE ACCIDENTAL ADVOCATE

Marion Mulder's early exposure to technology was a pivotal moment that set the stage for her future career as both a technologist and an advocate. Growing up in an era before personal computers were ubiquitous, Mulder's curiosity was sparked by the presence of a rare PC in her family home. This early interaction with technology laid the foundation for a lifelong passion. Her practical mindset, combined with a natural curiosity, led her to explore the possibilities that technology could offer.

In her university years, studying economics and business administration, Mulder encountered a classmate who was programming on an Amiga computer—an experience that further fuelled her interest in technology. At a time when computers were not widely used in academic settings, she was drawn to the potential of these machines to solve real-world problems. This inclination towards practical applications of technology is a

DOI: 10.1201/9781003566465-9

common trait among innovators who have gone on to make significant impacts in various fields. For instance, Radia Perlman, known as the Mother of the Internet similarly developed an early interest in technology through hands-on experience, which later led her to invent the Spanning Tree Protocol, a fundamental part of the Internet's infrastructure.

The spark of Mulder's interest came from watching a speaker, a trend watcher and pollster, come to her university to talk to the student body about the Internet. "I remember he had a Quick-Time VR photo (tool), and he had a floppy (disk), and he had bookmarks, and (showed us that we could) get them on a floppy. This was new. I thought, this is interesting: hang on, I need to know more of this, because this is he's onto something. I remember in this room of like, almost 100 people, the majority (said), 'why would I need a website? I already have a folder or a flyer, right?' But I thought (it was) smart, that I needed to do something that made me go find out courses I could do in this thing. So, I did multimedia engineering, a very hands-on course, where it's a program in Notepad to do HTML. But it has been very helpful" (Mulder, 2024).

Mulder's career is marked by several key milestones that showcase her ability to adapt and innovate in a rapidly evolving field. One of the most significant shifts in her career occurred when she transitioned from a role in internal audit to a focus on technology. This move was driven by her recognition of the inefficiencies in traditional processes and her desire to leverage technology to improve them.

One of Mulder's earliest successes in this new direction was her pioneering work in Lotus Notes, a collaborative platform that predated modern tools like Microsoft SharePoint. While working in finance, she was responsible for producing a manual for controllers that quickly became outdated after publication. This was problematic when faced with servicing points and outposts worldwide from The Netherlands. Recognising the need for a more dynamic and efficient solution, Mulder proposed using Lotus Notes to create a digital version of the manual. "I went to the office and said, 'Can I try and put this in Lotus Notes and see if this works?' and that was my first ever website and office automation in a company, and that really set up my career" (Mulder, 2024). This simple problem-solving approach to innovation not only streamlined the process but also laid the groundwork for her future career in technology.

This transition is reminiscent of other key figures in technology who identify inefficiencies in existing systems and use emerging technologies to address them. For example, Sheryl Sandberg, former COO of Facebook, transitioned from government service to the tech industry by recognising the potential of technology to solve large-scale organisational problems. Similarly, Mulder's ability to see beyond the limitations of current systems and to harness technology for practical applications is a testament to her forward-thinking approach.

Beyond her technical achievements, Mulder's passion for ethical technology evolved into broader workplace advocacy. Recognising the intersection of gender biases in AI with larger societal issues, she expanded her focus to include LGBTQIA+ rights and workplace diversity, helping create inclusive spaces not just within technology but across corporate cultures. Her work in this area is driven by a profound understanding of the ethical implications of technology and a commitment to ensuring that technological advancements serve everyone, not just a privileged few.

One of the key areas where Mulder has focused her advocacy is in addressing gender diversity in artificial intelligence (AI). She has been a vocal critic of the pervasive gender biases that exist within AI systems, particularly in how these technologies often default to female personas for virtual assistants. This practice reinforces harmful stereotypes and reflects broader systemic issues within the tech industry. Her advocacy aligns with broader efforts in the tech community to address these biases.

Mulder's journey with AI began when she noticed a startling pattern: many of the AI chatbots and virtual assistants being developed were designed with female personas. From Apple's Siri to Amazon's Alexa, these assistants were not only given female voices but were also framed within traditional gender stereotypes—nurturing, service-oriented, and submissive. She found herself asking a fundamental question "Why were these AI systems predominantly female, and what impact does this have on society's perception of women and gender roles?" (Mulder, 2024).

This phenomenon is a clear example of how biases present in human society find their way into the technologies we create. AI systems are trained on large datasets, so often include biased information drawn from historical and current societal norms (Buolamwini and Gebru, 2018). In this case, the pervasive stereotype that women are more suited for service-oriented roles was codified into the very design of digital assistants. As she puts it, "It's not just that chatbots are female—it's the underlying assumption that women should be in subservient roles that's problematic" (Mulder, 2024).

Mulder highlights that while it might seem like a benign design choice, these AI systems reinforce harmful stereotypes thus encoding gender bias into widely used technologies (West et al., 2019). In her advocacy work, she emphasises the need for diverse teams in the AI development process, stating "the design choices we make today will shape the future interactions of millions of people" (Mulder, 2024). Without diversity at the design table, the risk of perpetuating gender norms remains high, potentially influencing how users interact with these systems and reinforcing outdated gender roles.

To understand the depth of this issue, it's crucial to look at how AI systems are trained. At the heart of AI and machine learning systems are massive datasets, often culled from the Internet and other sources that reflect societal attitudes and behaviours (Caliskan et al., 2017). As these datasets are used to train AI models, any biases inherent in the data are learned by the system. For instance, if the data disproportionately represents women in caregiving or service roles, the AI will associate women with those functions, leading to design decisions that reflect those biases.

Mulder's work focuses on creating awareness around these embedded biases. She points out that the default to female personas for digital assistants isn't necessarily malicious but rather a reflection of ingrained societal stereotypes. "It's a mirror of society's existing gender roles, and the problem is that technology can amplify and perpetuate those roles unless we consciously decide to change it" (Mulder, 2024).

Joy Buolamwini, founder of the Algorithmic Justice League, has also highlighted the risks of biased AI, particularly in areas like facial recognition, which often performs worse for women and people of colour due to biased training data (Buolamwini and Gebru, 2018).

Buolamwini's and Gebru's research, alongside Mulder's advocacy, underscores the need for diversity in AI development, not just in terms of gender but across race, ethnicity, and cultural backgrounds (Crawford, 2021).

Mulder's approach to solving these challenges lies in ethical AI design. She argues that it's not enough to create functional systems—AI must be designed with a conscious understanding of its social and cultural impact. Ethical AI design involves creating systems that actively avoid reinforcing stereotypes and biases, and it begins with asking questions like, "just because we can, should we?" (Mulder, 2024). This principle is at the core of her critique of current AI systems.

As a game designer I have long been told that *this game is not intended for women, you women have games like The Sims. Let us have our shooters.* We know that this is an unacceptable view held by the minority in video games where the number of women playing video games is on the rise. As I write this 45% of all gamers worldwide are women. So why do we still insist on having women in servitude for our chatbots? Mulder noticed the disparity in technology around 10 years ago when working on a project. Through training in diversity, she already knew that the world of work was a boy's world, but she was shocked to see how they were creating girls inside tech infrastructure "I thought that (there's) something wrong here. This was not good. I don't mind chat bots being women, if that's a conscious choice, but the fact that it's done because it's a service and women are more service-oriented, that basically becomes stereotype enforcement, and that is not the kind of world I want to live in" (Mulder, 2024).

Female chatbots in AI are rooted in cultural stereotypes. Women have long been linked to service roles, leading companies to give virtual assistants female personas, seen as nurturing and approachable. Here's a deeper look at why most chatbots are designed with female personas:

1. **Cultural and Gender Stereotypes**

   - **Association with Service Roles:** Historically, women have been associated with service-oriented roles, such as secretaries, assistants, and customer service representatives. This stereotype has persisted into the digital age, leading to the creation of female personas for virtual assistants and chatbots. The idea is that a female voice or persona is more nurturing, polite, and helpful—qualities that align with the expectations of service roles.

   - **Perceived Softness and Approachability:** Female voices are often perceived as softer and more approachable. Companies might choose female voices for their chatbots because they believe users will find them more comforting and easier to interact with, particularly in customer service or support roles.

2. **Marketing and Branding Strategies**

   - **Target Audience Appeal:** Companies often design chatbots with a specific target audience in mind. Female personas may be chosen based on the assumption that they will appeal more broadly across different demographics, including both male and female users. For example, research has shown that male users may respond more positively to female voices in service roles, reinforcing the decision to use female personas.

- **Branding Consistency:** Companies may opt for female chatbots to align with their brand's image. For instance, if a brand is positioned as caring, friendly, or supportive, a female chatbot might be seen as a better fit to convey these attributes.

3. Historical Precedents in AI Development

- **Early AI and Virtual Assistants:** Early examples of AI, like Siri (Apple), Alexa (Amazon), and Cortana (Microsoft), were all given female voices and names. This set a precedent in the industry, making it the norm to default to female personas for AI assistants. The success of these early models influenced the design of subsequent chatbots, perpetuating the trend.

- **Ease of Continuity:** Once a trend is established in technology, it often continues due to ease of development and user familiarity. Developers and companies might choose female personas simply because it is what has been done before, and it feels like a safer choice.

4. Bias in AI Development

- **Representation of Developers:** The tech industry has historically been male-dominated, and this is reflected in the biases that can be unintentionally introduced during the development of AI. When teams lack diversity, the products they create can reflect the unconscious biases of their creators, including gender stereotypes.

- **Data Bias:** AI systems are often trained on large datasets that reflect societal biases. If the data used to train AI includes biased assumptions—such as the idea that women are more suited to service roles—this bias can be replicated in the AI's design and behaviour.

5. Ethical Considerations and Criticism

- **Reinforcement of Gender Stereotypes:** The widespread use of female chatbots has drawn criticism for reinforcing outdated gender stereotypes. Critics argue that by consistently placing female personas in subservient or service roles, technology perpetuates the notion that women are better suited to these tasks.

- **Calls for Change:** There is a growing call within the tech community to challenge these norms and to design AI systems that are more representative and less reliant on gender stereotypes. This includes creating gender-neutral or male chatbots, as well as ensuring diverse AI design teams.

6. Future Directions

- **Gender-Neutral AI:** Some companies and researchers are exploring the development of gender-neutral AI, such as the gender-neutral voice assistant Q, which was developed to challenge the binary gender norms in AI design. This reflects a broader movement toward creating technology that is more inclusive and representative of all users.

- **Ethical AI Design:** The trend towards ethical AI design is encouraging companies to consider the broader societal impact of their technologies, including the role that AI plays in perpetuating stereotypes. This involves rethinking how personas are assigned to chatbots and considering the potential implications of these choices.

Mulder is not alone in questioning the authenticity of Large Language Models (LLMs); Joanna Bryson is a professor of Ethics and Technology at the Hertie School in Berlin and advocates for the ethical development of AI. Bryson argues that AI systems are artefacts created by humans and, as such, should be subject to the same ethical scrutiny as any other human-made tool. Her work emphasises the importance of transparency and accountability in AI development, advocating that developers and organisations should be held responsible for the impacts of their AI systems. She is perhaps most famously known for her provocative essay titled *Robots Should Be Slaves* (2009), in which she argues that robots and AI systems should not be anthropomorphised or treated as moral agents.

Sarah Porter is an influential figure in the field of AI and technology, known for her work in advocating for responsible AI and gender diversity within the tech industry. She is the founder and CEO of Ada-AI, an organisation dedicated to addressing the ethical challenges and societal impacts of AI, with a particular focus on ensuring that AI technologies are developed and deployed in ways that are equitable and inclusive. Ada-AI focuses on increasing the representation of women and other marginalised groups in AI research, development, and leadership roles. This is based on the understanding that diverse teams are better equipped to identify and mitigate biases in AI systems, leading to technologies that are fairer and more inclusive.

One of Porter's key strategies is Design Thinking, a user-centred approach to problem-solving that emphasises empathy, collaboration, and iterative design (Brown, 2009). In the context of AI, Design Thinking encourages developers to ask: *Who are we designing for? How might this technology be experienced by different people? What assumptions are we making about users, and how might those assumptions create biases in the technology?* Here's a checklist I use when designing anything, my checklist comes from Game Thinking by Amy Jo Kim, I've placed tickable boxes beside each point so you can check against your designs:

☐ Start by identifying the problem. What gap can be found in current works, processes or in the environment?

☐ Define the problem clearly—who is affected, and how?

☐ Brainstorm potential solutions, even the wild ones. Mulder herself experimented with new tools like Lotus Notes, proving that innovation doesn't require perfection from the start.

☐ Build a small prototype. It can be as simple as creating a presentation or trying out a coding challenge.

☐ Test it, gather feedback, and refine.

Mulder also draws on Futures Thinking, a methodology that explores multiple possible futures to anticipate the long-term impacts of current decisions (Sardar, 2010). When applied to AI, Futures Thinking helps teams consider how today's design choices might shape future interactions. She advocates for scenario planning in AI development, asking teams to imagine worst-case and best-case futures based on their design choices. By doing so, they can better prepare for the unintended consequences of their technologies.

One of the most concrete suggestions Mulder makes is to explore gender-neutral AI. Instead of defaulting to female personas, developers could design AI systems that either have no gender or allow users to customise the persona to better reflect their own preferences. This would not only give users more control but would also break away from the assumption that digital assistants must conform to traditional gender roles (West et al., 2019).

Some organisations have already begun exploring these possibilities. For instance, Q, the first gender-neutral voice assistant, was developed to challenge the gender binary in AI design (Q, 2020) Projects like these show that it's possible to create inclusive technologies that don't rely on outdated gender norms.

However, Mulder cautions that simply creating gender-neutral systems isn't enough. AI must be inclusive by design, which means involving diverse teams from the start (Mulder, 2024). This includes not just gender diversity but diversity in race, socioeconomic backgrounds, and cultural experiences. She emphasises that the goal is not just to avoid bias but to create technologies that reflect the full spectrum of human experience (Buolamwini and Gebru, 2018).

In her work with the Workplace Pride Foundation, Mulder has consistently advocated for inclusive environments in the tech industry, and this advocacy extends to AI development. She believes that the gender imbalance in tech—the fact that most AI systems are developed by predominantly male teams—has a significant impact on the biases we see in technology: "when you don't have diversity in the room, it's easy to overlook the experiences and needs of marginalised groups" (Mulder, 2024).

Mulder's call to action for the industry is clear: build diverse teams, incorporate ethical design principles, and challenge the default assumptions that have shaped AI development so far (Crawford, 2021). By doing so, we can create AI systems that are not only more inclusive but also more reflective of the diverse world they're meant to serve.

Mulder's work as a futurist is deeply rooted in her belief that the future is not something that just happens to us but something that can be actively shaped. In her work, she emphasises the importance of understanding emerging trends, imagining possible futures, and making conscious choices to create the future we want. This approach is particularly relevant in the context of technology, where rapid advancements can sometimes lead to unintended consequences, especially when it comes to issues like bias in AI.

Futures Thinking is central to Mulder's consulting approach, particularly in AI and workplace diversity. For example, while working with a major European tech firm, she led scenario planning workshops that considered both the risks of unchecked AI bias and the potential of AI to promote inclusivity. These sessions resulted in actionable steps, such as redesigning chatbots to avoid reinforcing stereotypes and implementing ethical guidelines for AI development (Mulder, 2024). Through these applications, she equips companies to anticipate future challenges and opportunities, shaping a more inclusive and ethical tech landscape. She further emphasises the importance of considering not just the immediate technological benefits but also the long-term societal impacts. "It's easy to get caught up in the excitement of new technologies," and I agree that both her statements resonate, "but we need to ask ourselves: what kind of future are we building with these tools?" (Mulder, 2024).

Futures Thinking is a strategic methodology used to explore potential futures and guide decision-making in the present. Unlike traditional forecasting, which often focuses on a single predicted outcome, Futures Thinking encourages the exploration of multiple future scenarios—both positive and negative—based on current trends and signals (Sardar, 2010). The approach is particularly useful in fields like technology, where rapid advancements can lead to unexpected or unintended consequences.

One of the core techniques of Futures Thinking is scenario planning, which involves creating narratives of possible futures based on identified trends, risks, and opportunities. By imagining both best-case and worst-case scenarios, organisations can develop strategies that are resilient and adaptable to various outcomes (Sardar, 2010).

Mulder employs Futures Thinking as part of her consulting work with businesses and governments, particularly around the ethical implications of AI and digital technologies. "Futures Thinking allows us to take a step back from the immediacy of the present and look at how today's decisions will shape tomorrow's world" (Mulder, 2024). The practice enables organisations to anticipate technological disruptions and societal shifts, fostering a mindset of long-term responsibility rather than short-term gain. Several principles form the foundation of Futures Thinking, providing a structured approach to considering future possibilities:

1. **Scanning for Signals**: This involves identifying early signs of change or weak signals that might indicate emerging trends. For instance, the rise of AI chatbots and voice assistants signalled a shift towards more human-like interactions with machines, but also raised questions about gender bias and the portrayal of women in digital spaces (West et al., 2019). By scanning for these signals early, practitioners of Futures Thinking can begin to address potential challenges before they become entrenched issues.

2. **Scenario Planning**: Scenario planning is the heart of Futures Thinking. It involves crafting detailed narratives about different future possibilities, including best-case, worst-case, and most likely scenarios. This process helps organisations anticipate how

various factors—such as technology, politics, society, or the environment—might evolve. Scenario planning encourages teams to imagine futures where technologies like AI either exacerbate existing inequalities or help to create more equitable societies (Sardar, 2010).

3. **Backcasting**: Backcasting is a process that starts with imagining a desirable future and then working backwards to identify the steps needed to achieve that outcome. In the context of AI and diversity, Mulder advocates for backcasting to envision a world where AI systems are free from bias and then develop strategies to make that vision a reality. By understanding the future state we want to reach, organisations can set clear, actionable goals for the present (Mulder, 2024).

4. **Systems Thinking**: Futures Thinking requires an understanding of complex systems and the interrelationships between different factors. Technological advancements, societal changes, environmental challenges, and economic shifts are all interconnected. Systems Thinking helps futurists see how a change in one area, such as the development of AI, might have ripple effects across other sectors, like labour markets, education, and gender equality (Crawford, 2021).

5. **Ethical Considerations**: Mulder argues that ethical considerations are paramount in Futures Thinking. "It's not enough to create technology that works; it has to be technology that works for everyone," she states (Mulder, 2024). Ethical design, particularly in AI, requires developers to think critically about the societal impact of their innovations, ensuring that technologies promote fairness, inclusivity, and human well-being.

Futures Thinking is particularly relevant to the field of AI and digital transformation, where the pace of innovation often outstrips society's ability to fully understand or regulate new technologies. One of the key concerns that Mulder addresses is the ethical design of AI systems, where she emphasises that while AI holds the potential to revolutionise industries—from healthcare to finance—it also carries significant risks, particularly in terms of bias, surveillance, and privacy.

By employing Futures Thinking, Mulder helps organisations navigate the ethical complexities of AI. For example, she works with companies to imagine different scenarios where AI either reinforces existing societal biases or helps to dismantle them. In one scenario, unchecked AI development leads to systems that replicate and even exacerbate gender and racial inequalities. In another, AI is used to create more equitable decision-making systems by actively identifying and correcting biases in its data and algorithms (Buolamwini and Gebru, 2018).

Through these exercises, organisations are encouraged to think beyond the immediate benefits of AI—such as increased efficiency or cost savings—and consider the long-term societal impacts of their technologies. As Mulder notes, "the decisions we make today will shape the world we live in tomorrow. If we don't consciously choose to address bias and inequality in our systems, we risk building a future that replicates the injustices of the past" (Mulder, 2024).

Beyond AI, Futures Thinking also plays a crucial role in addressing broader challenges like sustainability and environmental impact. The concept of degrowth, which advocates for a reduction in consumption and production to achieve ecological balance, is increasingly becoming part of the Futures Thinking conversation (Latouche, 2010). Mulder is particularly interested in how digital technologies can be aligned with sustainability goals. "We need to think not only about the immediate environmental impact of data centres or AI development but also about the long-term consequences of a world driven by digital consumption" (Mulder, 2024).

This is where backcasting becomes a powerful tool. By imagining a future where technological innovation is in harmony with environmental sustainability, organisations can work backwards to determine the necessary steps to get there. This might involve investing in greener data centres, using AI to optimise resource management, or encouraging responsible digital consumption practices (Crawford, 2021). Mulder emphasises that sustainable innovation is not just about reducing harm; it's about actively creating technologies that contribute to the well-being of both people and the planet. "Technology should not only be efficient—it should also be ethical and sustainable" (Mulder, 2024).

Mulder's vision for ethical AI design is deeply intertwined with her work in Futures Thinking. Ethical AI requires developers to anticipate the long-term impacts of their systems and ensure that those systems promote inclusivity, fairness, and human well-being. Futures Thinking offers a structured way to explore the possible futures of AI, identifying potential risks and opportunities before they fully materialise.

In practice, Mulder uses Futures Thinking to guide organisations through the process of ethical AI design. By considering a range of possible futures, teams can better understand the ethical implications of their work and make decisions that align with their values. This approach encourages a proactive stance on ethics, rather than a reactive one. "We have the tools to create a better future, but it requires conscious effort and a commitment to long-term thinking" (Mulder, 2024). As she honed her technical skills, she became increasingly aware of how technology, when developed without diverse voices, could reflect and even reinforce societal biases. This realisation led her to not only design solutions but also advocate for those marginalised in the tech industry.

Advocacy that extends beyond gender diversity in AI and technology to include lesbian, gay, bisexual, transgender, queer or questioning, intersex, asexual, and more (LGBTQIA+) rights and workplace inclusion is something which is deep-rooted in Mulder's career. Her work in this area has focused on creating spaces where individuals from marginalised genders and sexualities can thrive in the often exclusive and male-dominated technology industry. At Workplace Pride and ING, Mulder championed policies to make tech workplaces inclusive and accepting of LGBTQIA+ individuals.

In the early 2000s, Mulder co-founded the LGBTQIA+ network at ING, and her work with Workplace Pride—an international platform advocating for LGBTQIA+ inclusion—helped raise awareness and foster conversations about diversity in workplaces, particularly in the technology sector. As she reflects on her own journey, she explains that coming out at work was not just a personal decision but a professional one, allowing her to be her authentic self and advocate more effectively for others facing similar challenges (Mulder, 2024).

Technology, despite being an innovation-driven field, has often been slow to adopt inclusive practices, particularly for those identifying as LGBTQIA+. Mulder's work has been pivotal in shifting this narrative by promoting the idea that inclusivity is not just a moral imperative but a business necessity. She believes that when individuals can bring their full selves to work, companies benefit from a diversity of perspectives that drive creativity and innovation.

One of Mulder's key contributions has been her role in developing diversity and inclusion (D&I) policies that ensure LGBTQIA+ individuals are represented and protected within corporate structures. "In many workplaces, people still feel that they have to hide who they are in order to succeed, especially in male-dominated industries like technology," she shares. "I wanted to help change that by creating environments where diversity is celebrated and where people can feel safe being themselves" (Mulder, 2024).

Mulder's work with Workplace Pride and ING demonstrates a focus on the intersection of personal identity and professional development, ensuring that LGBTQIA+ individuals have equal opportunities for career progression and leadership roles. Through these organisations, Mulder has championed initiatives that focus on LGBTQIA+ visibility, allyship training, and the development of inclusive workplace cultures. Despite progress in diversity and inclusion, LGBTQIA+ individuals in the technology sector still face significant challenges. Studies have shown that LGBTQIA+ employees often encounter discrimination, exclusion from decision-making processes, and barriers to career advancement (Cech and Rothwell, 2020). Furthermore, the hyper-masculine culture prevalent in many tech spaces can alienate those who do not conform to traditional gender or sexual norms (Jokinen and Smith, 2017). These systemic barriers can prevent LGBTQIA+ individuals from fully participating in or advancing within the technology industry.

Mulder has spoken openly about the struggles she faced as a woman and an LGBTQIA+ individual in the tech world. Early in her career, she felt isolated and uncertain about how to come out at work, given the lack of role models and support systems for LGBTQIA+ employees at the time (Mulder, 2024). However, these experiences also fuelled her commitment to creating inclusive spaces where minorities could thrive. One of the biggest challenges she identifies is the lack of visible LGBTQIA+ role models in the tech industry. Without representation at senior levels, it can be difficult for younger employees or those just entering the field to see a path forward. This invisibility perpetuates the exclusion of LGBTQIA+ individuals, reinforcing the notion that technology is a space where only certain identities are accepted or celebrated. To address this, she has focused on mentorship and leadership programs that elevate LGBTQIA+ voices within organisations.

Mulder's involvement with Workplace Pride has been particularly impactful in driving forward LGBTQIA+ inclusion in technology. Workplace Pride is an international foundation dedicated to improving the lives of LGBTQIA+ people in workplaces worldwide. The foundation works with businesses to foster inclusive environments, provide training on LGBTQIA+ issues, and create networks of support for LGBTQIA+ employees.

Mulder's advocacy has led to tangible changes in several organisations. At ING, she helped introduce comprehensive LGBTQIA+ support programs, fostering a more inclusive environment for employees. Her work with Workplace Pride resulted in corporate benchmarks that provide a framework for companies to assess and improve LGBTQIA+ inclusion. Many companies, including ING and several others across Europe, have since adopted these benchmarks, significantly shifting how diversity and inclusion are approached in the tech sector (Workplace Pride, 2019).

Her advocacy also extended to intersectionality, recognising that LGBTQIA+ individuals often experience multiple forms of discrimination based on their gender, race, or socioeconomic status. Mulder emphasises the importance of intersectional approaches in workplace policies, ensuring that inclusion efforts are not limited to gender or sexual identity but encompass all aspects of diversity (Mulder, 2024). Her efforts have led to tangible changes in many of the companies she has worked with. ING, for example, implemented comprehensive LGBTQIA+ employee support programs, including allyship training, mentorship opportunities, and resource groups. These initiatives created a more supportive environment for LGBTQIA+ employees, allowing them to participate fully in the workplace without fear of discrimination or exclusion.

A cornerstone of Mulder's advocacy is her focus on allyship—the role that individuals who do not identify as LGBTQIA+ can play in fostering inclusive workplaces. She believes that allies within technology companies can be powerful advocates for change by actively supporting their LGBTQIA+ colleagues and pushing for policies that promote inclusion. "True allyship is not just about saying the right things," Mulder explains, "It's about taking concrete actions to create a culture where everyone feels they belong" (Mulder, 2024).

Through Workplace Pride, Mulder has helped develop allyship training programs aimed at educating employees about the challenges LGBTQIA+ individuals face in the workplace and equipping them with the tools to support their colleagues. These programs emphasise the importance of listening, empathy, and advocacy, encouraging allies to take an active role in dismantling barriers to inclusion. Her journey mirrors that of other LGBTQIA+ pioneers in the tech industry, such as Edith "Edie" Windsor who was the lead plaintiff in the landmark Supreme Court Case United States v. Windsor, which overturned *Section 3 of the Defense of Marriage Act (DOMA)* and led to the legalisation of gay marriage. What's less well known is that Windsor was a computer programmer and an engineer, working with the UNIVAC at Combustion Engineering, Inc., and later at IBM in the 1950s and '60s, eventually becoming a senior systems engineer. Her work, like Mulder's, has been instrumental in advancing both technological innovation and LGBTQIA+ rights.

In addition to allyship, Mulder stresses the importance of leadership in creating lasting change. "Inclusion has to come from the top," this is such an important part of being able to succeed in careers where we represent the minority of personnel. "If senior leaders are not committed to creating an inclusive environment, it's very difficult to make meaningful progress" (Mulder, 2024). By engaging senior leaders in diversity and inclusion efforts, she ensures that these initiatives are not just token gestures but integrated into the core values and practices of the organisation. These experiences were not unique to Marion; many women in tech have faced similar challenges. For example, in a 2015 survey by the International Game Developers Association, it was found that women in the gaming industry often faced harassment and discrimination, underscoring the broader issues of gender inequality in tech. She has worked to bring diversity to the fore in large organisations or corporate structures where only 7% of companies in Europe are led by women (European Women on Boards, 2022) and represent only a third "of directors of boards of the largest listed companies across the EU" (EIGE, May 2023).

Mulder's advocacy which extends to inclusive design and development of technologies is relevant and quite unique. It's unusual to prescribe the functional with the social or psychological in this way but it makes sense. One of her key concerns is the ways in which technology—particularly AI and data systems—can reinforce harmful stereotypes or per-petuate discrimination. As she explains, "if the data we use to train our AI systems is biased, then the technology we create will be biased too. We need to be intentional about creating systems that are inclusive and fair" (Mulder, 2024).

Mulder continues to push for more inclusive data practices, ensuring that the needs and experiences of marginalised groups are considered in developing new technologies. She has been particularly critical of the ways in which AI systems often default to binary gender categories, excluding individuals who identify outside of traditional male-female frameworks (West et al., 2019). To address these issues, she promotes the inclusion of diverse voices in the design process, advocating for the creation of technologies that serve everyone, not just a privileged few.

Marion Mulder, Joanna Bryson, and Sarah Porter are women who are at the forefront of a critical movement to ensure that AI development is conducted in a way that is ethical, inclusive, and reflective of diverse perspectives. Their work is instrumental in shaping a future where AI technologies can contribute positively to society, without reinforcing the biases and inequities of the past.

I enjoyed interviewing Mulder for this book. Her journey showed me that I don't need to follow a conventional path to thrive in technology (absolutely not!). Whether curious about coding, design, or ethics, the future of tech is all our responsibility to get it right. Trusting ourselves and questioning biases we see in the technology around us is how we get this done. But trusting ourselves is such a human trait that sometimes we trust ourselves to be able to do anything even if it costs us our career. Even though it's not as black and white for my next subject, in her own words, she felt that she achieved more by not being her true authentic self. Warning, this is a sad story, but in a way, I hope by sharing the story of one of my game design heroines, I can at least show how diversity, equity, and inclusion are not a one-size-fits-all for our psyche, let alone inside our peer group.

DANIELLE BUNTEN BERRY: THE DANCE OF A THOUSAND INSTANCES

I grew up in game design, and although there are more women involved today, we are still navigating a traditionally male-dominated space. Over time, inclusivity in game design has increased, and we've seen role models like *Lara Croft* and *Commander Shepard* who have shown the industry that women's voices matter. But few names shine as brightly as Danielle Bunten Berry. A pioneer whose work fundamentally transformed multiplayer gaming; Berry's contributions are indispensable to understanding the evolution of interac-tive entertainment (Donovan, 2010). Her story is one of innovation, determination, and a profound understanding of what makes games truly engaging.

Berry belongs in this book because of her relentless pursuit of the perfect multiplayer experience and much more. As a gamer and technologist, her work is especially inspiring to me. Today, from *M.U.L.E.* to *Call of Duty Mobile*, games bring us together for both competition and conversation—things we take for granted but owe much to Berry's early innovations (Donovan, 2010). Games teach us about ourselves: how much we can think ahead, how we handle pressure, and how we interact socially. In my earliest days of gaming, I lived through the narratives of characters and connected with the story through non-player characters.

She was born Dan Bunten in 1949 and transitioned much later in her short life when she became Danielle. A native of St. Louis, Missouri, Berry's interest in gaming and technology began early. As Dan, she graduated with a degree in industrial engineering from the University of Arkansas and initially worked as a systems analyst. However, her true passion lay in creating interactive experiences (Levy, 1984).

Before her transition, Dan Bunten had already made significant contributions to the video game industry. Her first game, *Wheeler Dealers*, was a multiplayer economic trading game, one of the earliest computer games to focus on economic strategy. Designed for the Apple II, it wasn't a commercial success but was a significant step in her career. Bunten's continued interest in economic strategy led to the development of *Cartels & Cutthroats*, published by SSI, which allowed players to run their own businesses and compete in a market. Perhaps her most famous work, *M.U.L.E.*, a groundbreaking multiplayer game for the Atari 400/800, combined economic simulation with cooperative and competitive gameplay. It remains influential in game design to this day (Donovan, 2010).

Berry's groundbreaking *M.U.L.E.* was designed to be a multiplayer game that allowed up to four players to play simultaneously. The game was set on the fictional planet Irata, where players took on the roles of colonists trying to develop and prosper through resource management. The core mechanics included:

1. **Simultaneous Gameplay**: Up to four players could play on the same system, taking turns to perform actions within a shared game world. Each player controlled their avatar sequentially, contributing to a dynamic game environment where individual actions affected the group.

2. **Shared Economy**: Players engaged in various economic activities such as farming, mining, and trading. The in-game economy was dynamic, with supply and demand influenced by players' actions, requiring interaction, negotiation, and cooperation (Levy, 1984).

3. **Auction System**: One of *M.U.L.E.*'s most innovative features was its auction system, where players could buy and sell goods in real time. Berry often emphasised that the real value of multiplayer games lay not in simply defeating opponents but in the shared experience. In her game design philosophy, she believed that "a great multiplayer game fosters cooperation as much as competition" (Levy, 1984). This vision is most clearly seen in M.U.L.E., where players not only competed but also learned to cooperate and negotiate, turning the game into a social experience as much as a

strategic one (Donovan, 2010). This reflects her belief that games were about more than just competition; they were about human connection. In designing M.U.L.E., Berry was driven by a vision of creating environments where players not only competed but also learned how to cooperate, making the game a social experience as much as a strategic one.

4. **Random Events**: Random events like natural disasters and alien invasions affected all players, adding unpredictability and requiring players to adapt their strategies (Levy, 1984).

5. **Turn-Based Actions**: Players had a limited time per turn to perform actions such as deploying M.U.L.E.s (Multiple Use Labor Elements) or managing resources. This ensured each player had equal opportunities to influence the game (Donovan, 2010).

In the early 1980s, developing a successful multiplayer experience was no small feat. Berry faced several challenges due to the limited technology of the time. Multiplayer gaming on a single system was difficult, and Berry's ingenuity helped her navigate these barriers.

- **Single System Gameplay**: Since online gaming was not yet feasible, Berry designed *M.U.L.E.* for multiple players on a single system with shared input devices. This approach maximised the available hardware capabilities (Levy, 1984).

- **Optimising Graphics and Memory Usage**: Berry had to optimise the game's code to ensure smooth performance on early home computers with limited memory. Efficient sprite management and minimal graphical load were critical to keeping the game engaging despite hardware constraints (Donovan, 2010).

- **Balancing Competition and Cooperation**: *M.U.L.E.* balanced competition and cooperation by creating a shared economy with random events affecting all players. This interdependence required strategic thinking and collaboration (Levy, 1984).

Berry's innovations in multiplayer gaming had far-reaching implications. The principles she championed—balancing competition with cooperation, dynamic economies, and direct player interaction—are foundational to multiplayer game design. Modern games such as *Fortnite*, *World of Warcraft*, and *Minecraft* build upon these ideas, incorporating shared economies, cooperation, and competition as key elements (Kücklich, 2005).

- **Shared Economies in *Fortnite* and *Minecraft***: The shared economy in *Fortnite* manifests through in-game trading and resource management, which mirror the economic strategies of *M.U.L.E.* Players must decide when to share resources or prioritise their survival, echoing the cooperative competition Berry pioneered (Kücklich, 2005). Similarly, *Minecraft* allows players to collaborate on building projects while managing resources, often leading to complex in-game economies where trade and cooperation are essential for survival (Crawford, 2012).

- **M.U.D. (Multi-User Dungeon) and Social Gameplay**: M.U.D. (Multi-User Dungeon) gameplay emerged in the late 1970s and early 1980s as one of the earliest forms of online multiplayer interaction. These text-based virtual worlds allowed players to explore dungeons, solve puzzles, and interact with one another in a shared digital space, relying heavily on the imagination. Berry's innovations in multiplayer design—where interaction, strategy, and resource management were central—paved the way for the social dynamics found in M.U.Ds. These early M.U.D. environments laid the groundwork for massively multiplayer online games (MMOs) like World of Warcraft and platforms like Roblox, which focus on shared economies, collaborative building, and player interaction. Her influence is evident in these systems, as she foresaw how multiplayer experiences could go beyond competition to become spaces for storytelling and social bonding. These games reflect the social and economic interdependence that Berry introduced in *M.U.L.E* (Taylor, 2006).

- **Cooperation and Team Dynamics**: In games like *Among Us*, cooperation is essential but with a twist: players must work together to complete tasks while identifying impostors. This dynamic gameplay, combining cooperation with mistrust, builds on Berry's emphasis on creating interactive experiences where competition and collaboration coexist (Taylor, 2006).

- **Competition as Conversation**: Berry understood that competition could be more than just a struggle to win—it could be a form of social interaction, a "conversation" between players. Games like *Call of Duty* and *Fortnite* allow players to engage with one another through gameplay, testing strategies, and exchanging skills. This concept of competition as social interaction traces directly back to Berry's auction system in *M.U.L.E.* (Kücklich, 2005).

While Berry was pushing the boundaries of multiplayer game design, she was also navigating her personal identity as a trans woman in a male-dominated industry. Her transition in 1992, like her groundbreaking work, challenged conventions and norms, both in her life and her career (Berry, 1995). She openly discussed the challenges she faced during and after her transition, particularly the isolation and loss of relationships (Berry, 1995). Despite these personal difficulties, she remained committed to her vision of creating games that fostered connection and collaboration.

In her candid reflections, Berry offered advice to those considering gender reassignment, noting the significant emotional and social costs she experienced (Berry, 1995). Her story reminds us that even groundbreaking innovators face challenges when reconciling personal identity with professional life. Her legacy is not just in her technical innovations but also in her courageous journey toward living authentically.

Berry's work is deeply woven into the fabric of modern multiplayer gaming. Her pioneering efforts in *M.U.L.E.* and other titles set the standard for social interaction and economic systems in games. The multiplayer experiences she created have evolved into the global interconnected gaming communities we see today (Donovan, 2010).

Berry's courage in navigating her gender transition and the challenges that came with it solidified her role as a trailblazer for transgender individuals in gaming and technology. Her story serves as an inspiration not just for game designers but also for anyone marginalised in a male-dominated industry (Margolis and Fisher, 2002). Reflecting on her contributions encourages us to envision a future where diversity in the tech industry is celebrated, and where the resilience and authenticity of pioneers like Berry inspire future generations.

Where Berry's designs turned competition into shared experiences, Mulder's work extends these principles to technology's capacity for inclusivity. Both understood that the true value of technology lies in its ability to bring people together and challenge societal norms. Both women understood that technology, whether in games or AI, should not only function but foster human connection. Berry's belief that multiplayer games could transcend entertainment to create shared experiences is echoed in Mulder's insistence that AI should be inclusive, fair, and representative of diverse human identities.

By linking their legacies, we see how these two pioneers pushed for a more connected, empathetic future through their respective fields. Their work continues to inspire a generation of women in tech to shape technology with empathy and inclusivity at the forefront.

At the heart of both Berry's and Mulder's legacies is a powerful message: technology, when crafted with care, becomes a love language—one that speaks to our universal need for connection and recognition. As we look to the future, their work reminds us that the real power of technology lies not just in what it can do, but in how it brings us together, fosters understanding, and helps us build a more inclusive and interconnected world.

Danielle Bunten Berry and Marion Mulder have shown us that technology is more than just code, mechanics, or systems—it is a space for building human connections, challenging societal norms, and pushing boundaries. Their stories illustrate how deeply intertwined the technical and the personal can be, reminding us that innovation often comes hand in hand with resilience, identity, and empathy.

As we move forward, their legacies inspire the next generation of women to continue shaping technology not just as users but as creators and leaders. Whether it's designing multiplayer experiences that foster cooperation and competition or developing ethical AI systems that serve everyone, women have the power to redefine the landscape. Technology can be a powerful love language—one that transcends barriers and brings people together in meaningful ways.

For those stepping into the world of tech, Berry and Mulder's work serves as a reminder that inclusion and diversity are essential not just for the advancement of technology but for its capacity to truly connect and empower people across the globe. By embracing our unique perspectives and standing strong in the face of challenges, we can continue their work of making technology a tool for positive, lasting change.

For both Danielle Bunten Berry and Marion Mulder, technology became a way to bring people together. Berry's multiplayer games turned competition into an opportunity for conversation and connection, while Mulder's advocacy for ethical AI and gender inclusivity opened the door for a more empathetic, representative technological future.

Berry's design philosophy that "games should be fun because of the people you're with, not just the game itself" underscores how multiplayer games were about the joy of shared experiences. Similarly, Mulder's work with AI, particularly in challenging gender biases, is an example of how inclusive design can bridge divides and reflect the diversity of human experience.

Through their work, they demonstrated that technology, at its best, is a powerful love language—one that transcends mere function to become a means of communication, empathy, and understanding. Whether in a virtual game world or in the ethical design of AI systems, their contributions remind us that technology's true value lies in its ability to connect us to one another.

REFERENCES

Berry, D. (1995) *Special note to those thinking about a sex change: Personal reflections.* [online] Available at: https://ai.eecs.umich.edu/people/conway/TS/Warning.html#Dani (Accessed: 15 September 2024).

Brown, T. (2009) *Change by design: How design thinking transforms organizations and inspires innovation.* New York: Harper Business.

Buolamwini, J. and Gebru, T. (2018) 'Gender shades: Intersectional accuracy disparities in commercial gender classification', *Proceedings of the 1st Conference on Fairness, Accountability and Transparency*, 81, pp. 77–91.

Caliskan, A., Bryson, J.J. and Narayanan, A. (2017) 'Semantics derived automatically from language corpora contain human-like biases', *Science*, 356(6334), pp. 183–186.

Cech, E.A. and Rothwell, W.R. (2020) 'LGBT workplace inequality in the federal workforce: Intersectional processes, organizational contexts, and turnover considerations', *Industrial and Labor Relations Review*, 73(4), pp. 949–978.

Crawford, G. (2012) *Video gamers.* Oxon: Routledge.

Crawford, K. (2021) *Atlas of AI: Power, politics, and the planetary costs of artificial intelligence.* New Haven: Yale University Press.

Donovan, T. (2010) *Replay: The history of video games.* East Sussex: Yellow Ant Media.

European Women on Boards (2022). *Gender Diversity Index 2022.* [online] Available at: https://www.europeanwomenonboards.eu/gender-diversity-index-2022/ [Accessed 15 September 2024].

Jokinen, E. and Smith, J.M. (2017) 'Gender and technology in the workplace: Implications for women's career development', *Gender, Work & Organization*, 24(1), pp. 89–109.

Kücklich, J. (2005). Precarious playbour: Modders and the digital games industry, *Fibreculture Journal*, 5, pp. 1–5.

Latouche, S. (2010) 'Degrowth', *Journal of Cleaner Production*, 18(6), pp. 519–522.

Levy, S. (1984) *Hackers: Heroes of the computer revolution.* Garden City, NY: Anchor Press/Doubleday.

Margolis, J. and Fisher, A. (2002) *Unlocking the clubhouse: Women in computing.* Cambridge, MA: MIT Press.

Mulder, M. (2024) Interview by Kelly Vero. 2 September 2024.

Q. (2020). *Meet Q: The first genderless voice.* [online] Available at: https://genderlessvoice.com (Accessed: 15 September 2024).

Sardar, Z. (2010) 'The namesake: Futures; Futures studies; Futurology; Futuristic; Foresight—What's in a name?', *Futures*, 42(3), pp. 177–184.

Taylor, T.L. (2006) *Play between worlds: Exploring online game culture.* Cambridge, MA: MIT Press.

West, S.M., Kraut, R. and Chew, H.E. (2019) *I'd blush if I could: Closing gender divides in digital skills through education.* Paris: UNESCO.

Workplace Pride. (2019) 'LGBTQIA+ Inclusion Benchmark Report 2019.' *Workplace Pride.* Amsterdam.

Woman Thing/"This Is Not a 'Woman Thing'"

I'M SITTING HERE, CHATTING with my friend Jackie Maguire on Zoom. We try to catch up every Friday, but lately, life has been getting in the way. We've always been active talkers—despite her being in Arizona and me in Zurich, the time difference never really bothers us. Even though it's early morning for her and late afternoon for me, we always find things to laugh about. She's an artificial intelligence (AI) and cybersecurity analyst, so our conversations often dive into the nerdy world of tech. We've both seen so much in this evolving field, and as we enter this new era of AI, with its endless complexities and risks, it's comforting to have these deep discussions across thousands of miles, all thanks to video conferencing.

In this book, I've made a conscious effort, inspired by the women I know—some friends, some acquaintances—to showcase not just their achievements, but the broader impact those achievements have on regular people like me. I've spent much of my life searching for role models and didn't truly find them until I started working in video games. It was then that I discovered what opportunities existed for someone like me, a woman in technology, to succeed and lead. What inspires me most is that every day, new pioneers are emerging—and they happen to be women. I've strived to balance this book by highlighting not only well-known names but also women from diverse backgrounds—different cultures, religions, sexualities, and genders—who are shaping technology in ways that often get overlooked.

As I sit here reflecting on the long arc of women's contributions to technology—from the early pioneers like Aganice of Egypt and Hypatia of Alexandria to the incredible minds shaping today's world—one theme resonates clearly: the battle for recognition continues. The stories of women in ancient times reveal both the timeless power of curiosity and the relentless barriers to opportunity. Today, the battlefield has shifted, but the fight to be seen, heard, and acknowledged remains just as fierce.

In this chapter, we turn our gaze towards modern innovators—brilliant women who stand on the shoulders of giants. Their struggles mirror those of ancient mathematicians,

DOI: 10.1201/9781003566465-10

157

philosophers, and engineers, but their achievements come at a time when the stakes are higher, the technologies more complex, and the global reach of their contributions more profound.

Adele Goldberg is a computer scientist best known for her work at Xerox PARC, where she co-created the Smalltalk programming language, one of the first object-oriented programming (OOP) languages (Kay, 1993). Smalltalk was revolutionary in its approach to programming, introducing concepts like the graphical user interface (GUI) and having a major influence on modern software development, including languages like Java and Python. Goldberg's pioneering work in OOP and GUIs helped lay the foundation for personal computing and software engineering as we know it today. She was also a strong advocate for education and technology, co-authoring several books on programming. Her work on Smalltalk and her role in advancing OOP principles have had a lasting impact on software development and modern computing (Kay, 1993).

Adi Tatarko taught herself to code. Let's let that sink in. Many women, myself included are encouraged to do other things where programming is not necessarily readily available. When she experienced frustrations with her own home renovation, she coded a solution out of the problem and Houzz was born. Her leadership and innovative use of technology have disrupted the traditional home design industry, bringing digital transformation to an otherwise offline space (Tatarko, 2020). What began as a small online community has grown into a global platform with millions of users, connecting homeowners with designers, contractors, and architects. Her background in computer science and product development was key to the platform's rapid growth and success (BBC, 2019).

Amy Jo Kim is a renowned game designer and social gaming expert, who has made significant contributions to the design of innovative and genre-defining products. With a background in experimental psychology and neuroscience, she began her career as a programmer before transitioning into UX design, where her skills in building and fine-tuning systems came to the forefront. She was part of the early design teams for popular and impactful titles like *The Sims*, *Rock Band*, and *Ultima Online*, as well as platforms such as *eBay* and *Netflix*. Her experience in creating multiplayer social gaming environments provided her with a deep understanding of what it takes to create products that resonate with users and stand the test of time (Kim, 2017).

I'm a Kim fangirl. I read her book *Game Thinking* (2017) and fell in love with the idea of applying simple design techniques to anything from femtech to AI. Her work has evolved into teaching others through her unique user experience (UX) approaches, and Game Thinking, which she developed as a methodology to help entrepreneurs and innovators design successful, market-defining products. By merging her knowledge of psychology, systems design, and social gaming, she has become a vital voice in both the tech and gaming industries, inspiring the next generation of innovators to think strategically about user engagement from the earliest stages of product development (Kim, 2017). And yeah, she made some of our most favourite games!

Anita Borg (1949–2003) was a visionary computer scientist and a tireless advocate for women in technology. She founded the Institute for Women in Technology (later renamed the Anita Borg Institute for Women and Technology) in 1997 with the mission to increase the participation of women in computing and promote gender equality in the tech industry (Margolis and Fisher, 2002). She believed that women should be at the forefront of technological development, not just as users but as *creators*. Her work led to the creation of the Grace Hopper Celebration of Women in Computing, an annual conference that brings together thousands of women technologists to network, share knowledge, and support one another. Her advocacy extended beyond conferences, and you've probably heard of AnitaB.org but she put the success of the conferences into working with major tech companies to develop inclusive policies that addressed gender disparities in STEM fields. Throughout her career, she remained focused on the idea that technology must be shaped by diverse perspectives to better serve society. Her advocacy for women in technology and the founding of the Grace Hopper Celebration transformed how women engage with the tech industry, and her legacy continues to inspire women in computing to break barriers and drive innovation (Margolis and Fisher, 2002).

Arfa Abdul Karim Randhawa (1995–2012) was a Pakistani computer prodigy who became the youngest Microsoft Certified Professional at the age of 9. Her achievement at such a young age brought her international recognition, and she was invited to meet Bill Gates, who admired her talent and vision. She was an advocate for the role of women and girls in technology, even in a country where access to education and technology for girls is limited. Despite her short life, her legacy continues to inspire young girls across Pakistan and beyond to pursue careers in technology, where her accomplishments are widely recognised in the field of technology (AKTI, 2024).

Bertha Benz, wife of Karl Benz, is often considered one of the most influential figures in the early days of the automobile industry. In 1888, she made history by becoming the first person to drive a long-distance journey in an automobile, covering approximately 106 kilometres (66 miles) from Mannheim to Pforzheim, Germany (Sterling, 2018). Her journey was more than a mere road trip; it was a pivotal marketing move to demonstrate the reliability and practicality of her husband's invention, the Benz Patent-Motorwagen, the world's first true automobile, and transforming it from a curiosity into a viable form of transportation. She played an essential role in the success of the Benz company, not only by financially supporting her husband's endeavours—something we simply don't talk about enough—but also by providing crucial feedback on the mechanics and usability of the car. During her journey, she even repaired mechanical issues on the vehicle herself, evidencing her technical understanding. This journey proved that the automobile was not just a novelty but a reliable mode of transportation, significantly advancing the auto industry. Her long-distance drive is symbolic for any woman navigating the technology industry: she shows us that ingenuity and the pioneering spirit are not the only things that shaped the automotive industry (Sterling, 2018).

Brenda Romero is an award-winning game designer known for her work on the Wizardry series and her innovative contributions to game design and education. With a career spanning more than 30 years, she has become a leading voice in the gaming industry, particularly in advocating for diversity and inclusion. She has developed over 40 games and is recognised for her commitment to using games as a medium for storytelling and education (Romero, 2016). Romero's The Mechanic is the Message series, which includes games like

Train, explores difficult historical and social issues through gameplay, challenging players to reflect on the ethical dimensions of their choices. As an educator, she has taught game design at universities and worked to ensure that the next generation of game developers is more diverse and representative. "Games are about more than fun; they're about learning and connecting with people," she has said (Romero, 2016). She is still one of my career icons and leaning into her learning and vision is easy. She is a woman who continues to explore common design for fairer and equitable game experiences.

Camille Mendler is a renowned analyst and thought leader in the telecommunications industry, particularly in the areas of 5G and IoT (Internet of Things). As a principal analyst at Omdia, Mendler has been instrumental in providing critical insights into the development of 5G networks and their implications for businesses and consumers. Her work focuses on how 5G technology will revolutionise industries, including healthcare, manufacturing, and transportation. Her thought leadership has helped shape policy discussions around the global rollout of 5G and the ethical considerations of emerging technologies. Her analysis of the impact of 5G and IoT on global industries is well-regarded in the telecommunications sector (Mendler, 2012).

Carrie Anne Philbin is a British educator, author, and advocate for girls in STEM, known for her work with the Raspberry Pi Foundation. She is a passionate advocate for the neurodiverse community, openly sharing her experiences with ADHD. She has played a crucial role in developing resources to help teachers use digital technologies in the classroom, specifically aiming to make technology education accessible and inclusive for all students, regardless of neurodivergence. Through her YouTube series *Crash Course Computer Science* and her book, *Adventures in Raspberry Pi*, she has inspired countless young people to take up coding and computer science, especially those who may face barriers due to neurodiversity. Her work continues to push the boundaries for neurodiverse learners in the tech world (Philbin, 2017).

Carol Shaw is celebrated as one of the first female video game designers, recognised for her work at Atari and Activision during the early days of the video game industry. She was passionate about mathematics and computer science, earning a degree in Electrical Engineering and Computer Science from UC Berkeley (Lüsted, 2018), and afterwards joined Atari in 1978 designing one of the earliest video games, 3D Tic-Tac-Toe. She is best known for her creation of River Raid, a groundbreaking game that was not only a commercial success but also one of the first to feature complex scrolling environments, a technical innovation at the time. In a male-dominated industry, her success as a programmer and designer set her apart as a role model for women in gaming, showing that women could excel in the field of video game development. Her work as one of the first female video game designers revolutionised the gaming industry with her technical innovations, such as the development of River Raid, and she remains an influential figure in the history of gaming.

Deepa Madhavan is a trailblazing figure in fintech, currently serving as Vice President, India Country Head for Genesys, where she leads global data management and compliance initiatives. With a background in computer science, her path has been far from linear. We know that feeling well, don't we? Sometimes the things we studied at university don't seem to fit with our career until much later if at all.

Madhavan combined her technical expertise with strategic leadership to drive PayPal's innovations in data governance and privacy (Women Entrepreneurs Review, 2022). Her work was instrumental in ensuring PayPal's compliance with global data privacy regulations, enhancing the company's reputation for trust and security for millions of users worldwide. Her leadership extends beyond her technical responsibilities; she is a strong advocate for women in technology and finance, promoting mentorship programs that encourage women to take on leadership roles in the industry. "We need to pave the way for the next generation of women in tech by providing mentorship, opportunities, and most importantly, a sense of belonging," Madhavan said in a panel discussion on women in fintech (Madhavan, 2021). Maintaining a demanding career is not easy when we have to balance family life, but she reinforces the importance of work-life integration rather than separation by leading from doing. She believes that leadership requires empathy, and this is reflected in her approach to fostering inclusive teams where diversity of thought is encouraged. Her efforts to mentor women in fintech continue to inspire a more inclusive environment in the industry.

Debi Wood is an influential educator in computer science, with a teaching career that spans over two decades. She began her career in the mid-1990s, during a time when computer science education was just beginning to take root at the college level. As an IT educator, she has dedicated her life to empowering students with the skills and knowledge needed to thrive in a rapidly evolving technological world. Her teaching focuses on foundational programming languages and emerging technologies, helping to bridge the gap between traditional education and modern industry needs.

Let me tell you a story about Wood: I used to work with her. I was taking a break from my games career and working at a local college teaching young people how to understand applications inside platforms such as micro or web services. There were a million times that I wanted to quit because I was convinced teaching was something I was not good at. She didn't agree, so she conducted a small survey with the students and produced the findings. I stayed in teaching for a good long while after that and studied for my teach qualifications (just in case). If it wasn't for her, some of my former students might not have found their careers at EA, Nintendo and others. Wood's ability to stay current with advancements in technology has made her an enduring figure in computer science education for everyone.

Debjani Ghosh is one of India's most influential technology leaders, currently serving as the President of National Association of Software and Service Companies (NASSCOM). She has been instrumental in shaping India's technology landscape and has consistently broken barriers in an industry traditionally dominated by men. Before joining NASSCOM, she spent over two decades at Intel becoming the first woman to lead Intel South Asia operations, overseeing its growth across emerging markets like India, Indonesia, and Malaysia. Under her leadership at NASSCOM, she championed initiatives to accelerate India's digital economy and future-proof the country's workforce, and spearheading the FutureSkills initiative, which aims to upskill millions of Indian workers in areas like AI, big data, and cybersecurity by 2025 (NASSCOM, 2020). She has also been a strong advocate for women in tech, emphasising the need for systemic changes to support gender diversity in leadership roles. What opportunities might we have in technology without direct governance? "We must create workplaces that allow women to succeed by design, not by accident" (Ghosh, 2019).

Ghosh's influence is evident in India's evolving digital policies, particularly in advancing the skill set of the Indian workforce in emerging technologies. Her advocacy for gender inclusivity in the tech industry has sparked numerous initiatives focused on empowering women to take on leadership roles (NASSCOM, 2020). Despite her demanding career, she speaks openly about balancing work and family life. She highlights that successful careers for women should not come at the cost of personal fulfilment and family well-being. Her ability to advocate for policies that enable flexible, inclusive work environments is evidence of her holistic approach to leadership.

Diana Iracheta is a mechanical engineer and an outspoken advocate for women and minorities in STEM fields. Originally from Mexico, her journey into engineering was shaped by her own experiences as an immigrant and a woman in a predominantly male industry. She founded the platform LatinaEngineer.com to provide resources, support, and community for Latinx women pursuing careers in engineering (Tai, 2020). Through her work, she is breaking down barriers and advocating for greater diversity in engineering. She actively promotes STEM education for underrepresented groups and provides mentorship to young women aspiring to enter technical fields, and her advocacy has garnered a large following, making her an influential voice for Latinx representation in STEM.

Doris Cohen was a pioneering figure in aeronautical engineering, becoming NASA's first female aeronautical research engineer at the Langley Memorial Aeronautical Laboratory in 1939. Due to poor record keeping of particularly women of colour during this era, it is impossible to know when she was born and details about her life are also limited. Despite this, in a career spanning several decades, she made significant contributions to the field of aerodynamics, particularly in the study of airflow and flight dynamics. Her research provided critical insights into the behaviour of aircraft at high speeds, influencing both military and commercial aviation. She was also known for her groundbreaking research papers, including her 1941 publication on *The Effects of Turbulence on Airfoils*, which helped improve aircraft performance during World War II. In a male-dominated field, her work was nothing short of revolutionary, as she challenged the limitations placed on women in STEM. Despite facing societal barriers, her dedication and intellectual prowess paved the way for future generations of women engineers. Her pioneering research in aerodynamics had a profound impact on aviation and space exploration. As NASA's first female aeronautical engineer, and NACA's first female author and woman of colour author (she wrote almost 15 papers between 1941 and 1954); she broke barriers for women in STEM and contributed to advancements in flight technology (Shetterly, 2016).

Dorit Dor is Chief Technology Officer at Check Point Software Technologies, one of the world's leading cybersecurity companies. She has been instrumental in developing Check Point's firewall and intrusion prevention systems, which have become a standard in enterprise security solutions. She is a computer science expert and has been with Check Point for over two decades, playing a key role in the research and development of groundbreaking cybersecurity solutions. Her leadership has helped position Israel as a global leader in the field of cybersecurity (Check Point Software Technologies, 2020).

Dor's contributions go beyond product development; she has been a vocal advocate for diversity in tech, particularly in cybersecurity, where women remain underrepresented. She regularly speaks about the importance of encouraging more women to pursue careers in STEM fields, offering mentorship and promoting educational initiatives within the Israeli tech ecosystem (Dor, 2018).

Elena Bunina is a mathematician, data scientist, and business leader who served as the CEO of Yandex, one of Russia's largest tech companies, widely regarded as Russia's Google until 2022 (The Times of Israel, 2022). With a Ph.D. in mathematics, she initially made her mark in academia as a professor before joining Yandex in 2011 where she played a key role in growing Yandex's data science capabilities, overseeing both human resources and education initiatives aimed at training the next generation of data scientists and engineers in Russia. Since 2022, she has been a professor in the mathematics department of Bar-Ilan University in Ramat Gan, Israel, and a scientific advisor at the Y-Data school of data science in Israel. Her leadership has been particularly notable for promoting a culture of innovation and diversity, inspiring many women to pursue careers in technology and coding.

Ellen Sandor is a pioneering artist and technologist whose work in the realm of immersive art has pushed the boundaries of digital creativity. Known for her interdisciplinary approach, she has combined art, science, and technology to create groundbreaking 3D experiences. Her work in PHSColograms (Photography, Holography, Sculpture, and Computer Graphics) shows how art can intersect with emerging technologies to create new forms of expression. As the founder of the collaborative art group (art)n, her contributions have influenced the evolution of immersive and virtual reality art installations, merging the physical and digital worlds in unique ways. Her influence on immersive art and her pioneering use of technology in artistic creation is well noted (Fermilab, 2015).

Farzana Aslam is a distinguished physicist and astronomer whose research in space science and astronomy has made significant contributions to the field. Born in Wah Cantt, a small town in Pakistan, her work has focused on the study of star formation and the dynamics of galaxies and has also been involved in international collaborations that aim to better understand cosmic phenomena. As a woman in STEM, she has faced and overcome many barriers, using her platform to advocate for more women in the sciences. Her research continues to be influential in academic circles and has earned her recognition as one of the leading astronomers in her field (Coventry University, 2011). Her contributions to space science and her role in advocating for women in STEM are well documented.

Fei-Fei Li, one of the most prominent and influential figures in AI, is best known for creating ImageNet, a large-scale dataset that revolutionised the field of computer vision. Born in China and later moving to the United States, she became a professor of computer science at Stanford University and served as the Director of Stanford's AI Lab (Russakovsky et al., 2015). ImageNet was a pivotal innovation, enabling AI systems to *see* by recognising and categorising objects in images, which became a foundational tool for deep learning. She has been an advocate for the ethical use of AI, emphasising the need for diversity and inclusivity in the development of machine learning technologies. She co-founded AI4ALL, a non-profit organisation aimed at increasing diversity in AI by providing education and mentorship to underrepresented groups. Her work continues to shape the future of AI, ensuring that technological advancements are guided by ethical considerations and benefit all of humanity. Her advocacy for ethical AI development and diversity has had a lasting impact on the field (Russakovsky et al., 2015).

Grace Hopper, often referred to as The Mother of Computing, was a trailblazer in computer science and one of the most influential women in the history of technology. As a rear admiral in the U.S. Navy and a mathematician, she made pivotal contributions to the development of early programming languages, including the creation of COBOL, a language still used in business and government applications today (Beyer, 2012). Hopper's most famous innovation came when she developed the first compiler, a tool that translated high-level programming languages into machine code, making computers accessible to more people. Hopper is also credited with popularising the term *debugging* after she discovered a moth causing malfunctions in a computer system. Throughout her career, she tirelessly advocated for the importance of computer literacy, especially for women, and her impact on modern computing cannot be overstated. Her work paved the way for modern software development, and her advocacy for women in tech remains an inspiration (Beyer, 2012).

Hind Hobeika, a Lebanese entrepreneur and inventor, is the founder and CEO of Instabeat, a pioneering wearable technology designed for swimmers. Her innovation blends a passion for engineering with experience as a professional swimmer, making her one of the leading women in sports technology. Instabeat has been recognised globally for its potential to transform the way athletes engage with data to improve their performance (Hobeika, 2018).

Hobeika's journey into technology began with her background in mechanical engineering, where she specialised in fluid dynamics, which she applied to developing her product. Her work exemplifies how wearable technology can be used to enhance performance and safety, especially in sports. As an advocate for women in STEM, she has spoken about the challenges of being a female entrepreneur in the MENA region and how perseverance, technical expertise, and community support are essential for women breaking into male-dominated industries (Hobeika, 2019).

Jackie McGuire is a recognised thought leader in AI and cybersecurity, known for her deep expertise in developing advanced AI models and cybersecurity strategies to protect critical infrastructures. With more than two decades of experience in the technology industry, she has contributed to shaping how organisations use AI to enhance their cybersecurity protocols, mitigating threats in real time and predicting vulnerabilities before they can be exploited. Her leadership in developing innovative security solutions has placed her at the forefront of AI's role in modern cybersecurity, particularly in her work with multinational corporations and government bodies to safeguard sensitive data and networks (McGuire, 2019).

As an advocate for ethical AI, McGuire emphasises the importance of transparency, accountability, and fairness in AI systems. She has been instrumental in shaping policies that ensure AI technologies are used responsibly, particularly within cybersecurity frameworks, where bias and discrimination in AI algorithms could have significant consequences. She regularly speaks at international forums and conferences, sharing her insights on the evolving nature of cyber threats and the integral role AI plays in defence strategies.

Her thought leadership continues to influence the cybersecurity landscape, where AI is increasingly being used to automate threat detection and improve response times, protecting against the growing complexity of cyberattacks (McGuire, 2019).

Jess Wade is a British physicist and an active advocate for diversity in science, known for her work in materials science and her dedication to improving the representation of women and minorities in STEM. She works as a research fellow in the Department of Physics at Imperial College London, where her research focuses on the development of new materials for optoelectronic devices, such as organic light-emitting diodes (OLEDs). She has published extensively in her field, contributing to the understanding of molecular materials and their potential applications in technologies like flexible displays and solar panels (Karim et al., 2019). Her work in materials science has been recognised by several prestigious awards, including the Institute of Physics' Early Career Physics Communicator Award.

Beyond her research, Wade is perhaps best known for her advocacy efforts. She has written over 1800 Wikipedia pages to improve the visibility of women scientists and scientists of colour whose contributions have been overlooked in mainstream narratives. Her goal is to address the gender data gap and ensure that the accomplishments of these individuals are documented and accessible to a global audience. Her activism extends beyond Wikipedia, as she frequently speaks about the importance of representation in STEM and works to inspire the next generation of scientists through outreach activities (Wade, 2017). Her efforts have earned her widespread recognition, including a British Empire Medal in 2019 for her services to gender diversity in science.

Joy Buolamwini is an influential computer scientist and digital activist known for her work in addressing algorithmic bias, particularly in facial recognition systems. As the founder of the Algorithmic Justice League, she has been at the forefront of the fight against the ethical challenges posed by AI systems that reflect and perpetuate societal biases (Buolamwini and Gebru, 2018). Her groundbreaking research, which demonstrated that commercial facial recognition systems often misidentify women and people of colour, brought global attention to the issue of bias in AI. Her advocacy has led to significant changes in how tech companies develop and deploy AI systems, with several major corporations rethinking their use of facial recognition technology. She has testified before the U.S. Congress, calling for legislation to address the ethical implications of biased AI and championing the importance of transparency and accountability in AI development. Her work continues to inspire a growing movement aimed at creating ethical, inclusive, and equitable AI technologies. Through the Algorithmic Justice League, she promotes ethical AI practices and greater diversity in tech (Buolamwini and Gebru, 2018).

Karen Spärck Jones was a British computer scientist whose groundbreaking work in information retrieval and natural language processing (NLP) has had a profound impact on modern search engines. She is best known for introducing the concept of Inverse Document Frequency (IDF), a core idea in the field of information retrieval (Robertson, 2008). IDF is used to rank search results by the relevance of the document to the query, laying the foundation for the algorithms behind modern search engines like Google.

Throughout her career, she was also an advocate for the representation of women in computer science, emphasising the importance of equality in a male-dominated field. Her work on information retrieval and her development of IDF have been pivotal in the evolution of search engine technology, affecting how millions access information online today (Robertson, 2008).

Kateryna Yushchenko (1919–2001) was a pioneering Ukrainian computer scientist who made significant contributions to early computer programming. She is most famous for developing the Address Programming Language, one of the first high-level programming languages designed for computers in the 1950s. Her work laid the foundation for many future developments in computing, particularly in the areas of computer systems design and programming theory.

Yushchenko's contribution to programming was groundbreaking in the Soviet Union, where she became the first woman in Ukraine to earn a doctorate in physical and mathematical sciences with a focus on cybernetics. Her work on computer architecture and algorithms was instrumental in advancing the field of computer science in Eastern Europe. She is remembered as a trailblazer who helped shape the development of early computers and inspired generations of female scientists in Ukraine (Yushchenko, 1968).

Kimberly L. Tripp, often referred to as The Queen of Indexes, is a renowned expert in database management, specialising in Microsoft SQL Server. She is best known for her groundbreaking work in index tuning and database performance optimisation, a field that is critical for handling vast amounts of data in today's digital economy (Tripp, 2018). With over two decades of experience, Tripp has become a thought leader in the database management community, regularly sharing her expertise through workshops, conferences, and publications. She is the co-founder of SQLskills, a training company that helps database professionals enhance their skills in managing SQL Server environments. Her expertise in index tuning and database management has been instrumental in improving the performance of SQL Server databases. Her contributions to education and mentorship have made her a key figure in the world of data management (Tripp, 2018).

Kira Radinsky is one of Israel's most prominent data scientists and AI experts, recognised for her work in predictive analytics and machine learning. She gained international attention when she developed an algorithm capable of predicting major events, such as epidemics and political crises, based on historical data. Her work in predictive analytics has been transformative in fields ranging from healthcare to disaster prevention. In 2013, she co-founded SalesPredict, a company that used AI to improve business-to-business sales predictions, which was later acquired by eBay (Radinsky, 2013).

Radinsky continues to pioneer AI research, focusing on healthcare applications. As CEO and Chief Technology Officer of Diagnostic Robotics, a company that uses AI to assist in medical diagnostics, she is working to revolutionise how healthcare systems worldwide predict, diagnose, and treat diseases. Her contributions to AI and machine learning have positioned her as one of the leading figures in Israeli tech innovation (Radinsky, 2019).

Krista Kim is a contemporary artist renowned for her groundbreaking work in the field of digital and immersive art. Known for her exploration of the intersection between digital technology and art, she has been instrumental in promoting the idea of digital consciousness through her works. In 2021, she made headlines by selling a digital house titled *Mars House* as an NFT (non-fungible token), marking a significant moment in the convergence of art and blockchain technology. Her artistic vision focuses on using light and digital media to evoke a sense of tranquillity, and she is considered one of the foremost leaders in the NFT art movement (Martins and Wolfe, 2022).

Lakshya Sivaramakrishnan has established herself as a leader in software engineering and program management, currently serving as a Technical Program Manager at Google. Her work in the field of machine learning and AI has played a significant role in advancing Google's AI initiatives. Her career trajectory proves that we can be experts in managing complex technical projects while promoting inclusive work environments. Sivaramakrishnan's contributions to Google's AI and machine learning projects have helped the company stay at the forefront of technological innovation. (AnitaB.org, 2024)

Sivaramakrishnan is a strong advocate for women in engineering and has been involved in Google's Women in Tech initiatives, where she mentors young women pursuing careers in STEM. She underscores the importance of representation in technical fields and encourages women to pursue leadership roles, stating, "We need to ensure that women are not just participants in tech, but are empowered to lead and innovate" (Sivaramakrishnan, 2022). Her ability to balance technical excellence with a focus on diversity has earned her recognition in the industry. Outside of her professional work, she actively supports initiatives that provide resources and training to underrepresented groups in technology.

Latifa Al-Abdulkarim is a distinguished Saudi computer scientist and academic, recognised for her significant contributions to the fields of AI and legal reasoning systems. She is known for her work on the ethical governance of AI and for pioneering AI applications in legal systems, specifically through the development of Abstract Dialectical Frameworks (Al-Abdulkarim et al., 2016). This methodology enables AI systems to reason with legal cases by incorporating complex decision-making processes, making it possible for AI to assist in legal judgments in a structured and ethically sound manner.

Her role in AI research has been widely acknowledged, as she was featured in the *100 Brilliant Women in AI Ethics Hall of Fame* (100 Brilliant Women in AI Ethics, 2021). Additionally, Al-Abdulkarim has been recognised by Forbes for her pivotal role in shaping the 21st-century AI movement, where her work in AI ethics is lauded for ensuring the responsible development of AI technologies (Minevich, 2020).

Al-Abdulkarim has actively contributed to promoting the role of women in STEM, particularly in the Gulf region. She has been a key figure in advocating for gender diversity in AI and technology, which aligns with Saudi Arabia's broader goals for innovation and economic diversification under Vision 2030 (About Her, 2020). She has also represented Saudi Arabia in international forums, such as UNESCO, where she contributes to global dialogues about breaking gender biases in AI (UNESCO, 2021).

Marissa Mayer is best known for her tenure as the CEO of Yahoo, where she led the company through one of its most challenging periods. Before her role at Yahoo, she had a long and successful career at Google, where she was one of the company's earliest employees and played a key role in the development of some of its most iconic products, including Google Search and Google Maps (Vise and Malseed, 2006). As one of the few women leading a major tech company, her tenure at Yahoo was closely watched, with both her successes and challenges becoming a focal point of media scrutiny. Despite the obstacles, she managed to navigate Yahoo through a period of transformation before its eventual sale to Verizon. Her legacy includes her focus on data-driven decision-making and her advocacy for women in tech leadership roles. She has become a role model for women striving to break through the glass ceiling in the tech industry. Marissa Mayer's leadership at Yahoo and her early work at Google helped shape the modern internet, and made her an influential figure in Silicon Valley (Vise and Malseed, 2006).

Megan Smith, a leading figure in the field of technology and innovation, has had a profound influence on both the public and private sectors. Serving as the third Chief Technology Officer (CTO) of the United States under President Barack Obama, she worked tirelessly to leverage technology to address critical social issues and improve governmental functions. Before her role as CTO, she held senior positions at Google, where she contributed significantly to the development of key initiatives, including Google Earth and Google Maps, which have since become globally essential tools for geographical navigation and environmental awareness. Her ability to bridge the gap between technology and policy exemplifies her pioneering spirit, pushing forward the notion that technology can serve as a catalyst for social good and governmental transparency (Apte, 2019).

Beyond her work in government and the private sector, Smith has been a vocal advocate for inclusivity in technology. She co-founded Tech Jobs Tour, a project designed to bring more women, people of colour, and LGBTQIA+ individuals into the tech workforce. This initiative has travelled across the United States, connecting people with opportunities in an industry where diversity is still lacking. Additionally, she also founded and works with shift7, a social impact company, to continue her commitment to driving technological innovation that addresses societal challenges, such as climate change and economic inequality. Her contributions to technology and her commitment to fostering diversity within the industry have made her an iconic figure in modern technological leadership (Apte, 2019).

Sister Mary Kenneth Keller (1913–1985) was a pivotal figure in the early days of computer science. In 1965, she became one of the first women in the United States to earn a Ph.D. in computer science. Her groundbreaking work in the development of the BASIC programming language revolutionised access to computing for non-experts. She advocated for the idea that computers could be used for educational purposes long before it became a widespread belief. Her contributions helped lay the foundation for modern software development, making computing more accessible to students and professionals from various fields. She was also a nun and deeply believed that technology could help foster better education and societal progress.

Keller's belief in the power of computing to enhance education made her an early advocate for computer literacy. Her work at Dartmouth College, where she earned her Ph.D., and her subsequent efforts to integrate computers into academic curricula, were instrumental in the early use of computers in education. Her legacy is significant not only for her technical contributions but also for her role in opening the world of computing to a broader, more diverse audience (Croucher, 2023).

Lydia X. Z. Brown is an autistic disability rights advocate, attorney, and a prominent voice in technology ethics, particularly concerning the impact of AI on marginalised communities. She has extensively worked on issues related to algorithmic bias and the implications of AI for disabled people, particularly those with cognitive disabilities, and she focuses on ensuring that new technologies are built inclusively and ethically, with a particular emphasis on algorithmic justice.

In their work with organisations such as AI Now Institute and Georgetown Law's Institute for Technology Law & Policy, Brown has been instrumental in advancing conversations around the intersection of disability and technology. Her work has influenced the development of more ethical AI systems, ensuring they do not perpetuate biases against disabled people (Gooding et al., 2023).

Marta Kwiatkowska is a Polish computer scientist known for her groundbreaking work in probabilistic model checking, a field that combines computer science and mathematics to verify and improve the reliability of systems such as software, networks, and embedded devices. A professor at Oxford University, she is also a Fellow of the Royal Society and one of the most prominent figures in theoretical computer science today.

Kwiatkowska's research has been applied to diverse areas, including cybersecurity, autonomous systems, and biological systems. Her work has had a profound impact on the development of tools and techniques to ensure that safety-critical systems—like those used in medical devices and air traffic control—are reliable and secure. Her leadership in the field of formal verification has earned her numerous awards, and she remains a role model for women in STEM, particularly in the field of computer science (University of Oxford, 2020).

Mary Wilkes is best known for her work as a computer programmer and her role in developing the Laboratory Instrument Computer (LINC), which is considered one of the first personal computers (Ceruzzi, 2003). She was instrumental in creating software for the LINC, and she also famously used the LINC at home, making her one of the first people to use a personal computer outside of a laboratory setting. Her groundbreaking work in the early days of computing showed that computers could have practical applications in everyday life, paving the way for the personal computing revolution of the 1980s. Her contributions to the development of the LINC computer and her early advocacy for personal computing mark her as a pioneering figure in the tech industry (Ceruzzi, 2003).

Nergis Mavalvala, a Pakistani American astrophysicist, is renowned for her contributions to gravitational wave detection, which culminated in the groundbreaking observation of gravitational waves by the LIGO (Laser Interferometer Gravitational-Wave Observatory) collaboration in 2015. Born in Karachi, Pakistan, she pursued her education in the United States and became one of the key figures in the development of technology that enabled the detection of these ripples in space-time, a discovery that confirmed a major prediction of Albert Einstein's theory of general relativity (Abbott, Abbott and Abbott, 2016). In 2020, she became the first female Dean of the School of Science at MIT, a justification that scientific achievements and leadership really do pay off. Throughout her career, she has advocated for inclusivity in STEM, particularly for women and underrepresented minorities.

Her work in quantum mechanics and astrophysics continues to push the boundaries of our understanding of the universe, while her leadership at MIT is helping to shape the next generation of scientists. As a dean at MIT, she is a leading advocate for diversity in science and technology (Abbott et al., 2016).

Neelam Dhawan has made a name for herself as a formidable leader in India's technology sector, with over 30 years of experience in executive roles at HP, Microsoft, and IBM. She broke several barriers as one of the first women to lead a major tech company in India, becoming the Managing Director of Hewlett-Packard (HP) India in 2008 (Economic Times, 2018). Her leadership is notable for fostering innovation, scaling business operations, and driving digital transformation initiatives. Currently serving as an Independent Director on the board of ICICI Bank, she is known for her advocacy of diversity and inclusion, stressing that corporate India needs more women in leadership roles. She has been vocal about the need for organisations to create opportunities for women to rise to executive positions, stating, "A more diverse workforce leads to better decision-making, and we need to enable more women to break the glass ceiling" (Dhawan, 2019). Her work at HP, Microsoft, and IBM has also contributed significantly to the digitisation of businesses in India (Economic Times, 2018). Throughout her career, she has been balancing her work commitments with her role as a mother and believes that time management and a strong support system are crucial for women pursuing careers while raising a family. Her experience in overcoming industry gender biases has inspired a new generation of women in tech and business leadership.

Nivruti Rai is an influential figure in India's tech landscape, having served as the Country Head for Intel India. With over two decades of experience in the semiconductor and IT industries, she played a critical role in advancing Intel's initiatives in AI, 5G, and digital transformation in India. Her leadership has positioned Intel India as a hub for innovation, helping the company tap into emerging technologies and build strategic partnerships with Indian businesses and academic institutions. She has been a vocal advocate for women in STEM, often sharing her own experiences of navigating a male-dominated industry. "We need more women to not only join STEM fields but to rise to leadership positions where they can influence the direction of the technology industry," she said during a keynote address on gender diversity in tech (International Conference on VLSI Design and Embedded Systems, 2018). As a mother and a leader, Rai believes that balancing work and family is achievable with the right support structures in place, and she has advocated for policies that enable women to pursue both career and family aspirations. Today she is the MD and CEO of Invest India lifting a new generation of technologists by driving trade, framing policies and optimising growth.

Orna Berry is an Israeli scientist, entrepreneur, and policymaker and she has made extensive contributions to Israel's high-tech sector. She was the first woman to serve as Israel's Chief Scientist, where she was instrumental in advancing innovation policies that supported startups and R&D in the country. With a Ph.D. in computer science, she co-founded Ornet Data Communications, a company that developed some of the earliest Ethernet switches. The company was later sold to Siemens, marking a major success in

Israel's tech history (Berry, 1997). She is recognised not only for her technological contributions but also for her advocacy for women in tech and science, and is a pioneer in pushing for gender equality in Israeli tech and academia (Berry, 2003). Today, Berry serves as Director of Technology at Google Cloud.

Pankajam Sridevi is an influential leader in banking and finance, currently serving as Managing Director at Commonwealth Bank of India. With over three decades of experience in the industry, she has held senior roles at both ANZ Bank and Commonwealth Bank, focusing on driving digital transformation and enhancing operational efficiency. She is known for her ability to lead complex change management programs, often integrating cutting-edge technologies like AI and blockchain to optimise banking operations. She is also a strong advocate for workplace diversity and inclusion and has implemented several initiatives to increase the representation of women in leadership roles at Commonwealth Bank. "We need to create ecosystems where women can thrive, not just survive, in corporate environments," she remarked during a recent diversity forum (REVA Academy for Corporate Excellence, 2022). Her commitment to work-life balance is demonstrated by her ability to manage a high-stress executive role while raising a family, advocating for more flexible workplace policies to support other working mothers. She has been instrumental in driving digital transformation at Commonwealth Bank, making the institution more competitive in the digital age. Her advocacy for workplace diversity has helped create more inclusive environments for women in banking.

Radia Perlman is a computer scientist best known for inventing the Spanning Tree Protocol (STP), which is essential for the functioning of network bridges and switches (Perlman, 2000). Her contributions to computer networks have earned her the title Mother of the Internet. STP is used to prevent network loops in Ethernet networks, which is crucial for the stability and reliability of the internet and local networks. She has also contributed to network security and routing protocols, making her one of the most influential figures in the field of computer networking and her work continues to shape how data is transferred securely and efficiently across the globe. Her invention of STP and her contributions to network protocols have been foundational to the development of modern computer networking (Perlman, 2000).

Rasha Abu Safieh is the co-founder of GGateway, Palestine's first IT impact-sourcing social enterprise, is a successful venture supported by the World Bank. It serves as a regional outsourcing hub, creating hundreds of jobs for young people through IT outsourcing and remote work, helping to transform lives despite the challenging economic, political, and social conditions. By learning programming and digital skills, she believes everyone can pursue careers in technology, despite the challenges posed by living in a conflict zone. Her work has helped hundreds of women in Gaza gain access to resources and training, providing them with the skills to work remotely in global tech markets.

As one of the few female tech leaders in Gaza, Safieh has been a tireless advocate for women's empowerment through technology. She has spoken internationally about the importance of providing marginalised women with the tools to succeed in tech, using Gaza as an example of how technology can be a lifeline in conflict-affected areas

(StartSomeGood, 2023). Her efforts have been recognised for breaking down barriers to education and employment for Palestinian women, making her a key figure in the region's tech empowerment movement.

Raya Bidshahri, a neuroscientist-turned-edtech pioneer was the founder and CEO of Awecademy, a global online learning platform aimed at preparing students for the future by teaching them about emerging technologies. She centred her work around creating a new model of education that departs from traditional rote learning, focusing instead on critical thinking, creativity, and ethics in technology. Today she is the founder and CEO of The School of Humanity and by combining her passions of technology, philosophy and is also a strong advocate for the ethical development of technology and has spoken extensively on the importance of ensuring that emerging technologies like AI are used responsibly. She frequently highlights the need for a diverse range of voices in technology, particularly women and underrepresented groups, to ensure that these innovations benefit all of humanity. Her forward-thinking approach to both education and technology has made her a leading voice in the global edtech and futurist communities, impacting students across the MENA region and beyond (Bidshahri, 2019).

Renee Cummings is a leading voice in AI ethics and data activism, focusing on the intersection of AI, justice, and social equity. With a background in criminology and urban policy, she has dedicated her career to ensuring that AI technologies are developed and deployed in ways that do not exacerbate existing inequalities. As an advocate for responsible AI, she promotes the ethical use of AI in law enforcement, healthcare, and criminal justice (Stonier et al., 2023). Her work highlights the importance of diverse representation in AI development, emphasising that without the input of marginalised communities, AI systems will continue to reflect and reinforce societal biases. She has become a sought-after speaker on topics such as AI governance, algorithmic justice, and data ethics, advocating for greater accountability in how AI technologies are used, particularly in high-stakes areas like criminal justice reform. Her advocacy for ethical AI development continues to shape policy discussions around AI and social equity (University of Virginia, n.d.).

Sam Roach is a prominent figure in the gaming industry, known for her extensive expertise in engineering and development. Currently, she serves as the Global Head of Partner Engineering for Games and Entertainment at Unity, a role she has held since February 2024. In this position, she drives partnerships and technical innovation for one of the leading platforms in game development. Her previous roles at Unity include Senior Manager and Manager of Partner Engineering, where she led initiatives focused on integrating complex technical solutions to enhance game development capabilities.

Prior to joining Unity, Roach worked as an XR Developer at Make Real and Rewind, where she applied her skills in developing real-time features and immersive experiences. Her early career involved QA coordination and customer service at Space Ape Games, contributing to her well-rounded understanding of the gaming landscape. She holds a Bachelor of Science in Games Design and Development from the University of Greenwich, where she honed her technical skills in programming languages like C++, C#, and JavaScript. Her career trajectory highlights her expertise in managing innovative engineering solutions while supporting the broader gaming community.

Sara Hendren is an artist, design and engineering researcher, and professor who focuses on the intersection of disability and technology. While not a coder in the traditional sense, her contributions to assistive technologies have been groundbreaking. She teaches at Olin College of Engineering and is the author of *What Can a Body Do? How We Meet the Built World*, which explores how technology and design can better accommodate diverse bodies and abilities.

Hendren's work advocates for an inclusive design approach that considers the needs of people with disabilities from the outset, rather than as an afterthought. Her influence in both the tech and design communities has led to a greater focus on creating accessible technologies that serve everyone. Her focus on disability and technology challenges common perceptions of what innovation looks like (Hendren, 2020).

Dame Stephanie Shirley, also known as Steve Shirley, is a pioneering British entrepreneur and philanthropist who transformed the software industry in the 1960s by founding Freelance Programmers, a software company that primarily employed women. At a time when women were often excluded from technical roles, she created job opportunities for women programmers, many of whom worked from home, a revolutionary concept at the time (Shirley, 2019). Shirley's company played a critical role in developing software for major projects, including programming for the Concorde aircraft. Her advocacy for women in STEM has continued throughout her career, with her later years dedicated to philanthropy in the fields of autism research and education. Her story is one of resilience and innovation, as she not only broke down barriers for women in tech but also redefined what it meant to be an entrepreneur in the digital age. Her continued advocacy for women in STEM and philanthropy has had a lasting impact (Shirley, 2019).

Silvia Götti is a Swiss XR specialist, on the coding side, of course. She is currently blending her passions for archaeology and software engineering into a unique career path. More recently she was ICT Specialist for the Archaeology Service of Canton Bern, managing critical databases while also pursuing an archaeology degree at Bern University. Her career in IT includes experience in full-stack software engineering, where she worked on 3D and XR-related projects using JavaScript, and honing her skills in tools like Python, SQL. She also uses photogrammetry a lot, especially for AR development. Her diverse expertise positions her as an emerging leader in cultural heritage digitisation. But before her current role, she gained experience as an augmented reality developer and software engineer at various companies, including SO REAL DIGITAL TWINS AG. She is also a co-founder of the Flutter Meetup in Zurich and regularly gives talks on her innovative projects. With a strong foundation in both technical and cultural fields, she continues to bridge the gap between archaeology and modern technology, showcasing how digital tools can preserve and enhance our understanding of historical artefacts and data.

Susan Wojcicki (1968–2024) was the CEO of YouTube and had long been a prominent figure in the tech industry, having joined Google in its early days as the company's first marketing manager in 1999. She is often credited with the creation of Google AdSense, a tool that revolutionised the internet advertising landscape and became a major source of revenue for Google (Vise and Malseed, 2006). In 2014, she took over as the CEO of

YouTube, where she oversaw its growth into the world's largest video-sharing platform. Under her leadership, YouTube has expanded its influence in digital media, focusing on content monetisation, creators' welfare, and global reach.

As a working mother of five, Wojcicki was an outspoken advocate for work-life balance in tech, emphasising the need for family-friendly policies in corporate America. Her achievements in the technology sector have made her one of the most powerful women in the world, and she continues to push for greater diversity in tech leadership roles. Susan Wojcicki's contributions to digital advertising and online media have reshaped the internet economy. Wojcicki died on 9 August 2024, at the age of 56, after battling non-small-cell lung cancer for two years.

Tessy Thomas is an Indian scientist and engineer who made history as the first woman to lead a missile project in India. Known as the Missile Woman of India, she is the Director-General of Aeronautical Systems at the Defence Research and Development Organisation (DRDO), where she has played a pivotal role in the development of the Agni missile series, India's long-range nuclear-capable missiles (Srinivasan, 2012). Her work in missile technology has made her a symbol of women's empowerment in India's male-dominated defence sector, earning her numerous awards and accolades including the prestigious DRDO Scientist of the Year award. As a role model for young women aspiring to enter STEM fields, she has broken through significant barriers, proving that women can excel in even the most technical and demanding industries (Srinivasan, 2012).

Thuy Thanh Truong, often referred to as one of Vietnam's most influential tech entrepreneurs, was the co-founder of GreenGar Studios, a mobile app development company that gained international attention. Her work focused on building mobile apps for real-time collaboration, creating a platform where users could interact seamlessly across devices. She gained recognition not only for her technical skills in software development but also for her relentless drive to promote Vietnam's tech ecosystem. She later transitioned to healthcare technology, founding the company Tappy, which was acquired by the US-based company Weeby.co in 2015. She also founded Startup Viet Partners; a venture capital firm dedicated to nurturing the next generation of Vietnamese entrepreneurs in the tech industry.

Throughout her career, Truong was a pioneer who helped bridge the gap between Vietnam's growing tech talent and the global startup community. She was an advocate for fostering an entrepreneurial culture in Vietnam, believing that coding and technology could unlock new economic opportunities for the younger generation. Her legacy is particularly significant given her battle with lung cancer, which she fought while continuing to inspire others through her leadership and innovation in technology until her passing in 2020. Truong's impact remains a driving force in Vietnam's burgeoning tech landscape, proving that perseverance, innovation, and community can transform local industries (Morgan, 2020).

As I reflect on these remarkable women, I realise that history often tells us to sit down, shut up, and fall in line, and many do. But it's the outliers, the ones who don't fit neatly into those constraints, who change the game. These outliers aren't always rebellious by nature; sometimes they're simply curious and driven, like Herrad, Al-'Ijliyyah, or Van Schurman—women who sought to challenge ideas and forge their own paths.

Cavendish and Theano remind us that when we're onto something important, we must lead with conviction, regardless of opposition. Leadership in innovation requires courage, and not everyone is willing to take that stand. Hypatia did, and though her story ended in tragedy, it serves as a powerful reminder of the risks inherent in pushing against the status quo. Sometimes, standing up for what we believe comes with great costs, but it's those moments that drive progress forward, especially in technology.

As we continue to build on the foundations laid by these extraordinary women, I am inspired to contribute in my own way. Their stories are not just historical accounts; they are calls to action. They remind us that the journey towards recognition and equality is ongoing, and each of us has a role to play in shaping the future of technology.

REFERENCES

Abbott, B.P., Abbott, R. and Abbott, T.D., et al. (2016) 'Observation of gravitational waves from a binary black hole merger', *Physical Review Letters*, 116(6), pp. 061102.

About Her. (2020). *Latifa Al-Abdulkarim.* [online] Available at: https://www.abouther.com/tags/latifa-al-abdulkarim (Accessed 9 December 2024).

AKTI. (2024) *About Us.* [online] Available at: https://akti.com.pk/about-us/ (Accessed: 23 September 2024).

Al-Abdulkarim, L., Atkinson, K. and Bench-Capon, T. (2016) 'A methodology for designing systems to reason with legal cases using abstract dialectical frameworks', *Artificial Intelligence and Law*, 24 (1), pp. 1–49. doi:10.1007/s10506-016-9178-1. https://link.springer.com/article/10.1007/s10506-016-9178-1

AnitaB.org. (n.d.). *Lakshya Sivaramakrishnan: Speaker Profile.* [online] Available at: https://ghc.anitab.org/speaker/lakshya-sivaramakrishnan/ (Accessed 9 December 2024).

Apte, P. (2019) Interview: Megan Smith. [online] Available at: https://increment.com/teams/interview-megan-smith/ (Accessed: 23 September 2024).

BBC. (2019) *'Before we knew it this little website had 350,000 users'.* [online] Available at: https://www.bbc.com/news/business-48395181 (Accessed: 23 September 2024).

Berry, O. (1997) *Venturing in Israel.* July 10, 1997. [online] Available at: https://www.forbes.com/1997/07/10/venturing.html (Accessed: 23 September 2024).

Berry, O., European Commission, (2003). *Women in Industrial Research: A Wake-up Call for European Industry.* [pdf] Available at: https://genderportal.eu/sites/default/files/resource_pool/wir_final.pdf (Accessed 9 December 2024).

Beyer, K. (2012) *Grace Hopper and the invention of the information age.* Cambridge, MA: MIT Press.

Bidshahri, R. (2019) *Reimagining Education in the Exponential Age.* [online] Available at: https://singularityhub.com/2018/09/20/reimagining-education-in-the-exponential-age/ (Accessed: 23 September 2024).

Buolamwini, J. and Gebru, T. (2018) 'Gender shades: Intersectional accuracy disparities in commercial gender classification', *Proceedings of the 1st Conference on Fairness, Accountability, and Transparency*, 81, pp. 77–91.

Ceruzzi, P.E. (2003) *A history of modern computing.* Cambridge, MA: MIT Press.

Check Point Software Technologies. (2020). *Check Point Software Technologies Reinforces Leadership Team for Greater Execution and Innovation.* [online] Available at: https://www.checkpoint.com/press-releases/check-point-software-technologies-reinforces-leadership-team-for-greater-execution-and-innovation/ (Accessed 9 December 2024).

Coventry University. (2011). *Staff Profile: Dr Farzana Aslam.* [online] Available at: https://web.archive.org/web/20110218071840/http://www.coventry.ac.uk/cu/engineeringandcomputing/mathematicalsciences/staff/a/4803 (Accessed 9 December 2024).

Croucher, J.S. (2023) *IT girls: Pioneer Women in computing.* Stroud: Amberley Publishing.

Dhawan, N. (2019) 'Breaking the glass ceiling in corporate India: Insights from a female executive', *Forbes India Leadership Summit*, Mumbai.

Dor, D. (2018) 'Women in cybersecurity: Breaking barriers and leading the way', *Cybersecurity Leadership Forum*.

Economic Times. (2018) *Neelam Dhawan: A digital leader with a purpose.* Economic Times Digital. Available at: https://economictimes.indiatimes.com/industry/tech/tech-bytes/neelam-dhawan-profile (Accessed: 15 September 2024).

Fermilab. (2015). *Chicago Innovator Ellen Sandor is Fermilab's New Artist in Residence.* [online] Available at: https://news.fnal.gov/2015/12/chicago-innovator-ellen-sandor-is-fermilabs-new-artist-in-residence/ (Accessed 9 December 2024).

Ghosh, D. (2019) 'Building the future of women in technology: Breaking barriers in the digital age', *IEEE Women in Engineering Conference*, Bangalore.

Gooding, P., Brown, L.X., Myrick, K., Ubozoh, K.E.L.E.C.H.I., Horton, J., Bossewitch, J., Vásquez Encalada, A. and Katterl, S. (2023) *Digital futures in mind: Reflecting on technological experiments in mental health and crisis support.* Melbourne, AU: University of Melbourne.

Hall of Fame. (2021) *100 Brilliant Women in AI Ethics™.* [online] Available at: *https://womeninaiethics.org/the-list/hall-of-fame/* (Accessed: 23 September 2024).

Hauben, M. and Hauben, R. (1997) *Netizens: On the history and impact of Usenet and the internet.* New York: IEEE Computer Society Press.

Hendren, S. (2020) *What can a body do? How we meet the built world.* New York: Riverhead Books.

Hobeika, H. (2018) 'Pushing boundaries in sports tech with Instabeat.' *TechCrunch Disrupt*, San Francisco.

Hobeika, H. (2019) 'Challenges of being a female entrepreneur in MENA.' *Women in Tech Summit*, Beirut.

Intel. (2020) *Nivruti Rai: Leading innovation in India's technology landscape.* [online].

International Conference on VLSI Design and Embedded Systems. (2018). *Keynote Address.* [online video] Available at: https://www.facebook.com/esvlsid/videos/keynote-address/3081814395181646/ (Accessed 9 December 2024).

Karim, M.M.S., Ganose, A.M., Pieters, L., Leung, W.W.W., Wade, J., Zhang, L., Scanlon, D.O., & Palgrave, R.G. (2019). Anion Distribution, Structural Distortion, and Symmetry-Driven Optical Band Gap Bowing in Mixed Halide Cs_2SnX_6 Vacancy Ordered Double Perovskites. *Chemistry of Materials*, 31(22), pp. 9430–9444.

Kay, A. (1993) 'The early history of smalltalk', *Communications of the ACM*, 26(10), pp. 693–699.

Kim, A.J., 2017. *Game Thinking: Innovate Smarter & Drive Deep Engagement with Design Techniques from Hit Games.* Burlingame, CA: gamethinking.io.

Lüsted, M.A. (2018) *The most influential women in business.* New York: Rosen Publishing.

Madhavan, D. (2021) 'Creating pathways for women in Fintech.' *Women in Finance Summit*, London.

Margolis, J. and Fisher, A. (2002) *Unlocking the clubhouse: Women in computing.* Cambridge, MA: MIT Press.

Martins, L.B. and Wolfe, S.G. (2022) *Metaversed: See beyond the hype.* Hoboken, NJ: Wiley.

McGuire, J. (2019) *It's Time to Assess the Potential Dangers of an Increasingly Connected World.* [online] Available at: *https://www.darkreading.com/cyber-risk/it-s-time-to-assess-the-potential-dangers-of-an-increasingly-connected-world-* (Accessed: 23 September 2024).

Mendler, C. (2012) *Man vs. Machine: It's old history.* [online] Available at: https://www.forbes.com/sites/sap/2012/05/14/man-vs-machine-its-old-history/ (Accessed: 23 September 2024).

Minevich, M. (2020) *The Women defining The 21st century AI movement: Part 2 of 2.* Forbes. [online] Available at: https://www.forbes.com/sites/markminevich/2020/03/19/the-women-defining-the-21st-century-ai-movement-part-2-of-2/ (Accessed: 23 September 2024).

Morgan, H. (2020) *Remembering Vietnam's tech queen and what she taught us.* [online] Available at: https://www.forbes.com/sites/heathermorgan/2020/02/28/remembering-vietnams-tech-queen-and-what-she-taught-us/ (Accessed: 23 September 2024).

NASSCOM. (2020) Future Skilling for the Digital Economy. [pdf] Available at: https://skillsip.nsdcindia.org/sites/default/files/kps-document/NASSCOM%20future-skilling-for-the-digital-economy%202020%20%281%29_0.pdf (Accessed 9 December 2024).

Perlman, R. (2000) *Interconnections: Bridges, routers, switches, and internetworking protocols.* Reading, MA: Addison-Wesley.

Philbin, C.A. (2017). *Crash Course Computer Science Preview.* [online video] CrashCourse. Available at: https://www.youtube.com/watch?v=tpIctyqH29Q (Accessed 28 July 2024).

Radinsky, K. (2013) 'Using predictive analytics to forecast global crises.' *TEDx Jerusalem.*

Radinsky, K. (2019) 'AI in healthcare: Revolutionising diagnostics.' *Diagnostic Robotics.*

REVA Academy for Corporate Excellence. (5 March 2022). *Drives Success with Inspirational Leadership.* [online]. Available at: https://race.reva.edu.in/race-lab/drives-success-with-inspirational-leadership/ (Accessed 9 December 2024).

Robertson, S. (2008) 'Karen Spärck Jones: Contributions to information retrieval', *Communications of the ACM*, 51(12), pp. 91–97.

Romero, B. (2016) *The mechanic is the message: Games as social commentary.* Austin, TX: University of Texas Press.

Russakovsky, O., Deng, J. and Su, H., et al. (2015) 'ImageNet large scale visual recognition challenge', *International Journal of Computer Vision*, 115(3), pp. 211–252.

Shetterly, M.L. (2016). *Hidden Figures. Paperback edition.* New York: William Morrow and Company. 368 pages. ISBN 978-0-06-236360-2.

Shirley, S. (2019) *Let IT go: My extraordinary story—From refugee to entrepreneur to philanthropist.* London: Penguin.

Sivaramakrishnan, L. (2022) 'Leading with impact: A woman's journey in AI and technology', *Google Tech Talks*, San Francisco.

Srinivasan, S. (2012) 'Tessy Thomas: India's missile woman', *Defense Science Journal*, 62(2), pp. 91–98.

StartSomeGood. (24 August 2023). *Fireside Chat* [Instagram reel]. Available at: https://www.instagram.com/startsomegood/reel/CwUfD72uQ3s/?hl=en (Accessed 9 December 2024).

Sterling, D. (2018) *Driving ambition: The story of Bertha Benz and the first road trip.* Stuttgart: Motorpress.

Stonier, J., Woodman, L., Alshammari, M., Cummings, R., Dad, N., Garg, A. and Teeuwen, S. (2023) *Data equity: Foundational concepts for generative AI.* arXiv preprint arXiv:2311.10741.

Tai, A. (2020) *Interview: Diana Iracheta, manufacturing engineer, content creator, writer, & women-in-STEM advocate.* [online] Available at: https://www.femmerevamp.com/home/interview-diana-iracheta-manufacturing-engineer-content-creator-writer-women-in-stem-advoca (Accessed: 23 September 2024).

Tatarko, A. (2020) 'How technology can transform the home design industry.' *Global Tech Summit.*

The Times of Israel. (2022) *Report: Jewish CEO of 'Russia's Google' leaves country for Israel over war.* [online] Available at: https://www.timesofisrael.com/report-jewish-ceo-of-russias-google-leaves-country-for-israel-over-war/ (Accessed: 23 September 2024).

Tripp, K. (2018) *Index tuning for optimal performance in SQL server.* Redmond, WA: SQLskills Publications.

UNESCO. (2021) 'UNESCO convenes a global dialogue to break through bias in AI on International Women's Day.' *India Education Diary.*

University of Oxford. (2020). *Oxford Women in Computer Science Recognised for Their Impact.* [online] Available at: https://www.cs.ox.ac.uk/news/1697-full.html (Accessed 9 December 2024).

University of Virginia. (n.d.). *Renee Cummings*. [online] Available at: https://datascience.virginia.edu/people/renee-cummings (Accessed 9 December 2024).

Vise, D.A. and Malseed, M. (2006) *The Google story: Inside the hottest business, media, and technology success of our time*. New York: Delta Publishing.

Wade, J. (2017). *A Voice for Diversity in Science | Dr Jessica Wade | TEDxLondonWomen*. [online video] TEDxLondonWomen. Available at: https://www.youtube.com/watch?v=PUpOqdB6RDU (Accessed 9 December 2024).

Women Entrepreneurs Review. (2022). *Deepa Madhavan is named as the India Country Head by Genesys*. [online] Available at: https://www.womenentrepreneursreview.com/news/deepa-madhavan-is-named-as-the-india-country-head-by-genesys-nwid-2678.html (Accessed 9 December 2024).

Yushchenko, K. (1968) 'Address programming and early computer systems'. Soviet Cybernetics Review.

Index